A First Course in Economics

D.J. Thomas
M.A., B.Sc. (Econ.), Ph.D.

Bell & Hyman Limited
London

First published in 1979 by
BELL & HYMAN LIMITED
Denmark House, 37-39 Queen Elizabeth Street
London SE1 2QB

ISBN 0 7135 1093 5

Printed and bound in Great Britain at the Camelot Press Ltd, Southampton

Contents

PART THREE
PRODUCTION

PART FOUR
RESOURCES

PART FIVE

MONEY AND BANKING

PART SIX

THE INTERDEPENDENT WORLD

PART SEVEN

THE GOVERNMENT AND THE ECONOMY

Preface

The aim of this volume is to provide a text-book on Economics suitable for secondary school and college courses leading to the General Certificate of Education at the Ordinary Level. It is designed also for students taking the Economics examinations of the Royal Society of Arts and the London Chamber of Commerce (at the intermediate stages). It also provides a useful introduction for those taking Economics at Advanced Level in GCE and for those following Business Education Council (BEC) National Certificate or Diploma courses.

At the end of each chapter there are suggestions for practical and written work. The latter is divided into questions requiring short answers, and questions from recent GCE, RSA, and LCC papers requiring essay-type answers.

The Economics syllabuses of most examining bodies range over a wide field and a single text-book cannot possibly cover every detail. Accordingly, parts of the 'Suggestions For Practical Work' sections are aimed at encouraging individual research into topics that have not been given detailed treatment in the chapters.

With the agreement of the Publishers, I have made use of a certain amount of material from *A First Course in Commerce* where the subject matter is common to both commerce and economics syllabuses.

I wish to record my gratitude to Miss M. S. Lawrence for checking and typing the manuscript.

I wish to record my appreciation of the work done by Ms E. Foa in the preparation of this book.

I wish to thank the University of London School Examinations Department (U/L), the Joint Matriculation Board (JMB), the Associated Examining Board (AEB), the Oxford Delegacy of Local Examinations (Oxford), the Southern Universities Joint Board (SUJB) the Welsh Joint Education Committee (WJEC), the Oxford and Cambridge Schools Examination Board (Oxford and Cambridge), the Scottish Certificate of Education Examination Board (SCE), the University of Cambridge Local Examinations Syndicate (Cambridge), the Royal Society of Arts (RSA), and the London Chamber of Commerce (LCC) who have permitted the reproduction of questions taken from previous examination papers.

Grateful acknowledgment is made to the Controller of Her Majesty's Stationery Office for allowing the use of material taken from HMSO publications.

Tables

Figures

Part One
Introduction to Economics

1
The Meaning of Economics

Wants

People work in order to earn money for satisfying wants. There are some things which are wanted by everyone. They include food and drink, clothing, and shelter.

After people have sufficient food, clothing and house-room, they try to satisfy their other wants. For instance, some may want motor-cycles or cars; others may prefer better houses. If people were asked to write out lists of what they wanted, the lists would show a wide variety of different things.

If a person had no wants or if his wants could be satisfied without any effort on his part, he would not go to work. People work so that they may consume. They are *consumers*, that is they buy goods and services with the money earned.

Money is used, therefore, to satisfy wants and a person's *standard of living* is determined by the amount of goods and services that he may consume.

People who go to work are *producers* as well as being consumers. A miner produces coal, an insurance agent sells insurance and a solicitor sells his skill in handling legal matters. In fact, everyone who goes to work is helping to produce goods or, as in the case of the solicitor and the insurance agent, to provide services.

Production means the manufacture of goods and the provision of services, the aim of which is to satisfy people's wants.

Spending

People spend the money they earn in various ways. Here is a typical planned budget for a young wage-earner receiving a £30 net wage per week:

1

	£
Board and lodging	8.00
Lunches and fares to work	6.00
Clothes	4.00
Entertainment and miscellaneous expenses	5.50
Holidays, savings for	2.50
Regular savings	4.00
Total	£30.00

When a person plans his spending he arranges his wants in order of their importance to himself. The more important will have priority over the less important. Arranging wants in order of priority results in a *scale of preferences*. One person's scale will almost certainly be quite different from someone else's because each of us has individual tastes and preferences.

Wants are many and income is limited. (There is always some limit to what can be earned. For example, there is in a day only a limited time available for work. There are also limits to extra earnings available from promotion, obtaining additional qualifications and working overtime.) These facts mean that some wants will be satisfied only at the expense of others. For instance, a person may wish to visit a cinema *and* to buy a new tie. If he has sufficient money to satisfy only one of these wants he must choose one at the cost of the other. The real cost of the cinema visit, if he chooses that alternative, is not the cost of the ticket but the lack of the new tie which he has to do without. In economics this loss of the most desired alternative want is called *opportunity cost*.

The fact that people have to choose which of their wants to satisfy implies that there is an insufficient supply of goods and services in relation to wants. In the United Kingdom, where shops are well stocked with an abundant variety of merchandise, it may seem odd to claim there is scarcity. Nevertheless these goods are scarce in relation to the desire for them. For example, most people would like better houses, more domestic appliances, more frequent visits to the theatre and more holidays abroad. There seems to be an inexhaustible desire for more and better goods and services.

Whereas people's wants are many, the resources for satisfying them – raw materials, factories, machinery, labour – are limited. It seems unlikely that the production of unlimited quantities of anything will ever be possible, and certainly at present it is impossible to satisfy all the wants of every person. Consequently, to the economist goods and services are scarce because they are limited in supply.

Utility

What determines how a person spends his income? The economist would answer this question with the word 'utility'. This term means the amount of satisfaction derived by a person from buying goods and services. At the same time, an economist assumes that a person spends his income in those ways which provide him with the greatest amount of satisfaction.

There are a number of points to note about utility.

In the first place, it varies from person to person because people have individual tastes and preferences. For example, tobacco has considerable utility to a smoker but to the non-smoker it has none at all.

Secondly, utility is not constant and will vary for the same person at different times. For example, central heating has no utility to a householder on a warm summer day but on a cold wintry day it has considerable utility.

Thirdly, utility has no moral significance and it must not be confused with 'benefit'. For example, a person might be healthier and happier if he spent more on food or exercise and less on alcohol or amusements. However, economics does not study how people *ought* to behave; it is concerned only with *how* they do, in fact, behave. When a particular pattern of spending is described as giving a person the greatest utility, this simply means he prefers spending his money in that way to any other.

Fourthly, utility is subjective in that it denotes someone's personal estimate of satisfaction. For this reason, it cannot be objectively measured or counted.

Although a person has many wants, there is a limit to his want for a particular commodity at any one time. For example, a person wants only a certain quantity of bread, vegetables or entertainment at any one moment. Additional quantities tend to give less satisfaction than previous purchases. Thus as a person's stock of a commodity increases, his desire for more of it decreases.

Marginal utility

The extra satisfaction to be derived from owning an extra unit of a commodity is called its marginal utility. Generally, as consumption increases, marginal utility decreases. This statement is called the law of diminishing marginal utility. In a more formal way, it reads 'as more of a commodity is consumed, the less the utility derived from the consumption of an extra unit.'

For example, after returning home hungry from afternoon school, the first sandwich provides great satisfaction, and its marginal utility is very high. The second sandwich is also very welcome, but it does not yield so much utility as the first, while the third will provide an even lower level of satisfaction. Eventually the continued consumption of sandwiches becomes distasteful and marginal utility is negative.

Although the law is applicable for the majority of people in most circumstances, there are a number of exceptions to it. They comprise examples of marginal utility increasing as stock increases. For example, the miser obsessed with amassing unlimited amounts of money provides an exception to the law. Similarly ardent collectors of foreign stamps or coins, may find marginal utility increasing as their collections grow and their interest develops. In like manner, a keen football supporter or opera-goer or anyone else who has an intense interest in a particular activity or hobby may form an exception and find that 'the more one has, the more one wants'.

Marginal utility determines the order in which wants are arranged on a scale of preferences. A person tries to obtain the greatest value for money from his spending. Thus he buys less of goods that have less utility and more of commodities that provide him with greater satisfaction. He continues to adjust his expenditure, buying a little more here and a little less there, until he can get no gain in total satisfaction from any further adjustment. When this stage is reached, he has so distributed his expenditure that he would not willingly have spent even 1p more on one commodity and 1p less on another. In other words, in order to obtain maximum satisfaction from his total outlay, a person tries to equate the marginal utility of the last penny spent on each commodity.

Prices and value
In deciding how to spend their incomes, people have to consider the prices of goods and services available for purchase. Price is not the same thing as value. Something may have value (in the ordinary sense of the word) to a person because it yields him some degree of satisfaction. However, value in this subjective sense is not the concern of the economist. In economics, value is measurable and means always 'value in exchange'. It denotes the estimate which people place on goods and services and this is measured in terms of an exchange. For example, if one table exchanges for three chairs, the value of a chair in terms of tables is one-third. Value is, therefore, the rate at which one commodity exchanges for another.

In practice, values are invariably expressed in money and price is the market value of the commodity bought and sold.

The distinction between price and value is clarified by the following example. If the price of a chair is £6 and a table is priced at £24, then in terms of value, four chairs are a fair exchange for one table. The same would be true if the purchasing power of money changed, as for example, if the price of chairs were £12 and the price of tables £48; or if the price of chairs were £3 and tables were priced at £12. A price is, therefore, a measure of value in exchange.

Marginal utility and total utility

Having introduced the economic ideas of utility and marginal utility, it is possible now to explain how a situation can exist where a commodity which is a necessity to everyone (e.g. water) has a low money value, while others which are not vital necessities (e.g. diamonds or perfume) sell at a very high price. The reason is that marginal utility rather than total utility is measured by price. A person's desire for any good decreases as the amount consumed increases, and hence his willingness to pay for additional units of it falls progressively to zero as the point of satiation is reached. Water is a necessity of life and as such has a high total utility, but in European countries water is relatively abundant and therefore the marginal utility of an extra litre is small. Diamonds are scarce, however, and consequently marginal utility is high.

Opportunity cost and marginal utility

As noted earlier, the opportunity cost of satisfying a want is the utility which would have resulted from satisfying an alternative want. In practice people are usually able to adjust their spending so as to be able to avoid rejecting one alternative completely in favour of another. A consumer considers whether he will make do with a little less of one product so that he can have more of another or vice versa. In other words, choice is exercised 'at the margin' and estimates of opportunity cost involve comparing the satisfactions obtainable from marginal units of different commodities. In order to obtain maximum satisfaction from spending his income, a consumer tries to equate the marginal utilities of all his different purchases. We can say that the opportunity cost of every marginal pennyworth must balance exactly.

Wealth

Wealth is a stock of goods which possesses value in the sense used in economics, that is, value in exchange. Such goods have to be paid for and they are sometimes described as 'economic goods'. Free goods are those which have no price because supplies are so plentiful that everyone can have as much as he wants without making any payment. It is difficult to give many examples of free goods other than the air we breathe. In fact, free goods do not enter into the subject matter of economics at all because anything in unlimited supply presents no economic problems.

Ownership of wealth
Wealth is owned either privately or by the state.

Privately owned wealth includes possessions owned by individual people (e.g. houses, clothes, cars, household furniture, etc.) and those owned by business firms (e.g. factory buildings, machinery, raw materials, etc). Unlike a person's possessions, business wealth does not satisfy wants directly. Rather it is wanted to assist in the production of other things – cars, furniture and other consumer goods. Wealth used to produce more wealth is called *capital*.

Publicly owned wealth includes all property owned by the state or local authorities. It comprises assets under the control of the national-ised industries and also those such as libraries, hospitals, roads and harbours under the control of government departments or local authori-ties (see Fig. 1).

Summary
People have a wide range of wants and possess the means for satisfying only some of them. Incomes are limited and in order to enjoy some goods and services, it is necessary to do without others. Although this chapter has been mainly concerned with people as individuals, the problems of *scarcity* and *choice* extend beyond individuals and families to society as a whole. (The economic systems adopted by different societies or countries are examined in the next chapter.) Economics is the study of *how scarce resources are used to satisfy wants*. It studies the economic activities of individual persons and, in a broader context, it examines the mechanism by which the resources of countries are organised to meet the needs of their populations.

QUESTIONS

Write *short* answers to the following:

1 Why do people go to work?
2 Write down a person's three basic wants.
3 What is a consumer?
4 What do you understand by the phrase 'standard of living'?

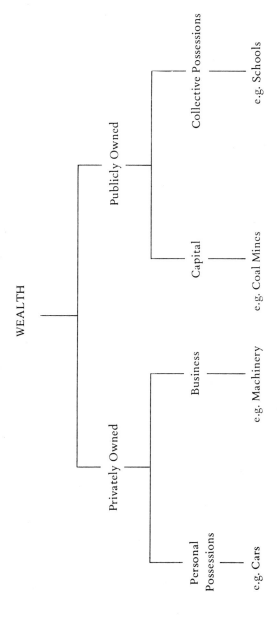

Fig. 1 Types of Wealth

5 Write down the meaning of 'production'.
6 Why does everyone have to make choices in their spending?
7 What is a 'scale of preferences'?
8 Write down the meaning in economics of 'utility'.
9 How do prices assist consumers to satisfy their wants?
10 What is the meaning of 'opportunity cost'?
11 Why does the economist say that all goods are scarce when there are well-filled shops throughout the country?
12 Name the resources which are used in production to satisfy wants.
13 What is the meaning of 'marginal utility'?
14 What is the meaning of 'value'?
15 What is the meaning of 'wealth'?
16 How would you classify the ownership of wealth?
17 Give a definition of economics.

Write answers to the following:

1 What is meant by 'economics'? Explain and illustrate the following terms as used in economics: utility, wealth, opportunity cost. (AEB)
2 What is meant by the concept of 'marginal utility'? Use this concept to explain how a rational consumer would distribute his expenditure between different goods. (Oxford)
3 What is meant by the principle of diminishing marginal utility? How far does it apply to money income? (JMB)
4 What is meant by 'diminishing marginal utility'? Why is water cheap relative to diamonds? (Oxford)
5 Why do economic problems occur? How may some of these problems be solved? (RSA)
6 What is the science of Economics? Give a reasoned argument for it as a subject of study. (RSA)
7 Distinguish between opportunity cost and money cost and explain why a consumer considers both when allocating his income between competing wants. (LCC)
8 Define 'opportunity cost' and explain the relevance of this concept to economic decisions you have taken. (LCC)
9 (a) Define the terms 'price', 'cost' and 'value' as used in economics.
   (b) Explain their interrelationship, using examples of different kinds of products. (U/L)

2

Economic systems

The economic problem

The resources for satisfying wants are limited and a community has to decide how to use the resources available to their best advantage, that is, to satisfy as many of its members' wants as possible. This is the economic problem.

In attempting its solution, a community has to make the following decisions:

(*a*) to select the goods and services to be produced;
(*b*) to decide the quantities in which they are to be produced;
(*c*) to determine how they are to be produced;
(*d*) to decide how they are to be distributed among the members of the community.

Factors of production

The resources available for use in producing goods and services are called the factors of production. They comprise

(*a*) human resources
(*b*) natural resources
(*c*) man-made resources.

In economics these three resources are known as

(*a*) labour
(*b*) land
(*c*) capital.

In return for its part in producing goods and services each factor receives an income. Labour is paid a wage or salary; land earns rent; and capital is rewarded by interest.

Production usually requires a combination of these three factors. In order to achieve this, there is a fourth factor which is called enterprise.

Without its managing and co-ordinating function, the other factors would lie idle and unused. The reward of the entrepreneur or organiser is profit.

Broadly speaking there are three economic systems which seek, in different ways, to solve the economic problem. They are

(a) private enterprise (which is sometimes called free enterprise, individualism or capitalism);
(b) collectivism (which is sometimes called state enterprise, socialism or communism);
(c) a mixed system (in which the state owns a number of industries and services but the greater part of production is carried on by private enterprise).

Private enterprise

Under a private enterprise system, business capital is in private hands. People are free to spend their incomes on the goods and services of their choice. All goods and services produced have market prices. Resources are allocated through the *price system*. The latter determines what goods are to be produced and in what quantities; how they are to be produced; and how they are distributed.

Functions of the price system

In the first place, the price system gives the ultimate decision to consumers as to what goods and services will be produced.

How does this process work?

Every time a consumer makes a purchase it is like registering a vote in favour of the continuing production of that article. As a retailer finds his stock diminishing, he re-orders from the wholesaler or the manufacturer. The latter makes further supplies.

On the other hand, if manufacturers find that orders for certain articles are declining because consumers' demand is falling, they will make fewer of them.

If consumers' demand for a particular article *increases rapidly* there will be a shortage of supplies in the shops. Scarcity will cause a rise in price. This will have two effects. First, the price increase will ration out the quantitiy available by reducing the number of buyers; secondly, the prospect of greater profits will encourage producers to increase supplies.

A *falling-off* in demand by consumers will have the opposite effect. Sellers will reduce their prices in an effort to clear their stock and a fall in price will have two results. First, the price reduction will encourage more buyers to make purchases; secondly, some manufacturers will be unable to make a profit at the lower selling price so they will stop production. Hence supplies will diminish.

Thus consumers' demand, acting through the price system, determines the assortment and quantity of goods produced. It is sometimes said that under a private enterprise system, 'the consumer is king'.

The second function of the price system is the distribution of scarce resources among competing producers.

Those industries which can offer the highest prices for the factors of production are able to attract supplies. On the other hand, industries which find that factor prices are too high to yield a profit from manufacturing are forced to contract. Thus production resources switch to industries whose goods are in more urgent demand.

The third function of the price system is to determine who should produce goods and services and which methods of production should be used.

These matters are decided by competition among different producers. Those who are more efficient because their costs of production are lowest will succeed in supplying a commodity at a lower price than their competitors. The inefficient will be forced out of business. In a similar way, competition determines the methods of production used. They will be those by which costs are reduced to the minimum.

Finally the price system determines the way in which the goods and services produced are distributed among members of a society.

The share of goods and services available to a person depends on the level of his income. Income is earned either by some form of labour or it is derived from the ownership of property. The amounts of these incomes are determined by the conditions of demand and supply in the markets for land, labour and capital. Wages, interest and rent are prices and their levels depend upon two factors, namely their supply, and consumers' demand for the products they help to make. If demand for a product is rising, firms engaged in its production will expand; their demand for factors of production will increase, and the incomes of the factors will rise. Conversely, if consumers' demand for a product is declining, then the incomes of factors engaged in producing that product will tend to fall.

An example will make clear the working of the price mechanism.

If consumers decide that they want more gloves than are currently being manufactured, and fewer shoes, there will be an increased demand for the stock of gloves on the market and a slackening of demand for shoes. As a result, glove prices will rise as consumers seek to buy more of them than are available and shoe prices will tend to fall as the public passes the shoe shops by. When glove prices rise, profits in that industry will rise too and as shoe prices fall, profits in that industry will fall. Consequently workers will be released from the shoe factories as output contracts and will move to the glove business where more workers will be required to produce a greater supply of gloves. The result is that glove production tends to rise and shoe production tends to fall. Through the price mechanism, society has changed the allocation of its productive resources to fit its new desires.

Advantages of the price system

   1   It is an automatic and self-regulating process.

No elaborate administrative machinery is required to operate the price mechanism and yet, by means of it, goods and services are produced and distributed to where they are most in demand. Adam Smith (who is generally agreed to be the founder of economic science) wrote in his *Wealth of Nations* (1776) of 'the invisible hand' which acting through each person's self-interest and the competition resulting therefrom, provided those goods that society wants, in the quantity that society desires and at the prices which society is prepared to pay.

   2   It offers freedom of choice to consumers.

Consumers express their particular tastes and preferences by the way their incomes are spent. Hence demand influences prices, and so consumers determine what is to be produced. If a producer does not make what consumers want then his rivals will. Thus it is the consumer who has the final say under private enterprise.

   3   It provides conditions in which initiative and enterprise can flourish.

The price system is based on the profit motive. It assumes that personal interest (or as Adam Smith called it 'the natural effort of every individual to better his own condition') is the root of all economic activity. When demand exceeds supply and prices rise, producers are encouraged by the prospect of making profits to increase supply. In a system where enterprise is rewarded in this way, people will be alert to opportunities of meeting new or increasing demands for goods and services.

Criticisms of the price system

The price system is open to criticism on a number of grounds.

   1   A system based on self-interest and the profit motive supplies only those needs which can find expression in terms of money. Goods go to those who are prepared to pay the highest prices. Consequently the rich may enjoy luxuries while the poor lack necessities. Thus a person with no money and without food has a desperate need, but under the price system he provides no 'demand' for food.

2   The price system does not recognise any sense of duty to the community. Only those goods and services offering a profit are produced and so it is doubtful whether vital services such as the judiciary, a universal system of education and the various social amenities such as libraries, parks and gardens would be made available.

3   The system may lead to some waste of economic resources. The transfer of resources from declining industries to those which are prospering may take a very long time. Labour and capital may be unemployed for years and consequently resources remain unused.

4   Competition is an essential requirement for the working of the price system and it may break down because of the development of monopoly situations. Generally the latter are harmful to society. For example, an employer may be the sole buyer of labour in a particular region and lack of competition provides him with an unfair bargaining power in fixing wage rates. Similarly if a producer is the only supplier of a particular product, then consumers are forced to pay the price asked for or go without. They cannot purchase elsewhere.

5   The exercise of the freedom to obtain the most advantageous return from resources may result in actions which are detrimental to the welfare of the community. For example, a builder may erect houses cheaply in order to maximise his profits and without regard for the safety of people who will live in them; a manufacturer may allow unpleasant fumes to pollute the district surrounding his factory rather than incur expenditure in preventing the nuisance. In a similar fashion if it is cheaper to use child labour than adult workers, then child workers will be employed without consideration of the effects on the health of the next generation.

Collectivism
Under a collectivist system, the allocation of resources is decided not by individual consumers through the medium of the price system, but by the government acting on their behalf.

In order to achieve this objective, the government has, first, to estimate consumers' wants and then decide which goods shall be produced and in what quantities. Usually the government appoints a number of committees to perform these tasks. For example, one committee may be asked to compile lists of all the commodities to be produced, such as, for example, so many million tonnes of wheat, and so many million metres of cloth. Another committee calculates the labour supply and other resources available. A co-ordinating (or central planning) committee will then have the task of allocating resources among different industries in order to produce the goods required.

In a collectivist system it is necessary for the government (a) to own the resources of land and capital, and (b) to control or direct the employment of labour.

Advantages
The advantages claimed for collectivism are that it cancels out many of the failings of private enterprise.

1 A minimum standard of living can be provided for everyone in the community. Under private enterprise where profit is the dominant motive in production, it is doubtful whether the poorer members of the community could obtain, for example, minimum standards of education or medical care. Through its control of resources, the state can provide these and other minimum requirements.

2 The waste of resources which may occur in a competitive system can be avoided. For example, under private enterprise, different railway companies may build a number of railway lines between the same two places. Consequently there is a waste of resources. When the government is in control the working of an industry can be planned as a whole and the wasteful duplication of railway lines (and similarly, gas mains, electricity cables, etc.) can be avoided.

3 Account can be taken of objectives other than profit. Under private enterprise, for example, a train service would be provided only if it was profitable to do so. Under collectivism, trains may be run on certain lines for the convenience of people living in the area, although the service may run at a loss. Similarly coal mines may be worked at a loss but be kept open in order to provide employment in certain areas.

4 Private monopolies do not exist under collectivism and so consumers cannot suffer from their harmful effects. The state itself is, of course, one huge monopoly but collectivists assume it will not act in a way that is contrary to the interests of the community.

Criticisms
A collectivist system can be criticized in the following ways.

1 It is practically impossible for the government to assess demand for each one of the host of goods and services that people want. Each consumer has highly individual tastes and where a community comprises a large number of people, a central authority could never assess accurately the state of demand.

The difficulty is overcome by the government making itself responsible for deciding what people need and what will be best suited for them. Thus consumers lose the freedom they enjoy under private enterprise to choose which wants they will satisfy.

2 Administrative machinery has to be set up (a) to collect and analyse information concerning the extent of demand and supply, (b) to allocate factors of production and (c) to enforce the decisions made. Thus a very large number of officials will be employed to carry out these tasks. The situation may result in bureaucracy and its attendant dangers such as, for example, much filling-in of forms, slow decisions and the possibility of bribery and corruption.

3 Collectivism involves planning by a central authority and this operation is subject to all the problems of management and control which arise in any large-scale enterprise.

4 The collectivist system may not stimulate the effort and initiative which exist under private enterprise. Thus the salaried officials of the collectivist system may give less drive and effort because their own capital is not at risk.

A mixed system
In the real world, economic systems that are based exclusively on private enterprise or exclusively on collectivism do not exist. The collectivist economies of communist countries incorporate some features of private enterprise, while the private enterprise economies of western countries contain some state enterprise and state control.

The economic system of the United Kingdom is described as a mixed economy. Some planning of production is undertaken by the government, directly or through its nationalised industries, and some – the greater part – is left to private enterprise. The government undertakes the following:

(a) The provision of essential services such as roads and communications, health, education and a range of social services.

(b) The organisation of basic industries such as coal, steel, electricity and gas.

In addition to producing goods and services the government provides a framework of law and regulations to check any harmful effects of private enterprise. For example, the Factory Acts and The Offices, Shops and Railway Premises Act (1963) control employees' working conditions; the Monopolies and Mergers Commission protects consumers from exploitation by large firms; and planning regulations control

15

the location of industry in accordance with the interests of the community as a whole.

Thus the economic system of the United Kingdom uses both collectivist methods and private enterprise in trying to solve the economic problem.

QUESTIONS

Write *short* answers to the following:

1 What is the 'economic problem'?
2 What are the main economic systems operating today?
3 List the questions to which an economic system seeks to find answers.
4 What are 'factors of production'?
5 How do people make choices under private enterprise?
6 Explain briefly how the consumer is sovereign under private enterprise.
7 What part does competition play under private enterprise?
8 How does the price mechanism ensure that an increased demand for gloves is met?
9 Write down the advantages of the price system.
10 What are the drawbacks of the price system?
11 Name the functions of the government in a collectivist system.
12 What are the advantages of collectivism?
13 List the drawbacks of collectivism.
14 What part does the government play in production in the UK?
15 How does the state protect its citizens against harmful effects of private enterprise in the UK?

Write answers to the following:

1 What is meant by 'the price mechanism'? What are its functions in the economy?   (AEB)
2 What do you consider to be the advantages of a mixed economy in which both private and public sectors exist?   (JMB)
3 Discuss the main ways in which different economic systems can allocate resources.   (JMB)
4 How would you explain to a visitor from the Soviet Union the main differences between the economic system prevailing in his own country and that existing in Britain?   (JMB)

5 Explain and discuss the methods by which resources are distributed in the economy. (RSA)
6 What do you understand by the term 'the price mechanism'? Give examples of its operation. (RSA)
7 'In a private-enterprise economy, consumers control what is produced.' Discuss this statement. (LCC)
8 Why are opportunities for making profits necessary, if the wants of consumers are to be satisfied in a private enterprise economy? (LCC)
9 What functions are performed by the price system in a private enterprise economy? (LCC)
10 How is the problem of allocating scarce resources between competing uses solved in a private enterprise economy? (LCC)
11 What is meant by the basic economic problem? How is the problem solved by the price mechanism in a free enterprise economy? (AEB)

PRACTICAL WORK

1 'The nineteenth century had opened with a feeling of contempt for government of every kind and with unbounded confidence in the virtue of economic liberty and individual initiative . . . The century closed amid a clamour for state intervention in all matters affecting economic or social organisation.'

Using reference books, discover the reason for the change of attitude to state intervention in the UK.

2 Find out the significance of the 1944 White Paper on Employment Policy in the development of state responsibility for economic affairs.

Part Two
Markets

3
Markets and Competition

Exchanges and markets

The process of distributing goods to consumers necessitates a number of exchanges. For example, the wholesaler buys from manufacturers and sells to retailers; the retailer purchases his stock from either a wholesaler or direct from a manufacturer and sells to consumers. Whenever exchange takes place between buyers and sellers a market is in operation.

In everyday speech the word 'market' may be used in two ways. First, it may describe the extent of the sale for some commodity as, for example, 'there is a wide market for used cars'. This use of the word has no relevance to the specialised definition of 'market' used in economics. Secondly, it may refer to a particular place where buyers and sellers meet regularly. For example, the weekly market held in country towns for the sale of local produce; the wholesale fruit, vegetable and flowers market at Covent Garden; the market for stocks and shares at The Stock Exchange, and so on. However, while markets are often found in particular places, the development and use of communications in modern times has made the gathering of buyers and sellers in one place less necessary. Thus people forming a market may communicate, for example, through a local newspaper advertising 'articles for sale'; through a car magazine advertising cars or components for sale; or by means of details of property for sale displayed in estate agents' windows. The use of telephone and telex make possible markets between buyers and sellers in different countries. World-wide markets exist in commodities such as oil and steel. Nevertheless, whatever the extent of a market – local, national or international – its essential feature remains. It is simply a group of buyers and sellers who wish to exchange goods or services.

Types of markets

Markets exist for all commodities and for all services. Some of the more familiar examples are listed below.

1 Financial markets These include the markets in short-term and long-term loans; the new-issues market; the market in existing securities; and the market for foreign currencies. They are dealt with more fully in Chapter 17.

2 The labour market Labour services are sold by workers and bought by employers. In its widest sense the market for labour services comprises employers' associations, trade unions, employment offices and the 'situations vacant' columns in newspapers and magazines.

3 Land Land is usually sold through estate agents and advertisements in newspapers and magazines.

4 Commodities Commodity markets are often held in a particular place or building. Many of the old-established commodity exchanges for raw materials and foodstuffs are found in London, but there are also important markets for cotton, fruit and corn in provincial centres such as Liverpool and Manchester. Commodity markets are conducted by brokers who act as agents for buyers and sellers. Buyers include manufacturers and wholesalers while sellers are the producers or growers of the commodity.

5 Consumer goods These markets are formed by the wholesale and retail trades. In the retail market the finished product is made available to consumers. The simplest form of retail market is the street market which is held regularly in many towns and villages on certain days. The permanent retail market is formed by the various kinds of shops.

The wholesale market extends over a much wider area than the retail market. Orders received from retailers by the wholesaler are passed on to the manufacturer and communication may take place by telephone and letter. There may be no central meeting-place for buyers and sellers other than the showrooms maintained by wholesalers and manufacturers for such of their customers as may be in the locality.

Perfect markets

The economic importance of markets lies in the fact that they are places where prices are determined. A measure of how well a market works is indicated by the variations in prices found within it. Ideally there is only one price within the market area, but this ideal is realised only if certain conditions are fulfilled. When these occur and a single price is established the market is said to be perfect.

The conditions necessary for the operation of a perfect market are as follows.

1   The number of buyers and sellers must be large enough to prevent a single one of them from influencing the market price. In other words, no consumer buys enough to affect the market price by buying more or by buying less; and no supplier sells enough to create scarcity by withholding supply.

2   Buyers and sellers have exact knowledge of what is happening in any part of the market. This does not necessarily mean that the market involves a small area, but it does emphasise the importance of communications. When buyers and sellers are in close touch with one another sellers know what prices are being offered by buyers, and buyers know what prices are being asked by sellers. It follows that buyers can purchase at the lowest price and sellers can sell at the highest price. The result of the efforts of buyers and sellers to obtain the best terms for themselves is the establishment of a single price throughout the market.

3   The commodity must be highly standardised, that is, each unit must be identical with another. As a result, buyers find that each seller is offering units of a product which are perfect substitutes for each other. There are no trade marks or brands so each supplier's product is identical to those of other suppliers.

4   Buyers and sellers must base their actions solely on price, that is, there is no preference shown for buying from or selling to any particular person. No consumer has a 'favourite' shop to which he remains loyal when the owner raises his price; neither do sellers have favourite clients to whom they give preferential prices or price reductions on large orders.

Since buyers are indifferent as to who sells the product, any slight fall in price in one place will attract all the buyers. Unless the seller raises his price to that asked elsewhere he will soon sell all his stock. Similarly any price rise deters buyers from purchasing from that supplier. Unless he reduces his price to that asked by other suppliers, his sales will be nil.

5   The commodity dealt in is easily transferable from one part of the market to another. This means that it can be transported cheaply and without difficulty over long distances. Easy movement means that changes in demand can be met promptly by suppliers.

When these conditions necessary for a perfect market are fulfilled, price differences for the same commodity are quickly eliminated so that one price tends to be established.

In practice these conditions are very difficult to achieve and it is doubtful whether any market under actual trading conditions fulfils all the requirements necessary for it to be judged 'perfect'.

However, some markets do approach fairly near to perfection. The markets for stocks and shares (stock exchanges) provide an example. Securities can be transported without difficulty; buyers and sellers on the various exchanges throughout the world can be contacted immediately by telephone and telex and so information is quickly and easily spread. Consequently price changes are rapidly circulated.

Another example is provided by some of the organised commodity markets in raw materials and foodstuffs. Where commodities such as wheat and cotton are capable of being graded into exactly defined classifications, then all units within the same grade can be considered as identical. There are many producers and many buyers and no single producer is large enough to influence the market price. As on a stock exchange, the buyers and sellers are professional dealers who have a sound knowledge of market conditions. They are aware of price changes in any part of the market and the result of their actions is the rapid elimination of price variations.

Imperfect markets
In contrast to the examples quoted above, most markets are to a lesser or greater extent imperfect.

The retail market, for example, is far from perfect. Few people have the time or take the time required to visit all shops to gain knowledge of where the lowest price is to be found. In the same way, retailers do not always know what other shopkeepers are charging for similar goods.

Moreover, buyers are influenced by considerations other than price when making purchases. Many people continue to buy at certain shops even though well aware that they are charging higher prices than their competitors. Customer loyalty may be created by such factors as service received in the past, a personal liking for the shopkeeper, or the fact that the dearer shop is more conveniently situated.

Furthermore, although two brands of goods offered for sale in a shop may be similar in composition, to the consumer they may seem to be quite different. This effect is achieved by advertising when it seeks to convince buyers that one particular brand is better than another. Competitive advertising increases the imperfection of a market by attempting to convince consumers that basically similar commodities are not perfect substitutes for each other. (Not all advertising produces this effect. Informative advertising which seeks to increase the knowledge of buyers and sellers helps to make the market more perfect.)

The markets for services are generally far from perfect. For example, the labour market tends to be narrow and local because labour is, generally, immobile. Workers are often reluctant, in spite of the attraction of a higher wage, to move to another locality or to a different country. Hence wage rates for the same kind of job may vary in different areas of the country. Again, where a consumer requires the personal services of doctors, solicitors, dressmakers, tailors and so on, both time and transport costs limit the extent to which either the consumer will travel to the producer or the producer will journey to the consumer. Hence prices charged for services of this kind are likely to vary between different areas.

The market for housing is imperfect because houses cannot be transported from the cheaper to the dearer part of the market. Consequently houses of a similar type may differ widely in price between one town and another, or even between different districts in the same town.

Finally, the market tends to be imperfect *(a)* where buyers and sellers are relatively few in number (as in the case of the market for antiques) and *(b)* where commodities cannot be graded easily into identical units (as in the case of flowers).

In reality, therefore, most markets are imperfect to some extent and different prices for essentially the same commodity exist in different parts of the market. Only where the market is composed of many professional dealers is it likely to approach perfection, that is, the establishment of a single price at any one time throughout the market.

Markets and competition

A market is made up of buyers who demand a commodity and sellers who wish to supply it. In the course of dealing, buyers *compete* with one another in demanding the commodity and sellers *compete* with each other in supplying it.

The state of competition in a market may be *(a)* perfect, *(b)* imperfect or *(c)* non-existent.

Perfect competition

Under perfectly competitive conditions, price is fixed entirely by the forces of demand and supply.

In order that there should be perfect competition, the main conditions necessary for a perfect market must exist, namely:

(a) many buyers and sellers;

(b) close contact between buyers and sellers;

(c) no discrimination in the form of favouritism or prejudice between buyers and sellers;

(d) a standardised commodity;

(e) easy transferability of the commodity.

In addition to these conditions, one further requirement is necessary for the existence of perfect competition, i.e.

(f) freedom of entry into the market. Buyers can switch from seller to seller, and the owners of the factors of production (land, labour, capital and enterprise) are able to move easily from one industry to another.

When perfect competition exists, the actions of individual buyers and sellers cannot have any effect on price. Consequently market price is fixed entirely by the forces of demand and supply, that is, the cumulative effects of the actions of buyers and sellers.

Hence a seller operating under perfect competition has to take the market price for granted. At this price a firm can sell any quantity it wishes. No cuts in price are required to boost sales, for however large a particular firm's output it is still only a small part of the total supply of the commodity.

Perfect competition is a theoretical model created by economists. It is not to be found in the real world but is used for comparison and contrast with actual conditions.

Perfect monopoly

Under perfect monopoly competition is non-existent and price can be influenced by the single seller.

Two conditions are necessary for perfect monopoly. They are

(a) a single producer

(b) no substitute available for the commodity produced.

Thus under monopoly the market is dominated by one seller who has complete control over the supply of the commodity. He cannot, however, control demand and so he cannot sell as much as he likes at any price he chooses. A monopolist is faced, therefore, with two choices. He can decide *either:*

(a) the quantity of the commodity he is prepared to sell – in which case the price will be determined by consumers competing with each other to buy the supply available; *or*

(b) the price at which his product is sold – in which case consumers will decide how much they wish to buy at that price.

Perfect monopoly is almost impossible to achieve in reality. It suggests a firm operating in the complete absence of competition, that is, without any substitutes for its product. This is unrealisitic because there are few commodities for which there is not some form of substitute. In any case, all goods are to some extent competitive because they compete one with the other for consumers' limited incomes. In this sense, therefore, all goods are, to some extent, substitutes for each other. and perfect monopoly could exist only if one firm controlled the supply of all the goods and services available.

Perfect competition and perfect monopoly

The main differences are as follows:

Perfect competition	*Perfect monopoly*
Large numbers of producers	A single producer
Identical units of product forming perfect substitutes for each other	No close substitute for the product
Producers have no control over price	Price can be influenced by the producer
Producers have no incentive to restrict supply	Producer may restrict output in order to raise price

Neither perfect competition or perfect monopoly are found in actual practice. However each serves a useful purpose by acting as opposite ends of a measuring rod with which to judge the competitive position of particular firms and industries.

Imperfect competition

Competition in the real world is not perfect for a number of reasons.

1 Commodities are not made up of identical units because of the use by producers of brands and trade marks.

Every producer has, to a greater or lesser extent, a monopoly of his own particular brand. For example, the proprietors of 'Green Meadow' butter are not monopolists as far as butter is concerned, but they are monopolists of Green Meadow butter. This is a commodity different from 'butter' and they are the sole supplier.

Brand advertising is employed to persuade consumers of the differences between, for example, Green Meadow butter and Brown Cow butter. If the advertising is successful, then the two brands will have different images in a consumer's mind and they will not be perfect substitutes for each other.

2 Suppliers may deliberately limit competition by joining together and sharing out the market, so that each enjoys a regional monopoly.

3 Entry to an industry may be difficult where a large capital outlay is needed to provide costly amounts of large-scale plant and machinery. Iron and steel, tyre manufacture, oil processing and vehicle manufacture are cases in point. This requirement limits the number of suppliers able to enter the industry and restricts competition.

4 New firms may be excluded from entering an industry by the conferment of patent rights on an invention. A person registering an invention at the Patents Office is given a monopoly of working it for a certain number of years. Copyright is somewhat similar and grants an owner the sole right to reproduce a literary or musical work. The purpose of these laws is to encourage research and invention and to give those who develop new ideas some opportunity to profit therefrom. Both patent right and copyright give rise, therefore, to imperfect competition.

5 Monopolies may be set up and controlled by the state for the provision of certain essential services such as gas, electricity and the postal services.

6 Monopoly is likely to develop if some natural product is found only in a restricted area. For example, a large proportion of the supply of gold and diamonds is concentrated in Africa. When this situation occurs, the market price can be kept high by restricting output.

Imperfect competition takes a number of different forms, ranging from near perfection to near monopoly, but two forms in particular should be noted. They are:

1 *Monopolistic competition* in which there is a large number of producers or sellers, but competition is made imperfect because the commodity is not standardised. The retail trade provides an example. A product is sold under a variety of brand names, and different retailers may stock different brands. Thus butter is not sold as such but in the form of 'Green Meadow' or 'Brown Cow' butter and so on.

2 *Oligopoly* is a form of imperfect competition where there are only a few sellers. (The word 'oligopoly' is derived from two Greek words meaning 'few' and 'to sell'). Each firm supplies a significant proportion of total output. If one firm cuts its prices, then its rivals are obliged to follow suit or they will lose business to the price-cutter. The constant danger of a price war may result in some kind of price agreement among the oligopolists. The dominant firm sets the price for the other sellers

and competition then takes the form of advertising, 'free gifts', and the like.

Examples of oligopoly are found in the soap and detergent industry where there are two giant producers; in the chocolate trade; and in the manufacture of cars.

Table 1 Types of Competition

Type	Producers	Commodity
Perfect competition	Many	Identical units
Imperfect competition		
Monopolistic	Many	Brands
Oligopolistic	Few	Brands
Monopoly	Single	Single

Advantages of monopoly and imperfect competition

1 Efficiency An industry which is under one control can be co-ordinated to make the best possible use of the capital equipment available. For example, with the nationalised industries, the duplication of gas, electricity or mail services can be avoided, whereas waste and inconvenience would result if competing suppliers each laid pipes or cables down every street or used scarce land to lay down railway tracks.

2 Savings in costs When separate firms come under one control, competitive advertising between them can be eliminated. Hence there is a saving in costs.

3 Planning Under perfect competition there is uncertainty regarding the future but the monopolist has no need to make guesses as to what are his competitors' future plans. Thus he is in a better position to plan long-term policy.

4 Standards A trade union or a professional association (which occupy near-monopoly positions as suppliers of labour) often lays down standards relating to the qualifications and professional conduct of its members. Thus before people can become, for example, accountants or solicitors, certain qualifications and experience must be gained. Similarly, trade unions prescribe periods of apprenticeship before admission to a craft. In effect, these measures maintain minimum standards of work and, in this sense, they are in the interests of consumers.

Disadvantages of monopoly and imperfect competition

1 Restriction of output The monopolist is not subject to competition from other producers and so he can restrict his output with the purpose of forcing up prices.

2 High prices   By restricting output, the monopolist causes prices to be higher than they would be under perfect competition.

3 Choice is limited   Under perfect competition, consumers' demand determines what goods and how much of each shall be produced. By restricting output the monopolist forces consumers to lose some of their freedom of choice.

4 Loss of efficiency   Competition forces firms to adopt any new production methods which will result in greater efficiency. A failure to do so results in the inefficient firm being forced out of business by its competitors. Under monopoly the supplier does not have to fear the competition of rivals and so the incentive efficiency is weakened. If new methods are costly to install, then the monopolist may be reluctant to make changes.

5 Waste of Resources   Product differentiation by means of branding divides up the potential market for the product into a number of artificial divisions. As a result, the advantages of large-scale production may not be available to individual firms. A firm selling its own brand may remain relatively small because the market is not large enough to justify production on a large scale.

Control of monopoly
When the state tries to maintain a private-enterprise economy, it has to prevent the exploitation of consumers by producers who possess some degree of monopoly power.

In Britain there are both public and private monopolies. The nationalised industries – gas, electricity, coal, etc., – are publicly owned monopolies. There are also large privately owned monopolies where one firm exercises a dominant influence in an industry. More common, perhaps, is an oligopoly situation where a small number of firms share the market. Most common of all is the existence of a large number of 'limited' monopolies, that is, suppliers of branded commodities.

Beginning in 1948, a number of Acts have been passed by Parliament which are designed to eliminate the disadvantages of monopolies. Legislation has not attempted to totally prohibit monopolies (in fact, they are approved when judged to be in the public interest). The aim has been to bring unfair competition under investigation and discussion for the purpose of assessing each case on its merits.

1 The Monopolies and Mergers Commission

The Commission had its origin in the Monopolies and Restrictive Practices Act 1948. Its function is to inquire into the existence of and effect on the public interest of monopolies in the supply of goods and services.

The Commission cannot begin inquiries under its own authority. It investigates matters referred to it by a government minister or the Director General of Fair Trading. (The Office of Fair Trading is a government agency which seeks to protect consumers against unfair practices). A reference to the Commission is not an automatic condemnation of the firms concerned. It is simply a request for a report on a particular situation in relation to the public interest. The reports made by the Commission indicate (a) whether its members consider the matter investigated to be against the public interest and (b) the action they consider to be appropriate.

The 'public interest' is rather a vague term but the Fair Trading Act (1973) attempted to give some guidance as to the meaning intended. It includes 'the maintenance and promotion of effective competition; the promotion of the interests of users of goods and services in respect of prices, quality, and variety; the promotion of technological innovation and reduction in costs; the encouragement of balanced distribution of industry and employment in the United Kingdom; and competitiveness in export markets'.

In making its investigations, the Commission has legal powers to secure evidence of witnesses and the production of documents, but it has no power to enforce its recommendations. Its reports are made to government ministers who lay these reports before Parliament and publish them. Any action to be taken upon the reports is the responsibility of the government.

A monopoly reference may be made where a firm either supplies or obtains at least one quarter of the particular goods and services in the United Kingdom.

Since its inception in 1949, the Commision has performed a valuable service in providing information on activities which work against the public interest. The Commission acts as a deterrent to monopolistic practices because the conduct of firms attempting them is likely to be subjected to an examination which is subsequently published. Few firms would wish to gain a reputation for acting against the public interest.

Generally, the reports of the Commission have shown that restraints on competition are very prevalent in British industry. The great majority of reports have criticised particular practices and have recommended changes by way of remedy. In most cases the industries concerned have given assurances that practices condemned by the Commission would be altered. Only rarely has the minister had to issue an order declaring any agreements or arrangements illegal. It should be noted that very few reports have found the monopoly situation in itself to be against the public interest.

2 The Restrictive Practices Court
The Restrictive Trade Practices Act 1956 established (a) a Registrar of Restrictive Trade Practices and (b) a Restrictive Practices Court.

A 'restrictive trading practice' is an action by firms to reduce competition. For example, producers may agree to supply only a restricted number of firms (called recognised dealers) on condition that those firms do not stock the products of any producer outside the group. The effect of the agreement is to restrict competition because new firms find difficulty in securing market outlets. Another example is a price agreement. Firms which are parties to the agreement fix common prices and agree not to compete on the basis of price.

The Act of 1956 declared that restrictive trade practices were against the public interest and any agreement between groups of firms to impose trading restrictions had to be notified to the Registrar. The latter is responsible for bringing agreements before the Court for consideration.

The Court was established as a division of the High Court and its purpose is to determine whether or not agreements are against the public interest. The judgement of the Court is binding on those concerned and so any agreement found to be undesirable must be immediately dissolved.

Many agreements by firms or trade associations were abandoned before investigation or replaced by agreements which were within the law. Of the registered agreements which were brought before the Court, the great majority have been judged to be against the public interest. The findings of the Court have been published whether or not agreements have been approved. The possibility of unfavourable publicity caused some agreements to be ended before investigation began.

The 1973 Fair Trading Act brought the registration of restrictive practices under the control of the Director General of Fair Trading. The Act also broadened the Registrar's powers to include service industries such as transport, finance and advertising.

The law relating to restrictive practices is now consolidated in the Restrictive Practices Act 1976.

3 Resale price maintenance

This term means that a manufacturer fixes the retail price of his products and insists that they are sold at that price. Hence the retailer's profit margin is determined by the manufacturer. The effect on retailing is to substitute competition in service for price competition.

In the past, resale price maintenance was enforced collectively by manufacturers cutting off supplies to retailers who had reduced the prices of the products of any one of them. In 1956 collective resale price maintenance was condemned as a restrictive practice and made illegal in the Restrictive Trade Practices Act. However, the Act permitted individual resale price maintenance so that an individual manufacturer could prosecute a retailer who broke an agreement to sell at a fixed price.

Eight years later, the Resale Prices Act (1964) declared individual resale price maintenance to be against the public interest and brought within the jurisdiction of the Restrictive Practices Court agreements to enforce individual resale price maintenance. At the same time, provision was made for suppliers to claim exemption for their products. Claims had to be registered with the Registrar and the Court decided in these cases whether or not resale price maintenance was against the public interest.

In fact, few cases were contested in Court and the great majority of resale price maintenance agreements were abandoned voluntarily.

The Resale Prices Act 1976 consolidates the law relating to resale price maintenance.

QUESTIONS

Write *short* answers to the following:

1 Define the term 'market'.
2 Give three examples of markets which have particular locations.
3 Give two examples of world-wide markets.
4 Briefly describe the markets for consumer goods.
5 What is the characteristic feature of a perfect market?
6 List the conditions necessary for the existence of a perfect market.
7 Name markets which approach perfection in the real world.
8 What is the characteristic feature of an imperfect market?
9 Explain briefly why the retail market is imperfect.

10 Give other examples of imperfect markets.
11 Explain the difference between 'markets' and 'competition'.
12 How is price determined under perfect competition?
13 List the conditions necessary for perfect competition.
14 What are the conditions necessary for perfect monopoly?
15 Perfect competition and monopoly are economists' 'models'. What are their uses?
16 Why cannot a monopolist sell as much as he likes at any price he chooses?
17 List the main differences between perfect competition and monopoly.
18 Explain briefly why competition in the real world is imperfect.
19 What is the principal feature of imperfect competition?
20 Name two forms of imperfect competition.
21 List the advantages of monopoly and imperfect competition.
22 Describe briefly the disadvantages of monopoly and imperfect competition.
23 How would you describe the aim of monopoly legislation in Britain?
24 How is the term 'monopoly' interpreted in making a reference to the Commission?
25 A criticism which has been made of the Monopolies Commission is that it 'lacks teeth'. What do you think the critic meant?
26 What is the effect of a 'restrictive trading practice'?
27 What are the functions of (a) the Registrar of Restrictive Trade Practices, (b) the Restrictive Practices Court?
28 What is the meaning of Resale Price Maintenance?
29 In what way does RPM restrict competition?
30 What action was taken by the Acts of (a) 1956 and (b) 1964 against RPM?

Write answers to the following:

1 What do economists mean by a market? What conditions in a market lead to (a) rising prices and (b) falling prices? (U/L)
2 Explain what is meant by (a) imperfect competition and (b) monopoly. .Why are pure monopolies very rare in practice? (JMB)
3 Various assumptions must be made for there to be perfect competition in an industry. Discuss what they are and whether they are at all realistic. (JMB)

4 What are monopolies? How does the government seek to control private monopolies? (U/L)

5 How would you distinguish between a perfect and an imperfect market? By what means and for what purpose may a manufacturer create an imperfect market for his products? (JMB)

6 'Monopoly is neither good nor bad. It entirely depends on the circumstances.' Discuss this statement. (JMB)

7 What is a monopoly? Are there any reasons why monopolies should be subject to state control? (Oxford)

8 Compare the functions of the Monopolies Commission, and the Restrictive Practices Court. (Oxford and Cambridge)

9 What are the conditions required for perfect competition and perfect monopoly? Why are these not fulfilled in practice? (JMB)

10 What is a market? How does it operate? Give examples. (RSA)

PRACTICAL WORK

1 Imagine that you wished to buy or sell the following:

(a) a second-hand car
(b) a country mansion and estate
(c) a caravan holiday
(d) a racing pigeon
(e) an antique piece of furniture

Find out which organisations or publications would supply you with market information.

2 Imagine you are a manufacturer of a consumer good. List the ways in which you could make the market more imperfect to your own advantage. State which of the methods you suggest are illegal.

3 Select a product, e.g. cosmetics, soap, toothpaste, petrol and examine (a) how a producer of a particular brand attempts to make it different from similar brands (e.g. distinctive wrapping, gift tokens), (b) how advertising is used to encourage sales of a particular brand (e.g. use of sex appeal, health qualities).

4 Make two lists showing (a) the advantages and (b) the disadvantages of branded goods.

5 Examine one of the Reports of the Monopolies Commission. You should find the Reports available in a public library. The range of commodities reported on includes electrical lamps, matches, tyres,

electrical car components and detergents. Notice how a Report provides a detailed account of the economic structure of the industry investigated.

4
Demand and supply

In the previous chapter on Markets, it was explained that the function of a market is to determine price. A price is fixed through the interaction of the forces of demand and supply. The purpose of this chapter is to examine demand and supply.

The meaning of demand
In economics the word 'demand' means an effective demand. A want or a need for something is not a demand unless it is backed by money and can be made effective. For example, a person's demand for a car is related to the money he has available to spend on it. He may *want* a car costing ten thousand pounds, but if he can afford only one thousand pounds, then his *demand* will be effective only at that price. In addition, a definition of demand must include the time period involved, i.e, a year, a month or a week – in order to provide some indication of the time required to sell the amount demanded at each price.

Generally, less of a commodity will be sold at a high price than at a low price. This is because, as price falls more and more people can make their wants effective, but as price rises, only those within the higher income groups can continue to afford to purchase. It is possible, therefore, to draw up a schedule for a particular commodity showing the quantities demanded per week (or other period of time) at different prices. For example, a demand schedule for coffee might be as follows:

Demand Schedule for Coffee

Price of coffee per kg (£)	Quantity demanded per week (kg)
1.60	1000
1.40	2000
1.10	5000
1.00	8000

Price of coffee per kg £	Quantity demanded per week (kg)
0.80	9600
0.60	14000
0.40	16000
0.20	20000

Thus, when coffee is £1.40 per kg, total weekly demand will be 2000 kg; when price falls to 60p per kg, weekly demand rises to 14 000 kg.

A demand schedule can be plotted in the form of a graph showing a demand curve (Fig. 2).

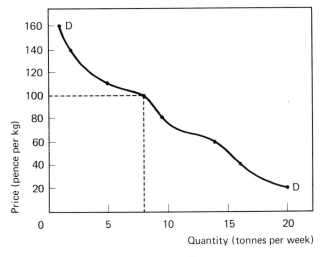

Fig. 2 A Demand Curve

It is possible to read off from the graph the quantity that will be sold at any particular price. For example, if the price was £1, then the quantity sold would be 8000 kg. The graph illustrates clearly that the demand for a commodity extends as price falls and contracts as price rises.

Elasticity of demand
The effect on demand of a price change is greater for some commodities than for others. The demand for some commoditites will change very little even though there is a considerable change in price. For example, most people buy as much bread as they need and a reduction in price will

not cause them to buy any more. Similarly, the price of bread would have to rise to a very high level indeed before there was any noticeable effect on demand. On the other hand, a fall in the price of 'luxury' items, such as new-season strawberries, usually results in a considerable expansion of demand while an increase in the price of strawberries may cause potential buyers to purchase other kinds of fruit. In this case, therefore, demand will vary considerably with changes in price.

When a relatively small change in the price of an article leads to a relatively large change (or 'stretching') in the quantity demanded, then demand is said to be *elastic*. Demand is *inelastic* when little or no change (or 'stretching') in demand results from a change in price, however marked is that change. Thus elasticity of demand is a term used to describe how sensitive the quantity demanded is to a change in price.

Measurement of elasticity

Elasticity of demand is calculated as follows:

$$\text{Elasticity of demand} = \frac{\text{Percentage change in the quantity demanded}}{\text{Percentage change in price}}$$

Where elasticity of demand is greater than one, demand is elastic (the higher the value, the more elastic the demand is said to be); where it is less than one, demand is inelastic; where it is equal to one, demand is said to have unit elasticity.

Elasticity of demand can be illustrated by reference to the demand schedule on page 35.

1 When price falls from £1.60 to £1.40, demand expands from 1000 to 2000 kg. Therefore

$$\text{Elasticity of demand} = \frac{\dfrac{1000}{1000} \times 100}{\dfrac{20}{160} \times 100} = \frac{100}{12.5} = 8$$

Thus at a price of £1.60 demand is *elastic* because it is greater than one and a fall in price causes a more than proportionate change in the quantity demanded.

2 When price falls from 40p to 20p, demand expands from 16 000 to 20 000 kg. Therefore

$$\frac{\dfrac{4000}{16000} \times 100}{\dfrac{20}{40} \times 100} = \frac{25}{50} = \frac{1}{2}$$

Thus at a price of 40p demand is *inelastic* because it is less than one and a fall in price causes a less than proportionate change in the quantity demanded.

3 When price falls from £1 to 80p, demand expands from 8000 to 9600 kg. Therefore

$$\text{Elasticity of demand} = \frac{\dfrac{1600}{8000} \times 100}{\dfrac{20}{100} \times 100} = \frac{20}{20} = 1$$

Thus at a price of £1, demand has *unit elasticity* because it is equal to one and a fall in price causes the same proportionate change in the quantity demanded.

Factors influencing elasticity of demand
A number of factors influence the elasticity of demand for a particular commodity at a certain price.

1 Substitutes
Where a close substitute is available within the same price range, demand for a commodity will tend to be elastic. If the seller of such a commodity raises his price, consumers will turn to the substitute. For example, the demand for coffee tends to be elastic because fairly close substitutes for it exist at approximately the same price. On the other hand, the demand for cigarettes is inelastic because there is no close substitute. The demand for a particular brand of cigarettes will be elastic, however, because there are a number of very close substitutes in the relevant price range.

2 Consumers' incomes
Generally, the higher a person's income,. the more inelastic will be his demand. Thus a £500 increase in the price of cars will not worry the rich man, though those less well off may be unable to buy.

Another important influence is the proportion of a consumer's income which is spent on the commodity. The smaller the proportion of total income spent on a commodity, the more inelastic will be the demand for it. For example, the price of a box of matches, or a tin of mustard or a daily newspaper might rise considerably before demand was noticeably affected.

3 Habit

Some commodities such as tobacco and alcoholic drink are habit-forming, and demand will tend to be inelastic over a fairly wide range of prices. In Britain the prices of both tobacco and alcoholic drink have been greatly increased by taxation, but demand has been relatively unaffected. Smoking and drinking seem to be acquired habits which consumers are reluctant to change. Hence demand tends to be inelastic.

4 Durability

Owners of durable consumer goods such as television sets, washing machines and cars replace them from time to time with new models. Thus a fall in the price of cars or television sets will encourage existing owners of these goods to buy new replacements as well as attracting new buyers. Thus the demand for durable goods tends to be elastic.

Practical importance of the concept of elasticity

1 Pricing policy

Whenever a firm considers changing the prices of its products, it has to take account of the effect of the proposed price change on consumers' spending. For example, a reduced selling price may result in a lower total revenue because demand is inelastic. The price reduction causes a less than proportionate change in the quantity demanded, as illustrated below:

Price	Quantity demanded	Total revenue
£1	1000	£1000
90p	1050	£ 945

On the other hand, if demand is elastic, then a reduction in price should result in a greater total revenue, because the price-cut causes a greater than proportionate change in the quantity demanded, as illustrated below:

Price	Quantity demanded	Total revenue
£1	1000	£1000
90p	1200	£1080

Similar considerations arise when a firm contemplates an increase in selling price. If demand is inelastic, consumers will continue to buy as much as before the price rise, and so revenue will increase. However, if demand is elastic, consumers' demand will fall and total revenue likewise.

2 Taxation

The government takes account of elasticity when considering changes in taxation. The main purpose of a tax on a commodity may be either (a) to raise its price in order to reduce consumers' demand or (b) to raise revenue.

The first aim is likely to be successful if demand for the commodity is elastic, but the second (and more usual) aim is best achieved by taxing goods which have an inelastic demand. For this reason, tobacco and alcohol are taxed heavily.

Changes in demand

Elasticity is used to measure changes in amounts demanded resulting from changes in price. When the quantity demanded varies with changes in price, it is said to extend or contract.

However, a *change in demand* (as opposed to a *change in the quantity demanded*) means that either more or less is now demanded at each price. These movements of demand are independent of price changes and not related to elasticity. They are caused by some change in conditions such as a change in population, a change in income, or a change in fashion or taste. These conditions are called the conditions of demand.

A change in demand is illustrated in Fig. 3. The state of demand before the change is shown by the curve DD. An increase in demand means that the curve D^1D^1 replaces the curve DD. The new demand curve shows that an increased quantity is demanded at any given price. For example, at price OP, the quantity demanded increases from OQ to OQ^1. If the new curve had been to the left of the original curve (DD), this would have shown a decrease in demand so that less was demanded at any given price. This is illustrated in Fig. 4. When demand falls from DD to D^1D^1, at price OP the quantity consumers wish to buy is reduced from OQ to OQ^1. It can be seen that a smaller quantity is now demanded at each price, thus:

1 Extensions or contractions of demand are caused by price changes and occur independently of changes in the conditions of demand. They are represented by movements up or down the same demand curve.

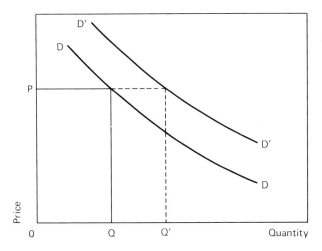

Fig. 3 An Increase in Demand

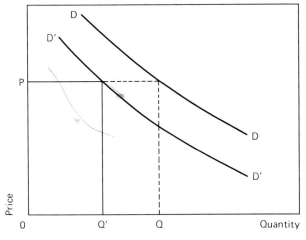

Fig. 4 A Decrease in Demand

2 Increases or decreases in demand are caused by changes in the conditions of demand. They are represented by a new demand curve.

The conditions of demand

There are many kinds of changes which can cause a shift of the demand curve to right or left. The following are the more important of these changes.

1 Changes in income

The more money a person has available for spending, the greater the total amount of goods and services that he can buy. Changes in income can take place when (a) wages, salaries, dividends or interest rise or fall, or (b) taxes on income are altered. Thus an increase in tax on personal incomes reduces the net amount earned and hence the amount available for spending.

Rising incomes will result in a general increase in demand for most goods and services of a 'luxury' nature such as cars and durable household goods. On the other hand there may be little effect on the demand for inexpensive foods such as bread and potatoes. Some commodities may actually suffer a decline in demand because additional income permits the purchase of more expensive alternatives. For example, while the demand for colour television has increased in the United Kingdom, the demand for black-and-white sets has declined.

A fall in incomes has opposite effects to those outlined above.

It is important to remember that 'incomes' refers to (a) *disposable* income, that is, money remaining after taxes have been deducted, and (b) *real* income, that is, income in terms of the goods and services it will buy.

2 A change in the size and distribution of the population

Four kinds of change may be noted.

(a) *An increase in total population* will result in a rising demand for houses, gas, electricity and water services and so on. If the increase in population is the result of large-scale immigration, then the introduction of new customs may change demand. Thus people from India and Pakistan who settled in Britain have increased the demand for foods such as curry in certain areas of the country.

(b) *Age distribution* An increased proportion of old people in the population will result in an increased demand for the assortment of goods and services that old people want. On the other hand, a higher proportion of young children brings an increased demand for goods required for children, such as cots, play-pens and toys. Similarly, an increased proportion of young persons brings a high demand for goods primarily required for teenagers.

(c) *Geographical distribution* As a result of changes in the regional distribution of the population some areas may experience a general increase in demand for goods and services while others suffer a decrease.

(d) *Sex distribution* An increase in the number of boys in the population will mean more items like football boots demanded; if there are more girls, then more dolls and so on.

3 Changes of taste or fashion

The demand for some commodities and services is very sensitive to changes in taste or fashion. Clothing, foods, beverages and entertainment are particularly affected. For example, changing tastes in entertainment have caused many cinemas to be converted to bingo halls. Alterations in clothing fashions cause frequent changes in demand. The influence of advertising is very important and a successful advertising campaign will cause changes in tastes and preferences.

4 Changes in the distribution of incomes

Inequality of incomes between different groups of people may be reduced (a) by taxation, (b) by subsidising basic foodstuffs and (c) by public expenditure in the form of child benefit allowances and social services. The effect of these measures is to raise the purchasing power of the poorer sections of the community. Thus there may be a decrease in demand for goods and services bought by people with large incomes (such as country estates and luxury yachts) and an increase in demand for cheaper luxuries (such as holidays abroad) which have been brought within the price range of those who could not afford them before.

5 Changes in prices of other commodities

The demand for one commodity may change as a result of a change in the price of some other commodity, but the type of change depends on the relationship between the commodities.

(a) *Joint demand* One commodity may be complementary to another, and so the two commodities may be jointly demanded, as for example, cars and petrol. A change in the price of one commodity will affect the demand for both. Thus a fall in the price of cars may result in more cars being bought and consequently an increase in the demand for petrol.

(b) *Substitutes* If one commodity is regarded as a substitute for another, then a rise in the price of one will cause a rise in demand for the other. For example, if the price of coffee is raised, then consumers may demand more tea. On the other hand a fall in the price of one may reduce the demand for the other. Thus a drop in rail fares may lead to a decline in the demand for long distance coach travel

(c) *Other commodities* Incomes are limited and so all goods and services are, to some extent competing for a person's income. If, for example, despite a general increase in the price of food, people continue to buy as much as before the price rise, then there will be less to spend on other goods and services. Hence demand for other things will fall.

The meaning of supply

In economics the word 'supply' means the quantity of a particular commodity which is offered for sale over a particular period of time at a certain price. Supply may not be the same as the total amount of a commodity that actually exists. Rather, it is that proportion of the entire stock which is made available for sale at a particular price.

Suppliers will offer a commodity for sale only if it is profitable to do so. Generally more will be supplied at a high price than at a low price. When price rises, producers already engaged in the industry will expand their output as far as possible. Producers in other industries who see the price of the commodity rising may decide that more profit is to be earned by switching from their current line of production. As a result of these actions there is an increase in the total supply. However, if price falls, those producers with the highest costs now find that they can no longer make a profit, and they discontinue production. Total supply falls as the market price falls. It is possible, therefore, to draw up a schedule for a particular commodity showing the quantities supplied per week (or other period of time) at different prices. For example, a supply schedule for coffee might be as follows:

Price of Coffee (£ per kg)	Quantity offered for sale per week (kg)
1.60	20 000
1.10	16 800
1.00	14 000
0.80	9 600
0.60	8 000
0.40	4 000
0.20	1 000

Thus at a supply price of £1, 14 000 kg of coffee will be supplied. From this supply schedule a supply curve can be drawn. It is possible to read off from the graph the quantity that will be put on the market at any particular price. For example, if the price was 60p then the quantity available for sale would be 8 000 kg. The graph in Fig. 5. illustrates clearly that the higher the price, the greater the quantity which will be supplied.

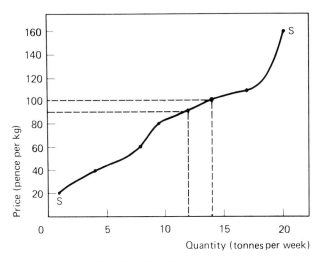

Fig. 5 A Supply Curve

Elasticity of supply

The readiness of suppliers of commodities to respond to changes in price depends on the nature of the commodity. For example, the supply of many manufactured commodities can be more easily adjusted to price changes than the supply of agricultural products such as meat and cereals. The supply of the latter may be subject to a long growing season, but the supply of factory-made articles can be altered relatively quickly by extra shifts or working short time, etc.

In the same way that elasticity of demand measures the response of demand to price changes so elasticity of supply measures the changes in the quantity supplied brought about by changes in price.

If a change of price causes a more than proportionate change in supply, then supply is *elastic*. On the other hand, if a change of price causes a less than proportionate change in supply, then supply is *inelastic*.

Measurement

Elasticity of supply is calculated as follows:

Elasticity of supply = $\dfrac{\text{Percentage change in the quantity supplied}}{\text{Percentage change in price}}$

Where the elasticity of supply is greater than one, supply is said to be elastic; where it is less than one, supply is inelastic; where it is equal to one, supply is said to have unit elasticity.

44

Elasticity of supply can be illustrated by reference to the supply schedule on page 43. For example, if as a result of a rise in price from £1 to £1.10 the quantity for sale increases from 14 000 to 16 800 then

$$\text{Elasticity of supply} = \frac{\dfrac{2800}{14000} \times 100}{\dfrac{10}{100} \times 100} = \frac{20}{10} = 2$$

Thus at a price of £1, supply is elastic because it is greater than one and a rise in price causes a more than proportionate change in the quantity supplied.

Factors influencing elasticity of supply
Elasticity of supply depends upon the ease with which producers can change output in response to alterations in price. The actual speed and degree of response to price changes is related to the following factors.

1   Time involved in the production process
Generally, the longer the period required to produce a commodity, the less responsive to price changes will it be. Additional supplies can be obtained almost immediately only where (a) stocks are carried in order to meet changes in demand, or (b) firms are producing below full capacity. In the latter case, it is possible to produce more by using existing plant and machinery more fully and either extending overtime working or taking on extra labour. These considerations apply mainly to manufactured goods. The supply of raw materials will, however, remain fairly inelastic because the output of crops, vegetable products and minerals cannot be increased quickly. For example, it takes approximately twelve months to increase the supply of wheat; a significant increase in the size of dairy and beef herds takes several years; rubber trees take up to seven years to reach maturity; while the supply of oak wood may remain inelastic for a hundred years.

2   Availability of factors of production
An increase in supply will be difficult if highly skilled labour is scarce or there is a shortage of machinery. When there is a shortage of labour skills, it may take several years for the number of workers to be increased, depending on the time needed for training.

3   Ease of entry into the market
Supply is increased by existing firms expanding output, and by new firms being drawn into the industry. Supply will be reduced by existing

firms contracting output, and by some firms leaving the industry. Thus elasticity may be influenced by the ease with which firms can enter or leave the market. Some examples of barriers are as follows: (a) entry may be controlled by professional associations or trade unions; (b) large amounts of expensive capital equipment may be required so that new firms find difficulty in obtaining sufficient finance.

Changes in supply

The amount of a commodity offered for sale at any given time may expand or contract in response to price changes. A change in output is represented by a movement along a particular supply schedule. For example, in Fig. 5 as a result of a rise in price from 90p to £1 the amount supplied increases from 12 000 to 14 000 kg. The degree to which a supplier can adjust the quantity offered for sale is described as elasticity of supply.

However, the supply of a commodity may alter although there has been no change in price. This is because the *conditions of supply* have altered. An *increase* in supply means that more is now supplied at all prices and as a result the whole supply curve moves to the right. This is shown in Fig. 6. A new supply curve (S^1S^1) has replaced the original

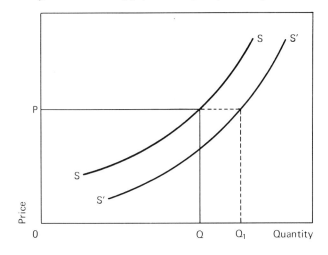

Fig. 6 An Increase in Supply

curve and at a price of *OP*, producers are now supplying the larger quantity OQ^1. A *decrease* in supply means that less is supplied at all prices and the supply curve moves to the left. This is demonstrated in Fig. 7. A

46

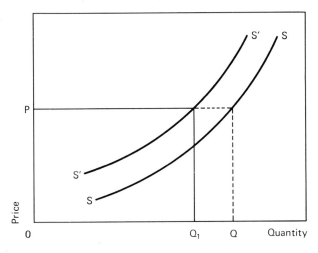

Fig. 7 A Decrease in Supply

new supply curve (S^1S^1) has replaced the original curve and at a price of
OP, producers are now supplying the smaller quantity OQ^1, thus:

1 Extensions or contractions of supply are caused by price changes
and occur independently of changes in the conditions of supply. They
are represented by movements up or down the same supply curve.

2 Increases or decreases in supply are caused by changes in the
conditions of supply. They are represented by a new supply curve.

Alterations in the conditions of supply may occur for the following
reasons.

1 *Changes in the average costs of production*
The cost of producing a commodity can change in two ways:
(*a*) the prices of the resources used may alter. For example a rise in
wages or in the cost of raw materials will increase production costs so
that firms will be willing to supply the same quantity of the commodity
only at a higher price level. Unless price does rise, the supply coming on
to the market will be reduced because those producers with relatively
high costs will no longer be able to make a profit. Thus they will be
forced out of business and total supply will fall.
(*b*) Technical improvements such as the invention of a new machine or
the development of a new method of production may make possible a
big expansion of output at lower cost and so increase supply.

2 *Changes in weather conditions*
The output of agricultural products cannot be estimated accurately

47

because of variations in weather conditions. For example, storms, floods, droughts and hurricanes will affect the supply of certain crops.

3 Taxation and subsidies

A tax levied by the government on commodities is likely to raise their prices. In effect, such a tax is equivalent to an increase in the cost of production and so will result, generally, in a decrease in supply at each price level. A tax reduction will have the reverse effect, and so will subsidies. If the government gives a subsidy to producers of certain commodities, then more will be produced at each price than would otherwise be the case.

4 Changes in the prices of other commodities

If the price of certain commodities increases so that their production becomes more profitable, then suppliers will divert resources to take advantage of these new opportunities. Thus the quantities supplied of the commodities whose prices remain unchanged will fall. For example, butter and cheese compete for a supply of milk. If the price of butter rises and makes butter-making more profitable than cheese-making, then the supply of cheese will fall.

Demand, supply and price

Each commodity or service has a demand schedule and a supply schedule. By comparing the two schedules it is possible to see that at one price the same quantity will be supplied as is demanded. Returning to the example of the demand for and supply of coffee and combining the market demand schedule (page 34-35) with the supply schedule for the industry (page 43) the following table can be compiled:

Price (£ per kg)	Quantity demanded per week (kg)	Quantity supplied per week (kg)
1.60	1000	20 000
1.40	2000	18 000
1.10	5000	16 800
1.00	8000	14 000
0.80	9600	9600
0.60	14 000	8000
0.40	16 000	4000
0.20	20 000	1000

From this table it can be seen that if the price of coffee is 80p per kg the same quantity is both demanded and supplied. At this price, therefore, demand and supply are said to be in equilibrium and 80p is the

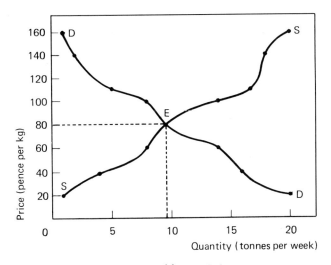

Fig. 8 Equilibrium Price

equilibrium or *market price*. This can be shown by plotting both demand and supply curves on the same graph. At the point where the two curves cut, with price 80p per kg, demand and supply are equal.

At prices higher than the equilibrium price, the quantity supplied exceeds the quantity demanded and competition between sellers will tend to force down the price; at prices lower than the equilibrium price the quantity demanded exceeds the quantity supplied and competition between buyers will tend to force up the price. Only at the equilibrium price is there no tendency for the price to change.

Changes in the conditions of demand and supply

In examining the effect of a change in one of the conditions of demand and supply, it is necessary to assume that *other things remain unchanged*. It is true that in the real world, other things rarely remain static, but the assumption is necessary if the effects of changing one demand or supply condition are to be analysed.

An increase in demand
Suppose there were an increase in the demand for coffee because, for example, a rise in the price of tea causes more people to drink coffee. The demand curve moves (as has already been noted) from D to $D^1 D^1$. The new demand curve ($D^1 D^1$) now cuts the supply curve at E^1, giving a new equilibrium price which is higher than the previous price. Sooner or later the effect of the price rise will be to increase the supply. *Thus an*

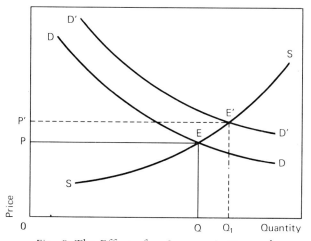

Fig. 9 The Effect of an Increase in Demand

increase in demand tends to increase price and also the quantity supplied. (Fig. 9)

A decrease in demand

Suppose there is a decrease in the demand for coffee because, for example, another drink became fashionable. The result is a fall both in price and in the quantity supplied (Fig. 10).

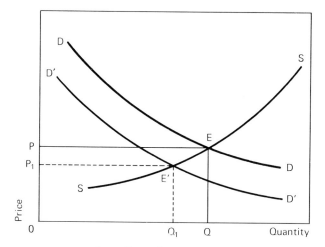

Fig. 10 The Effect of a Decrease in Demand

An increase in supply

Suppose there is an increase in the supply of coffee because, for example, the invention of a new harvesting machine reduces the costs of production. The supply curve moves to the right (as has already been noted) and indicates that a larger quantity will be supplied at each price. The change in supply causes price to fall from *OP* to *OP¹* and the quantity demanded increases from *OQ* to *OQ¹*. *Thus an increase in supply tends to lower price and to increase the quantity demanded* (Fig. 11).

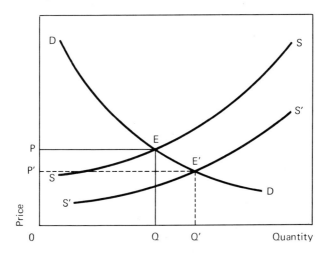

Fig. 11 The Effect of an Increase in Supply

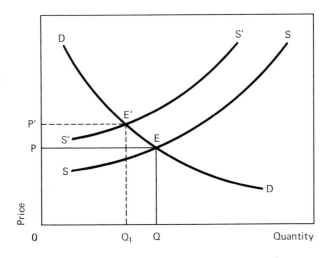

Fig. 12 The Effect of a Decrease in Supply

A decrease in supply

Suppose there is a decrease in the supply of coffee because, for example, the harvest has been poor. The result is a rise in price and a reduction in the quantity demanded (Fig. 12).

Applications of demand and supply analysis

Price fixing

Figure 13 shows the demand and supply curves for a commodity. The equilibrium price is OP and the quantity supplied is OQ. Suppose that the government imposes a maximum price of OP^1. At this price the quantity demanded will be OQ^2 but suppliers will offer for sale only the

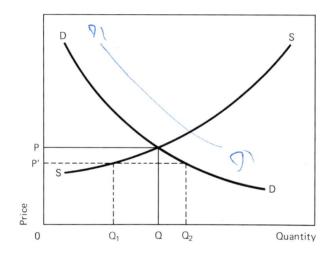

Fig. 13 Price Fixing

quantity OQ^1. Thus the quantity demanded at this controlled price exceeds the quantity supplied by Q^1Q^2. As a result, there would be shortages in the shops and some customers would have to go without. If a price is fixed in this way by the government then the fairest method of distribution is by a system of rationing.

Effect on supply of taxes on commodities

The demand and supply schedules for a certain commodity are as follows:

Price (£) per unit	Quantity demanded	Quantity supplied
7	180	400
6	220	340
5	260	260
4	280	220

The market price is £5.

Suppose that the government imposes a tax of £1 on each unit. A market price of £7 now represents a *supply* price of £6 (i.e. £6 plus £1 tax). Thus the supply schedule after the introduction of the £1 tax is as follows:

Price (£) per unit	Quantity supplied (after tax of £1 per unit)
7	340
6	260
5	220
4	180

A producer selling goods at a market price of £7 receives only £6 and at this supply price, he is prepared to offer only 340 units.

The schedules can be plotted on a graph as shown in Fig. 14.

The effect of the tax is to move the supply curve to the left, demonstrating that the quantity supplied falls.

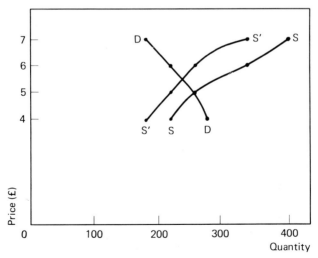

Fig. 14 Effect of a Commodity Tax

The price system

All goods and services are scarce in relation to the demand for them. The central problem of economics is how to share out these limited supplies among the people wanting them. In an economy based on private enterprise, this is done by the price system and the function of price is to balance demand with supply. The system of prices responds to changes in demand; allocates existing supplies; and directs the production of future ones.

In this chapter consideration has been given to the forces which determine prices. Below is a summary of the 'laws' of supply and demand. These 'laws' are generalisations based upon experience of everyday life. Each one must be qualified by the assumption that 'other things remain unchanged'.

1 Demand extends as price falls and contracts as price rises.

2 Supply extends as price rises and contracts as price falls.

3 If demand exceeds supply, then price will tend to rise.

4 If supply exceeds demand, then price will tend to fall.

5 Price tends to reach the level at which demand equals supply.

6 An increase in demand will tend to increase price and increase the quantity supplied.

7 A decrease in demand will tend to reduce price and reduce the quantity supplied.

8 An increase in supply will tend to reduce price and increase the quantity demanded.

9 A decrease in supply will tend to raise price and reduce the quantity demanded.

QUESTIONS

Write *short* answers to the following:

1 How is price determined?

2 Define the meaning of 'demand'.

3 What is a demand schedule?

4 Explain briefly the meaning of 'elastic' demand.

5 How is elasticity of demand calculated?

6 List the factors which influence elasticity of demand.

7 Describe briefly the practical importance of the concept of elasticity to (a) a firm and (b) the government.

8 How does a change in demand differ from a change in the quantity demanded?
9 List the principal causes of changes in demand.
10 Define the meaning of 'supply'.
11 What is a supply schedule?
12 What is the meaning of elasticity of supply?
13 How is elasticity of supply calculated?
14 List the factors which influence elasticity of supply.
15 How does a change in supply differ from a change in the quantity supplied?
16 List the main causes of changes in supply.
17 What is an equilibrium price?
18 What is likely to happen (a) when price is higher than the equilibrium, (b) when price is lower than the equilibrium?
19 Assuming other things remain unchanged, what is the effect of an increase in demand?
20 Assuming other factors remain unchanged what is the effect of an increase in supply?
21 Draw demand and supply curves for a commodity and show the effect of the government imposing a maximum price.
22

Price per unit (£)	Quantity supplied	Quantity demanded
10	150	100
9	120	120
8	110	140

(a) What is the equilibrium price?
(b) What is the effect on supply of a tax of £1 per unit?

Write answers to the following:

1 What is meant by *demand*? What factors determine the demand for new motor cars? (WJEC)
2 An advertisement states: 'There is no substitute for wool'. How would the introduction of a new substitute influence the market for wool? (U/L)
3 Explain and illustrate elasticity of supply. What determines the elasticity of supply of potatoes? (AEB)
4 What is meant by 'elasticity of demand'? What factors affect the elasticity of demand for tinned salmon in Britain? (AEB)

5 The following figures are extracted from a schedule of demand and supply:

Price (£)	Quantity demanded	Quantity supplied
9	10 500	8 500
10	10 000	10 000
11	9 500	11 500

(a) Calculate the *elasticity of demand* when price rises from £10 to £11.

(b) Calculate the *elasticity of supply* when price falls from £10 to £9.   (AEB)

6

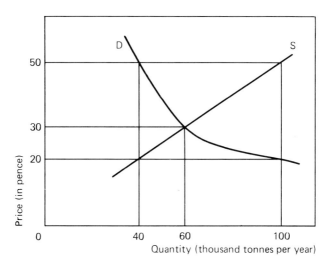

The diagram above shows a supply curve and a demand curve.

(a) What is the equilibrium price?

(b) Other things being equal, what is the effect on supply of a government regulation fixing a maximum price of 20p?   (AEB)

7

In the diagram on p. 57 D^1 and S^1 are the original demand and supply curves for a manufactured product, x.

Other things being equal, and starting from D^1, S^1 each time:

(a) Which curve could illustrate the effect on demand of a successful advertising campaign for x?

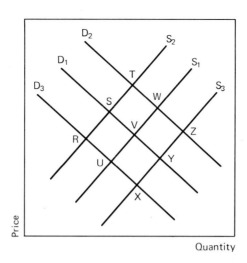

(b) Which curve could illustrate the effect on supply of a sharp increase in the price of raw materials used in the manufacture of 'x'?

(c) What would be the new equilibrium point if consumers' incomes increased while at the same time there was a fall in manufacturers' costs? (AEB)

8

Price (£) per unit	Quantity demanded	Quantity supplied
7	90	200
6	110	170
5	130	130
4	140	110

(a) What is the equilibrium price in the market to which the above demand and supply schedule refers?

(b) If the government imposes a tax of £1 on each unit, how many units would the suppliers be prepared to offer at a market price of £6 per unit? (AEB)

9 Would you expect the price of a good to rise when there is an increase in the demand for it? (Oxford)

10 Does an increase in the supply of a good necessarily produce a fall in its price? (Oxford)

11 What are the main factors determining the price of (a) beer and (b) cars? (Oxford)

12 What do you understand by 'the laws of supply and demand'? Have they any practical application?   (SCE)
13 What do you understand by supply? If demand remains unchanged, but the supply of fresh fish is increased, how will this affect its price? How would this change affect the demand for other foods?   (U/L West Africa)

PRACTICAL WORK

1 Make lists of conditions that affect (a) demand and (b) supply in addition to those listed in the chapter.
2 One factor which may change demand is the age distribution of the population. What goods and services are demanded most (a) by old people and (b) by young people in their teens?
3 On page 42 mention was made of joint demand. Draw up a list of pairs of commodities in joint demand, e.g. salt and pepper, bread and butter.

Part Three
Production

Goods and services are produced in order to satisfy people's wants. Production in a modern economy is based upon the principle of the division of labour, which has certain advantages with regard to costs and output. In addition it facilitates the organisation of production on a large scale.

The actual unit of production may take the form of the sole trader, the partnership, the joint-stock company or the co-operative society. All of these business units exist under private enterprise. Public enterprise exists when the state undertakes the production of goods and services and this is seen most clearly in the case of the nationalised industries.

Producers will organise production so as to reduce costs to the lowest possible level. Firms will be located, therefore, in certain places because cost advantages are to be gained there. Another major decision concerns the size of the firm. Changes in output bring changes in costs.

The aim of production is to satisfy consumers' wants and this is not achieved until the product is in the possession of the consumer. The work of distributing goods from factories and docks is undertaken by wholesalers and retailers – the final links in the chain of production.

5

Production

The meaning of production
Production means the manufacture of goods and the provision of services, the aim of which is to satisfy people's wants.

Many goods and services are valued in terms of money but some are not. For example, a housewife satisfies the wants of her family by cleaning the house and preparing meals, but as she is not usually paid a wage or salary for this work, it is difficult to place a monetary value on her services. Similarly the value of work which people do for themselves, such as home decorating or growing vegetables cannot be easily measured in terms of money. Nevertheless these services undoubtedly satisfy wants and must be included within the meaning of production.

However when economists calculate the money value of production, they are obliged to include only those goods and services which are paid for. Transactions which are not measurable because they are not priced have to be excluded from the calculation. Thus although a housewife is just as much a producer as her wage-earning husband, for practical purposes her services are disregarded when totalling up the value of production.

Since the aim of production is to satisfy the wants of people, it is not complete until a commodity has actually reached the person who wants it. Thus people such as wholesalers and retailers who work in distribution, and others who are engaged in the movement of goods through transport, finance and insurance, are all part of the process of production.

In everyday speech the word 'production' is often restricted to mean 'making something' and workers are described as 'productive' and 'non-productive'. The former include, for example, machine operators, bricklayers and carpenters because they create products. Non-productive workers include, for example, managers, advertisers, bankers and shopkeepers. These people are judged to be non-productive because they do not assist directly in manufacturing goods. Hence, it is important to remember that in economics, all work which is directed towards satisfying people's wants is considered to be productive.

The organisation of production

Most people earn their living by doing one particular job only. A man is an accountant, or a carpenter, or a welder, and he specializes in his particular occupation. Workers are specialists because industry is organised on the basis of the division of labour, that is, the production of an article is divided into a large number of different operations. Thus in the making of a pair of shoes, nearly one hundred distinct operations take place.

Workers are employed to perform one particular operation and they become specialists. A visit to a factory will help the reader to understand the system. As the product moves slowly along the assembly line each worker performs a particular task. When the product reaches the end of the line, it is ready for despatch to customers.

Historically, the system of division of labour began in the dividing-up of the day's work among the members of the family. It extended with the growth of towns to the specialisation of individual trades, and with the development of the factory system it came to mean the division of work into a number of processes, each being performed by a different worker. The development of foreign trade has enabled countries to specialise in producing certain commodities, so that division of labour has been established on an international scale.

The system of the division of labour has certain advantages and drawbacks.

Advantages of the division of labour

1 Specialisation leads to increased production. In the early days of the car industry one man built an entire engine. Henry Ford split the work into 84 operations, each of which was performed by a different man. The result was that the output of 84 men was trebled. When workers are specialists, repetition of the same operation increases speed and skill and more goods are produced.

•2 Various abilities can be used to the full. For example, it is far more beneficial for everyone when a brain surgeon can spend his time in the operating theatre rather than having to give part of the day to making his own clothes or repairing his car. It follows also that the simplification of tasks resulting from specialisation means that firms are able to find a proportion of suitable jobs for disabled persons.

3 When a process is broken down into a series of specialised and simplified tasks, a job takes a shorter time to learn, and workers feel less reluctant to train for a new job.

4 From an employer's point of view, the specialisation of processes means that output can be measured very accurately. If the assembly line is moving at a given speed then so many products will be coming off the line every hour. Thus a day's or a month's or a year's output can be estimated fairly accurately.

5 Finally, no time is lost between the performance of the various processes as would be the case if one man was responsible for making the complete product.

Disadvantages of the division of labour

Whilst production based on the specialisation of jobs has certain benefits, its adoption has some serious drawbacks.

1 A worker who performs the same task each day is, sooner or later, going to find his work monotonous. Firms have tried to combat

boredom in various ways, ranging from the provision of 'piped' music to the granting of a rest period during a part of every hour, but the problem remains.

On the other hand, the greater output of goods and services resulting from the specialisation of jobs has raised the standard of living and enabled workers to enjoy far more leisure than their fathers and grandfathers enjoyed. As production is further expanded, the working week is likely to get even shorter and, probably, annual holidays will be longer.

2 The goods produced under a system of specialisation are usually standardised products. This is evident in the design of cars, furniture, and houses. Whether or not standardisation is a disadvantage is really a matter of opinion. After all, a consumer can pay extra for a house or a car built to his particular requirements.

3 A more important disadvantage is that instability of employment may result from the application of the division of labour. Workers in one industry are very often dependent on those before them in the process of production. Thus a prolonged stoppage in the coal or steel industries may throw thousands of other workers out of work because supplies of raw materials stop. The same is true within an industry. Interdependence in car manufacture is such that the decision of a handful of workers to strike can put thousands of men out of work within hours.

Limitations to the division of labour

The extent to which the principle of specialisation can be applied is dependent upon two factors, namely (a) a suitable system of exchange and (b) the extent of the market.

People will specialise only if they can easily exchange the goods they make or the service they provide for goods and services made by other people. In early times exchange took place by barter, i.e. the exchange of goods for goods. However, barter is a clumsy, time-wasting and often quarrelsome method of exchange. Its drawbacks were overcome by the introduction of money as a medium of exchange (see page 187). In a modern economy the use of money permits people to exchange their labour for a wage which in turn is exchanged for a wide range of goods and services. Thus a system of production based on the specialisation of jobs is dependent on an efficient system of exchange.

A second factor which determines the extent to which division of labour can be applied is the market for the particular product.

The greatest degree of specialisation will occur in the production of those commodities for which there is a large demand. For this reason, some chain stores are able to grade clothes into a few standard sizes in order to mass-produce them. Hence the manufacture of the garments can be split into a large number of separate operations each performed by a different employee. On the other hand where demand is not large enough to justify the standardisation and mass production of goods, the division of labour cannot be applied. For example, a tailor may make clothes to the individual requirements of his customers but he cannot grade them to a few standard sizes. Hence division of labour cannot be applied because an individually tailored garment is not a standard article for which there is a wide demand.

The extent of the market depends not only upon the size of demand but also upon the existence of good transport facilities for the distribution of goods from producers to consumers. Good transport facilities make possible the sale of more goods. The distribution to consumers of the greatly increased output of manufactured goods during the time of the Industrial Revolution was made possible by the construction of roads, canals and railways. Developments in sea and air transport created world markets and made possible the division of labour on an international scale. Countries specialise in producing a few only of the things that they could produce and exchange their surplus requirements for the surpluses of goods produced by other countries.

Changes in input and output

An entrepreneur combines the factors of production – land, labour and capital – in order to obtain the maximum advantage from their use.

The relationship between the input of factors of production and the consequent returns (output) is expressed as follows: *if the quantity of a factor of production, used in combination with a fixed quantity of another factor, is continually increased, output per unit of the variable factor increases, reaches a maximum and then declines.*

This law which is based on physical facts, is derived from observation and experience. Its operation is inevitable in all branches of economic activity and two examples will make this clear.

1 In agriculture the fixed factor is the plot of land and an increase in cultivation as the result of the use of more labour or of more capital (e.g. machinery, fertilisers or drainage) results, after a certain point, in a less than proportionate increase in the quantity of produce grown. If, for example, the number of men working is continuously increased, then ultimately the increase in total output due to each man will diminish, if for no other reason than that they get in one another's way.

The results obtained by increasing the amount of labour employed in growing barley on a fixed area of land are represented in Table 2. The figures in this hypothetical example are of no importance – the significance lies in the relationships between them. Column *1* shows the variations in the numbers of men employed and column *2* indicates the total outputs resulting from the employment of these different numbers of men. Column *3* shows the average output per man and is obtained by dividing total output by the labour force.

As the number of men is increased from one to eight, the total output continues to increase but this is not true of average output, which rises to a maximum and then starts to fall. This movement is seen clearly in Fig. 15.

Table 2   The Law of Eventually
Diminishing Returns

1 Labour force	*2* Total output (tonnes)	*3* Average output (tonnes)
1	60	60
2	140·	70
3	240	80
4	440	110
5	650	130
6	840	140
7	910	130
8	960	120

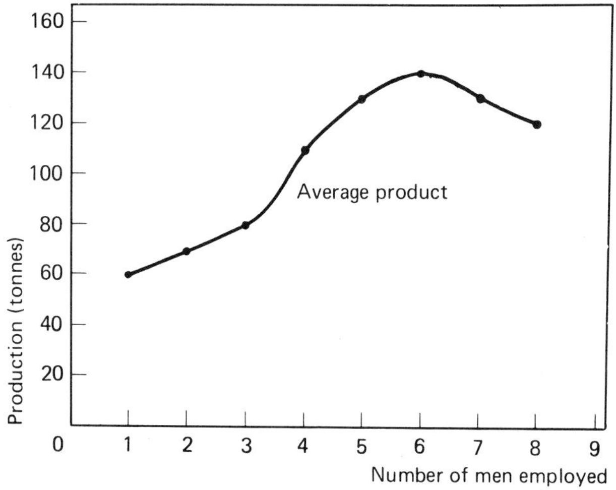

Fig. 15 The Law of Eventually Diminishing Returns

It is assumed that the workers employed are exactly alike as regards the quantity and quality of their work. Hence changes in average output are due to the changing proportions between the fixed factor (land) and the variable factor (labour).

Up to the point where six men are employed, average output increases. Up to this point the fixed factor has been under-utilised, but now that there is maximum average output per man employed the situation of maximum returns to the variable factor has been reached. As more men are added the total output still rises but by a smaller and smaller amount. The fixed factor is now being overworked in combination with the variable factor.

2   The same effect can be seen if in a factory of given size and equipment the number of workers is increased from zero. A certain minimum number will have to be employed to provide essential services such as power, heat and ventilation before machinery can be operated. Then, as further workers are added and the process of manufacture can begin, output per head of all employed will increase. Finally, if numbers are continually increased it will not be possible to keep everyone working at full capacity. There will not be enough tools and equipment to go round and sharing them will cause time to be wasted. Inevitably, output per head will decrease.

Whereas in agriculture, land is the constant factor used, in manufacturing, the fixed factor may be labour, capital or enterprise. Nevertheless, the returns to additional applications of the variable factors will ultimately diminish. If this principle did not operate in industry, all the shoes, for example, required by a community could be produced by one firm by increasing either the labour force or the capital equipment. It is, of course, no more possible to do this than it is to supply all the crops required from a single plot of land, because there is a limit to the output of one firm.

Thus production may be carried on under conditions of *increasing* returns, *constant* returns, or *diminishing* returns. Looked at in another way it can be said that input of factor per unit of output diminishes, reaches a minimum and then increases. From whichever viewpoint, it is clear that there comes a point when a business can increase output only at a greater cost per unit of output.

The costs of production
The total costs of a business firm consist of total fixed costs plus total variable costs.

Fixed costs are those costs which do not vary over a fairly considerable range of output. For example, once a factory has been built and machines have been installed, their cost will remain constant whether the firm is working at full capacity or only one quarter capacity. Even if the firm sells nothing at all, these fixed costs still have to be met. Similarly a retailer who pays £80 per week as rent for shop premises will have to pay the £80 regardless of the amount of the weekly takings. If he employs a salaried assistant the amount of the salary will have to be paid however many customers come into the shop. Other examples of fixed costs are rates, cleaning, interest payments on loans, and depreciation. The term depreciation requires a brief explanation. Every year it is necessary to set aside money for the replacement of a firm's assets, mainly plant and machinery. The need for replacement is largely due to (a) the wearing out of machinery and plant through use in production and (b) obsolescence, i.e. becoming out of date. Capital loses value or depreciates for both of these reasons. When firms set aside a fixed sum each year to cover depreciation, this money is a fixed cost.

Variable costs are those expenses of production which are directly related to output. For example, the cost of raw materials, charges for fuel and power and the wages bill all change when the volume of output changes. Thus if more goods are produced, these costs will also rise. On the other hand if fewer goods are produced, these expenses will decline.

Average cost is a term which refers to the average cost of producing each unit of output. It consists of average fixed costs and average variable costs. When output is small, average cost will be high because the fixed costs will be spread over a smaller number of units of production. As output rises, average cost will fall because the fixed costs are being distributed over a larger output. The fall will continue as long as there are increasing returns to the variable factors of production. When the optimum (or 'best') output is reached, average cost is at a minimum. Beyond that optimum, diminishing returns and increasing costs will cause average costs to begin to rise.

Marginal cost is the change in total costs when output is increased or decreased by one unit. Since total fixed costs are already incurred and do not alter, marginal costs will represent only those additional variable costs which contribute to changes in output. When marginal cost is below average cost, average cost is falling; when marginal cost is above average cost, average cost is rising. At the optimum output, marginal and average costs are equal.

The relationship between total, marginal and average costs is illustrated by Table 3.

Table 3 Cost Relationships

Output	Fixed costs (£)	Variable costs (£)	Total costs (£)	Average costs (£)	Marginal costs (£)
10	100	20	120	12	–
20	100	120	220	11	10
30	100	200	300	10	8
40	100	260	360	9	6
50	100	300	400	8	4
60	100	320	420	7	2
70	100	390	490	7	7
80	100	460	560	7	7
90	100	620	720	8	16

QUESTIONS

Write *short* answers to the following:

1 What is the meaning of 'production' in economics?
2 Which goods and services are excluded from a measurement of production?
3 Why are these goods and services excluded?
4 Why are people who work in distribution classed as producers?
5 What does the division of labour mean?
6 List the advantages of specialisation.
7 Give three disadvantages of the division of labour.
8 Name two factors which determine the extent of the application of the division of labour.
9 Define the term 'fixed costs'.
10 Give three examples of fixed costs.
11 Why do firms set aside a fixed sum each year to cover depreciation?
12 Give three examples of variable costs.
13 Define the term 'average cost'.
14 Why is average cost relatively high when output is small?
15 Why does average cost fall as output rises?
16 What is marginal cost?

Write answers to the following:

1 'Division of labour is determined by the extent of the market.' With the aid of examples explain this statement. (WJEC)

2 Explain what is meant when it is said that most of the advantages of division of labour are economic while most of the disadvantages are personal and social. (JMB)

3 What is meant by division of labour? Why is it so important in a large-scale enterprise? (Cambridge)

4 What is meant by 'mass production'? Why is mass production used in the manufacture of cars but not in their repair? (Cambridge)

5 What economic advantages are offered by the division of labour? (Oxford)

6 What do you understand by 'the division of labour'? Show how its successful application depends upon (a) an efficient transport system and (b) money. (Oxford)

7 How does specialisation in production involve risks to (a) an individual worker (b) an individual employer, and (c) a geographical region? (U/L)

8 How does the statement 'A doctor driven by a chauffeur in a mass-produced car' illustrate the division of labour? What different aspects of the division of labour does each part of the statement imply? (U/L)

9 The following information refers to the costs and output of the production department in a manufacturing firm during a particular five-day working week:

Number of workers employed	50
Number of articles produced	10 000
Weekly wages of each worker	£20
Rent, rates, depreciation, etc.	£130
Power	£100
Raw materials	£500

(a) Calculate the variable costs incurred during the week.
(b) Calculate the average daily output per worker. (AEB)

10 The following figures refer to output and total cost of a manufactured commodity:

Output	Total cost (£)
0	100
1	120

Output	Total cost (£)
2	134
3	144
4	152

(*a*) What are the fixed costs?

(*b*) (i) What is average cost when total cost is £152? (ii) What is the marginal cost of the third unit? (AEB)

11 In what way does the cost to a firm of producing a good, per unit of output, vary with the amount it is producing? (Oxford)

12 What is the difference between 'fixed' and 'variable' costs? Make use of this distinction to analyse the cost of running a car. (Oxford)

13 When is division of labour uneconomic? Give examples. (RSA)

PRACTICAL WORK

1 Divide the following list into (*a*) fixed costs and (*b*) variable costs.

Rent of factory	Pensions to former employees
Fuel bills	Raw materials
Postage	Repairs to buildings
Transport charges	Interest on debenture
Rates	Wage of weekly workers

2 (*a*) Calculate the average output for the conditions given.

Labour force	Total output (tonnes)	Average output (tonnes)
4	100	
5	130	
6	162	
7	196	
8	228	
9	252	
10	270	
11	286	
12	288	

(*b*) Using the data above draw curves on a graph to show total output and average output.

3 (a) Complete the table below.

Output	Fixed costs (£)	Variable costs (£)	Total costs (£)	Average costs (£)	Marginal costs (£)
1	100	15	115	115	—
2	100	27	127	63.5	12
3	100	37	137	45.6	10
4	100	46	146	36.5	9
5	100	53	153	30.0	7
6	100	63	163	27.1	10
7	100	75	175	25.0	12
8	100	90	190	25.7	15

(b) Using the data above draw curves on a graph to show (i) total costs and (ii) average costs.

6

Business Firms
Private Enterprise

In Britain goods and services are produced by undertakings which are either privately or publicly owned. Publicly owned undertakings are operated by the state or by local authorities.

In this chapter the various forms of private ownership are described. They are: the sole proprietor; partnership; the joint-stock company; and the co-operative society. Each form of organisation has particular characteristics of ownership, control, raising of capital and disposal of profits.

1 The sole proprietor

The trader in business on his own is known as a sole trader or proprietor. This is the simplest and most common form of business in Britain. A large proportion of shops and service trades (such as plumbers, electricians and shoe repairers) or establishments (such as cafes and launderettes) are under the control of sole proprietors.

The term 'sole proprietor' does not mean that no one else works in the business except the owner. Many sole proprietors employ assistants or apprentices. Rather the term means that a single person is responsible for raising the capital and controlling the business. He takes all the profits resulting from his work or bears the responsibility if his business suffers a loss.

Capital

When a person begins his own business, he must estimate how much capital will be necessary to obtain premises, equipment and a stock of goods. Having arrived at a figure he must consider ways of raising money.

The sole proprietor's own savings provide the most satisfactory form of capital. The use of his own savings reduces the sole proprietor's costs because interest payments will have to be paid on borrowed money.

Personal savings may be supplemented by loans of money from friends or relatives; from a bank; or from a building society if the proprietor intends to buy premises. Finally, it may be possible to obtain credit from suppliers. The purchase of stock on credit is similar to obtaining a loan from the supplier for the length of the period of credit.

Once a sole proprietor has established himself, he may develop his business by ploughing back much of the profit made each year, thereby increasing his capital out of savings.

Advantages of the sole proprietor

1   A man who is independent is likely to put more effort into his work than someone working for others in return for a wage or salary. Self-interest is a powerful driving force and the reward for effort belongs wholly to the owner.

2   A small business can be effectively managed by the owner. He has no need to consult partners or directors and decisions can be made and put speedily into effect.

3   The sole proprietor is in personal contact with his customers. Consequently he is in a very good position to appreciate their requirements and also to assess whether or not they are credit-worthy. In addition, he is able to gain custom by his own personality and reputation.

4   In a small business a more personal relationship is possible between the proprietor and his employees. In the larger forms of business organisation a lack of understanding frequently exists between management and workers. The close relationship between employer and employee in a sole trader's business enables each of them to better understand the other's point of view.

Disadvantages of the sole proprietor

1   The proprietor is personally liable for any debts incurred by the business. This liability extends to the full extent of his private possessions so that he might even have to sell his house and furniture.

2   Control of the business by one person may hinder the development of the firm. A man might be, for example, a first-class carpenter, but he may lack managerial ability, or facility in dealing with accounts, and the business may not prosper because of the owner's deficiencies. The success or failure of a sole proprietorship depends on one man, whereas in the case of the larger organisations the personal element is not so evident.

3   Scarcity of capital may limit the growth of the business.

Sole proprietorships are suitable for a person with limited capital. When a sole trader's business increases and prospers, he may decide the time has arrived to form a partnership or a private company.

2 Partnerships
There are two types of partnership. They are:

An Ordinary Partnership
Ordinary Partnerships are governed by the Partnership Act of 1890 and to some extent by the Companies Act 1967.

The Limited Partnership
Under the Limited Partnership Act of 1907, a limited partner's liability for the debts of the firm is restricted to the amount of capital he has invested in the business. However, in a limited partnership there must be at least one ordinary partner whose liability is unlimited. This type of partnership is quite rare.

Organisation
A partnership is a group of people who carry on business with the purpose of making a profit. Generally the number of partners may vary from a minimum of two to a maximum of twenty. However, the Companies Act 1967 created an exception to these numbers and unlimited membership is available to ordinary partnerships of solicitors, accountants, stockbrokers and stockjobbers. Unlimited membership is available to limited partnerships of surveyors, auctioneers, valuers and estate agents.

People who form themselves into a partnership should draw up a Deed of Partnership Agreement, which sets out in written form the terms and conditions of the partnership. The Deed should include such items as

(a) the names of the partners
(b) the amount of capital contributed by each
(c) the arrangements for sharing of profits or losses.

The Deed is not a legal necessity when a partnership is formed but it has the advantage of being a written agreement should a dispute over the terms of the partnership arise. If there is no Deed of Partnership Agreement, then the rights and duties of the partners are determined by the Partnership Act 1890. For example, if there is no written agreement as to sharing profits or losses, the Act lays down that they shall be shared equally.

All the partners have equal powers and responsibilities. For example:

each partner may bind the firm in any contract made on behalf of the partnership;

each partner is entitled to take an active part in the management of the firm;

all the partners are together liable for the debts of the firm to the full extent of their private possessions.

Advantages of partnerships

1   The formation of a partnership increases the capital available to an existing sole proprietorship so that the business may be expanded.

2   The management of the business can be improved by introducing partners with specialist skills. For example, a qualified accountant could be admitted as a partner in order to take charge of the financial side of the business.

3   The admission of new partners may introduce new ideas and thinking into the business, so that the efficiency of the firm is increased.

4   Business decisions can be taken rapidly because partners are working in the business together, and a close and personal contact is possible with both customers and employees.

Disadvantages of partnerships

Partnerships suffer from a number of drawbacks compared with the larger forms of business organisation.

1   Like sole traders, ordinary partnerships are subject to unlimited liability so that all the partners are responsible for the debts of the firm. However, under a limited partnership, only one partner need take this risk, but in return for having their liability limited to capital invested, limited partners lose the right to take part in the management of the business.

2   Any partner may bind the firm in trading contracts and in this way commit the other partners. Thus a partner with faulty business judgement or low integrity could ruin the business by his unwise actions.

3   Like the sole proprietorship this type of business lacks continuity of existence. A partnership is automatically dissolved on the death or bankrupty of a partner. Similarly by giving notice to the others, a partner can dissolve the partnership at any time.

4   Except for firms of accountants, solicitors, stockbrokers and stockjobbers (see the earlier section on Organisation of a Partnership, page 73) the number of partners is limited to twenty. The amount of capital subscribed by even twenty partners may not allow the business to expand to its fullest extent.

5   Finally, the consent of all the partners is required for admission of a new partner, and individual obstinacy could very well hinder the development of the partnership by refusing the admission of very desirable 'new blood'.

Scope of partnerships
Partnerships exist in undertakings where professional skill is of greater importance than the amount of capital. In many kinds of manufacturing, expensive equipment is necessary so that the partnership is not a suitable type of organisation. However, many professional people such as doctors, dentists and solicitors, work in partnerships. People who sell services require relatively little capital compared to those who undertake the production of goods. Some professional people work in partnerships because rules made by their governing bodies do not allow members to form limited companies.

3 Limited companies

The limited company is a very popular form of business organisation in this country. It can be described as a group of persons who have joined together in order to carry out some kind of business enterprise, the actual management of the firm being in the hands of a director or board of directors. The capital of the company is divided into shares, normally £1 shares, and profits are divided among the shareholders in proportion to the number of shares held. Sometimes a limited company is called a 'joint-stock company', indicating that a number of people have contributed to a common stock of capital to be used for a business purpose. The word 'limited' means that each member's liability for the debts of the business is limited to the amount of his shares. There are two kinds of limited companies, namely, private and public.

Private companies

Organisation
1   A private company can be set up with a minimum of two members. The maximum number is fifty (this does not include members who are in the employment of the company).
2   Each shareholder has limited liability, that is, if the company fails the shareholders are responsible for the debts only up to the amount they hold in shares.
3   This type of company cannot invite the public to subscribe capital.
4   Shares cannot be transferred without the consent of the other

shareholders. The directors have power to disapprove any proposed transfer of shares. As a result of this rule, shares in private companies cannot be bought or sold on a stock exchange.

5 Despite the term 'private' this type of company has to send a complete set of its accounts each year to the Registrar of Companies.

Uses

The limit of fifty shareholders makes this type of company unsuitable for an undertaking requiring large amounts of capital. The owners of small or medium-sized 'family' businesses often form themselves into a private company. As the minimum number of members is two, a husband and wife can be the two shareholders. Only one director need be appointed. Clearly, a private company with limited liability for each shareholder has distinct advantages over a partnership.

Public companies

Organisation

1 At least seven persons are required to form a public company and there is no upper limit to the number of members. The number of shareholders may be very large indeed and as it would be impossible for them all to manage the business, a committee or board of directors is elected to carry out this task. Thus, (as is the case with a private company) the control of the public company is delegated to directors. Similarly, a meeting of shareholders must be called at least once a year and at the meeting the accounts of the company must be submitted to the shareholders for their approval. Shareholders can criticise the directors and vote on proposals put forward for discussion.

2 Each shareholder has limited liability.

3 Shares are freely transferable and can be bought and sold on a stock exchange.

4 An appeal can be made to the public to subscribe capital.

5 A copy of the accounts must be sent every year to the Registrar of Companies.

Formation of a limited company

People who wish to form a company must carry out certain legal requirements.

In the first place, the name, objects, amount of the authorised capital, and certain other information must be stated in the *memorandum of association*. This is a document which is sent to the Registrar of Companies. There must be at least two subscribers for a private company and at least seven for a public company. The memorandum forms the legal framework or charter of the company.

In addition to the memorandum, the Registrar requires a statement of the rules for the internal arrangement and the management of the company. These are laid down in the *articles of association,* which deal with such matters as procedure in calling meetings of shareholders, procedure for the division of profits and so on.

When the memorandum and articles have been inspected by the Registrar, he will issue a *certificate of incorporation* which gives the company a legal existence. A private company can now commence business, but a public company still has to obtain its capital from the public before it can start business.

The document inviting the public to subscribe capital in the form of shares is known as the *prospectus.* It gives essential facts on which investors may judge the prospects of the company. In order to safeguard investors against false or extravagant claims about the company, a copy of the prospectus has to be sent to the Registrar.

The prospectus must state the minumum amount of capital that is necessary to enable the company to start business. When the Registrar is satisfied that this minimum amount of capital has been subscribed he will isssue a *trading certificate* entitling the company to commence business.

The capital of a public company
Capital may be classified as either *share capital* or *loan capital.*

Share capital
When a company is formed it can issue shares up to the amount written into the memorandum of association. This figure is known as its authorised capital (authorised capital is also known as nominal capital or as registered capital). The directors may, however, decide to issue only part of the authorised capital so that a reserve is available for issue at some future date. The part of the authorised capital for which the company invites public subscription is known as the issued capital.

If the whole of the authorised capital has been issued, and it is desired to increase the amount of authorised capital, then application may be made to the Registrar of Companies for permission to do so.

The capital of a public company is divided into two main kinds of shares, namely, preference and ordinary shares.

Preference shares
This type of share has first claim on any profits and carries a fixed rate of dividend (such as or 7 or 8 per cent), which has to be fully paid before

any dividend is paid on other types of shares. If the company goes into liquidation, preference shares receive repayment of their capital before other shareholders. As preference shareholders run less risk they have less favourable voting rights than other shareholders.

Most issues of preference shares are cumulative, which means that if there are insufficient profits in any year to pay the preference dividend it is carried forward or 'accumulated' until the company is able to pay.

There are also participating preference shares, which receive not only a fixed dividend but in addition, if profits are sufficient, receive an additional dividend after payment has been made to subordinate classes of shares.

Most shares cannot be bought back by the company, so that a shareholder who wishes to dispose of his holding must sell through a broker on a stock exchange. Redeemable preference shares are the only type of shares that can be re-purchased by the company. However, they are repaid when the company decides to do so, and not when shareholders want them to be.

The various types of preference shares may be combined in one type; for example, cumulative participating redeemable preference shares.

Ordinary shares

These shares are often referred to as 'equities'. Usually they do not carry a fixed rate of dividend and their holders are paid dividends only after the claims of preference shareholders have been met. Ordinary shares are also last in line for return of the money invested if the company goes into liquidation. If profits are good then the ordinary share dividend will be high. On the other hand, in bad years the dividend may be low or even non-existent. Holders of ordinary shares, therefore, bear most of the risk and in consequence have superior voting rights in the company.

A third type of share is more risky still. *Deferred shares* (or founder's or manager's shares) do not receive any dividend until all other types of shares have been paid a certain amount first. Deferred shares are taken up by the promoters of a company because of the valuable voting rights attaching to them. This class of share is comparatively rare.

Methods of issuing shares

There are four ways in which a company can issue shares.

1   The first is termed an *offer for sale*. The issue of shares is purchased by a merchant bank or a stockbroker and then all or part is offered to the public at a slightly higher price.

2   The second method is by means of a *placing*. Thus a stockbroker may buy a block of shares from a company in order to resell to his

clients. This method is normally used only in the case of smaller companies.

3 A company which is already in existence may offer additional shares to its shareholders at a price lower than the current market price. The offer is termed a *rights issue*.

4 The method most frequently used is a *public issue*, which is often done through a merchant bank. Investors are invited through the prospectus to apply for stated amounts of the shares at fixed prices. There are a number of stages in a public issue of shares:

(*a*) On *application* investors are required to send a sum of money (e.g. 25p) for every £1 share applied for. If the issue is oversubscribed some investors will have to go without or applicants will receive only part of the total number of shares applied for.

(*b*) *Allotment* takes place when the directors decide the number of shares to be allotted to each applicant. Letters are sent out to applicants, stating the number of shares allotted and requesting payment of the amount due on allotment (e.g. 25p).

(*c*) The balance owing (e.g. 50p) is payable by a number of *'calls'*. Thus a first call for another 25p may be made and later, a second and final call for 25p. Sometimes uncalled capital is used to provide a reserve of additional capital. The shareholders are liable for the amount of uncalled capital and the balance is payable when the directors 'call' for it.

Payment for shares may, therefore, be spread over a period of months. Once the full value has been paid no further claims can be made on shareholders because their liability is limited to the capital invested.

Each shareholder is issued with a share certificate showing the number and class of shares held.

Loan capital
In addition to share capital, a company may raise funds by borrowing.

Debentures may be issued on the security of the company's property. Debentures are not shares and the holders are not members of the company and do not have voting rights. They are creditors and must be paid their fixed rate of interest whether the company makes profits or not and before any dividend is paid on shares. If the company fails to pay interest or repay the loan, debenture holders may sell the business in order to recover their money. Loans without security are often referred to as *loan stock*.

Thus debentures and loan stock bring capital into the company without extending the basis of ownership.

Finance corporations are an important source of long-term loan capital. Examples are as follows.

(*a*)   The Finance Corporation for Industry (FCI) which provides loans for larger companies in excess of one million pounds.

(*b*)   The Industrial and Commercial Finance Corporation (ICFC) which assists smaller firms by providing loans (or ordinary share capital) up to one million pounds. Both FCI and ICFC are backed by the same holding company known as Finance for Industry (FFI).

(*c*)   Technical Development Capital Limited, which is owned by the ICFC and provides finance for the commercial development of worthwhile technical innovations involving greater risks than existing organisations are prepared to take.

These three institutions (*a*) – (*c*) above are jointly owned or have the backing of the Bank of England and the commercial banks or insurance companies.

(*d*)   Equity capital for Industry Limited is privately owned and provides ordinary share capital for small and medium sized companies.

Another method of raising money is to *mortgage* the property owned by the company. A mortgage deed is drawn up and the money borrowed on the security of the property is repaid, with interest over a period of years.

Finally, *government aid* in the form of loans or grants is available to firms which will expand in areas of high unemployment (see Chapter 13).

All of the forms of loan capital outlined above provide *long-term* finance, often over twenty years or more.

Temporary increases of capital may be provided by the following means:

1   An extension of credit facilities from suppliers. The purchase of stock on credit for a number of months is the same thing as obtaining a loan from the wholesaler for the length of the period of credit.

2   A bank overdraft. This is a form of loan granted for periods up to twelve months. The banker will then, if necessary, consider renewing borrowing facilities (see Chapter 16).

Finally, in addition to raising capital through share issues or by borrowing, a company may increase its capital by 'ploughing back' a proportion of the profit made each year.

Advantages of public companies

1   Larger amounts of capital can be raised than is possible with other forms of business organisation. Capital running into many millions of

pounds may be raised from a great many people and this form of business organisation assists production on a large scale.

2 Unlike sole proprietorships and partnerships, the public company has a continuous existence. It exists as a legal person quite apart from the individuals who hold the shares, and is unaffected by the death of even the largest shareholder.

3 All the shareholders enjoy limited liability. This privilege encourages people with only small sums available for investment to subscribe to the joint 'stock' of capital.

4 Legal regulations safeguard the interests of shareholders and persons dealing with the company. For example, when a company is formed, the memorandum and articles of association must be inspected by the Registrar of Companies before a certificate of incorporation is issued. Again, at the end of each year of trading, a copy of the accounts must be submitted to the Registrar, and this publicity is a safeguard against fraud.

5 Shareholders may dispose of their shares easily and quickly through the London and provincial stock exchanges. This fact encourages people to invest and makes it easier for companies to obtain new capital.

Disadvantages of public companies
Despite their many advantages, public companies suffer from a number of drawbacks.

1 The personal element which may be characteristic of smaller business units, is lacking. Employees often feel that they are mere 'units' of labour and that the company's profit is more important than their welfare. In fairness it must be pointed out that many companies have acknowledged this criticism. Personnel departments have been set up in an effort to bridge the gap between management and employees. Welfare schemes and social amenities also represent the efforts of companies in this direction.

2 The major concern of most shareholders is the amount of dividend. Consequently they may show little interest in other important factors such as employees' working conditions, export performance and modernisation of equipment.

The Stock Exchange
When an investor has subscribed capital to a public company, he cannot withdraw his investment by asking the company to buy back the shares. In order to get his money back he must find a buyer and the simplest way

of doing this is to employ a stockbroker. A broker buys and sells shares of behalf of members of the public in a market called The Stock Exchange. The London Stock Exchange is the most important market in shares in Britain although the major provincial financial centres (such as Birmingham, Liverpool and Manchester) also have exchanges.

In addition to shares, there are two other classes of securities dealt in on The Stock Exchange, namely stocks and bonds.

Stock consists of the capital of a company or the amount of a government or local authority loan. Stocks are usually quoted per £100 nominal value, but fractions may be bought or sold, whereas shares are not divisible.

Bonds are usually issued in multiples of £100. They consist of loans to a company, the government or a local authority.

The Stock Exchange is a market for second-hand shares and whenever a company makes an issue of shares it will apply for a *quotation,* that is, permission for the shares to be bought and sold on the Exchange. A company that fails to secure a quotation would be unable to attract investors because its shares would not be marketable. The grant of a quotation facilitates the raising of new capital by companies.

Business inside The Stock Exchange is conducted by members of the Exchange who are either brokers or jobbers.

Brokers are agents acting for members of the public. Brokers are paid by means of a commission charged on purchases and sales of shares.

Jobbers are dealers in shares and since there are so many different issues, they tend to specialise in particular kinds such as banks, steel, oil and so on. Jobbers make a profit (known as the 'turn') from the difference between their buying and selling prices.

Share Prices
The prices of stocks and shares change frequently. The Daily Official List published by The Stock Exchange and the lists printed in daily newspapers show the prices at which bargains were made on the Exchange.

The market price indicates the level of demand for the shares. The supply of a particular share is virtually fixed by the company's memorandum of association which lays down the amount of the authorised capital. Thus if supply remains unaltered and demand increases, then the price of the share will rise. Similarly if demand falls, so will the price. The factors affecting demand for a particular share include investors' expectations of the level of future dividends; rumours of mergers or take-over bids; and political conditions.

4 Co-operative retail societies

The first successful society was founded in 1844 by a small group of working men who became known as the Rochdale Pioneers. At a time when wages were low and living conditions poor these men put all their savings together and set up shop for themselves. Each took his turn in serving during his free time and any profit made was divided up among the group. In this way they provided the basic necessities of life at prices below those asked in other shops. The venture was successful and other societies grew up on the same lines. Today there are many co-operative retail societies of varying size.

Organisation of the co-operative movement
The co-operative movement has a three-tiered structure.

1 *The local retail societies* Many have branches throughout their areas selling groceries and meat. The central premises in the High Street may be in the form of a department store selling a wide range of articles. There may be supermarkets and self-service shops. Milk, bread and coal may be delivered to members' homes.

2 *The Co-operative Wholesale Societies* The Co-operative Wholesale Society operates in England and Wales and the Scottish CWS operates in Scotland. The Societies make bulk purchases from growers and manufacturers, and stock and distributes goods for the retail societies. The latter buy from the wholesale societies in the same way as a shopper buys from the local retail society. Dividends are paid to the retail societies on the basis of their purchases.

3 *The Co-operative Production Societies* These are owned by the wholesale societies, and include tea plantations, dairies and a large number of factories making a wide range of consumer goods. The majority of goods sold by the retail societies are produced by the production societies.

Organisation of a retail society
Each society is in business on its own and the success or failure of one society does not concern the others.

In order to join a society a person must contribute at least £1 of share capital (he can contribute any sum up to £1000). Shares earn a fixed rate of interest. Each member is entitled to vote on decisions affecting the running of the society and to draw dividend on his purchases at the society's shops.

The rate of dividend varies according to the profit made by the local society and is higher in some districts than in others.

A committee is elected by the members to manage the society and appoint the manager and staff. Meetings of members are held several times a year and each member has one vote.

Advantages

1 A co-operative society has a private market consisting of its own members.

2 The societies provide educational, social and welfare facilities for members and their families. Choirs, youth clubs, dramatic societies and similar activities are organised. The movement has its own political party, the Co-operative Party, which works closely with the Labour Party. These activities provide societies with a solid body of support in their trading.

In spite of these favourable factors and the attraction to customers of earning dividend on purchases, the co-operative movement is losing trade to other big shops. Why is this so?

Diffficulties of the co-operative movement

1 Many societies are too small to allow the introduction of bulk buying and centralised systems of management. In other words, they cannot obtain the advantages of large-scale operation which are enjoyed by their competitors, the chain stores and supermarkets.

2 About thirty per cent of the goods sold are from non co-operative sources. The societies are, therefore, acting as distributing agents for their competitors.

3 Most members do not exercise their right to attend meetings and vote. Consequently a society may be controlled, in effect, by a small number of members. The management committee may consist of people elected because of their loyalty to the ideals of the co-operative movement, rather than for their business abilities. Inefficiency in the society's business may continue unrecognised, and the business experience and drive which is necessary to meet the competitive power of other forms of retailing may be lacking.

4 The bulk of the movement's share capital is supplied by the members who are free to withdraw their funds on demand. Large-scale withdrawals of shares have created capital problems. This is a basic weakness in the movement's financial structure.

In recent years, attempts have been made to solve some of these problems. Some smaller societies have merged with their neighbours in order to become bigger and more effective. Attempts to ease the capital problem have produced plans to raise money from the investing public.

Retail co-operative societies differ from public companies as follows:

	Retail Co-operative	Public Company
OWNERSHIP	The owners are the customers	The owners are not necessarily customers
	Localised ownership	Possible national/international ownership
	Shareholders may contribute up to £1000 capital	There is no limit on a member's shareholding and one or a few shareholders may hold the majority of shares
	Shareholders receive a twofold income, (a) interest on share capital (b) dividend on purchases	Shareholders receive a share in the profits according to the size of their shareholding
CONTROL	Each shareholder has one vote irrespective of the capital	Usually the shareholders have votes in proportion to their capital holdings
	A society is managed by a committee elected by the shareholders	Control is by an elected board of directors
RAISING OF CAPITAL	Normally one type of share with fixed interest. Share capital can be withdrawn from the society at short notice.	Different types of shares receive share of profits. A company does not normally repay capital and a holder must dispose of his shares by selling them to someone else
	Remains constant in value	Quoted on stock exchange and may vary in value
DISPOSAL OF PROFITS	Profits shared among owner customers; traditional dividend or dividend stamps. Many employees are members	Profits distributed among owners who may buy little or nothing from the business. May have profit-sharing schemes for employees

QUESTIONS

Write *short* answers to the following:

1 Name the simplest and most common form of business organisation in Britain.
2 List the possible sources of a sole proprietor's capital.
3 Write down the advantages enjoyed by a sole trader.
4 There are two types of partnership. They are _____ .
5 How did the Companies Act 1967 affect the maximum number allowed in a partnership?
6 What is a Partnership Deed of Agreement?
7 Name the major drawback of partnerships.
8 Briefly describe the characteristics of businesses organised as partnerships.
9 What is the meaning of 'joint stock' companies?
10 Why is a company described as 'limited'?
11 In what sense can a private company be said to be 'private'?
12 Name the types of undertaking for which a private company is (*a*) unsuitable, (*b*) very suitable.
13 Write down the minimum number of members necessary to form a public company.
14 Name the two documents which must be sent to the Registrar by the promoters of a company.
15 Which two documents must be issued by the Registrar to a public company before it can begin trading?
16 Name the document advertising a public issue of shares.
17 Write down three kinds of preference shares.
18 Give two reasons why investors may prefer to hold ordinary shares rather than preference shares.
19 Write down three stages in buying shares from a company.
20 Define a debenture.
21 Write down the two kinds of members of The London Stock Exchange.
22 What is a quotation?
23 How does The Stock Exchange assist in the raising of new capital?
24 State the three tiers of the Co-operative Movement.
25 Write down as many examples as possible of how a co-operative retail society differs from other forms of retailing.
26 Name the two sources of income available to members of a co-operative retail society.
27 List some of the problems of the co-operative movement.

Write answers to the following:

1 What are the main features of a partnership? In which kinds of economic activity is the partnership common? (WJEC)

2 Distinguish between the different types of stocks and shares issued by a joint stock company. What are the advantages to the company of issuing each of these kinds of securities? (AEB)

3 What advantages are derived from converting a partnership into a joint stock company? (JMB)

4 Discuss the most important features of a Public Joint Stock Company from the point of view of an individual shareholder. (JMB)

5 Describe the organisation and functions of the Co-operative Movement and indicate some of its major problems. (Cambridge)

6 Sole trader, partnership, private limited company, public limited company, and co-operative societies are different types of business concerns. Choose any *two* of these types and compare their characteristics, paying particular attention to the provision of capital, ownership and the type of business for which they are best suited. (Cambridge)

7 Mr Coop is a member of a retail co-operative society and Mr Doe is an ordinary shareholder in a public limited company. Describe the main differences between the rights and responsibilities of Mr Coop and Mr Doe. (Cambridge)

8 Show how the existence of (a) limited liability, and (b) The Stock Exchange help public companies to raise money from the public. (WJEC)

9 What is the role of the London Stock Exchange in our economy? What are the factors which determine share prices on the Exchange? (AEB)

10 Describe and discuss the most important sources from which a Public Joint-Stock Company may get the capital it needs in order to expand. (JMB)

11 What are the main ways in which firms in the private sector of British industry are owned and controlled? (Oxford and Cambridge)

12 How do growing firms finance their expansion? (Oxford and Cambridge)

13 What are the main differences between a public and a private joint-stock company? Why do both types of company continue to exist? (SCE)

14 What are the main differences between a private limited company and a public limited company? Explain the procedure by which a private company becomes a public company. (U/L)

PRACTICAL WORK

1 Try to discover examples of (a) sole proprietorships, (b) partnerships, (c) private companies, (d) public companies in the area where you live.

2 Follow the prices of shares in a public company known to you. This information is available in the financial section of national newspapers. Record the prices daily for a month and try to discover the reason for any noticeable rise or fall. Make an imaginary investment in the firm and calculate each week the gain or loss from the sale of your shares.

3 A prospectus for the issue of shares or loan stock is often printed in an abridged form in newspapers. If you can find one, cut it out, read it, and keep it for reference.

4 Find out the differences between (a) chartered companies, (b) statutory companies and (c) registered companies.

5 If you live near London, you should enjoy a visit to the Visitors Gallery at The Stock Exchange.

6 Using encyclopaedias or other reference books, write an account of the development of the joint-stock company from the 16th century to the present day.

7 Obtain a copy of the Companies Act 1948 and look up Table A (Specimen Articles) and Table B (Specimen Memorandum).

8 Try and discover when the co-operative retail society in your area was formed. List the types of shops owned by the society. Are there banking and insurance services run by your local co-operative movement?

7

Business Firms
Public and Mixed Enterprise

1 State undertakings

Undertakings operated by the state are organised as public corporations (Table 4). Some corporations such as the British Broadcasting Corporation and the Port of London Authority were established before the Second World War (1939–45). During 1945–1951 several industries were nationalised and these also were organised as public corporations. Nationalisation means the taking over, by the state, of established undertakings which were being run as private concerns. They comprised major sections of the fuel and power, transport and steel industries and are now organised as follows:

Power	*Transport*
National Coal Board	British Rail
The Electricity Council	British Waterways Board
British Gas Corporation	National Freight Corporation

The iron and steel industry was first nationalised in 1951 under the Iron and Steel Corporation of Great Britain, but in 1953 it was denationalised. In 1967 the industry was nationalised again under the British Steel Corporation.

The Bank of England, the Post Office and British Airways are also state undertakings. The Bank was nationalised in 1946 but as the Central Bank, it had worked closely with the government for many years. The Post Office, throughout its long history, has been a public institution. Until 1969 it was operated as a government department but it is now a public corporation.

The British National Oil Corporation was created to enable the state to exercise its participation rights in the exploitation of Britain's offshore oil resources.

Table 4   The Main Public Corporations

Finance	Fuel and power	Raw materials	Transport	Communications
Bank of England	National Coal Board	British Steel Corporation	British Airways	The Post Office
	British Gas Corporation		British Rail	British Broadcasting Corporation (B.B.C.)
	Electricity Council		National Freight Corporation	Independent Broadcasting Authority (I.B.A.)
	Atomic Energy Authority			
	British National Oil Corporation			

Organisation and control

Although there are certain differences of detail in the organisation of nationalised industries, the bodies which control them are all public corporations.

The chairmen and members of a public corporation are appointed (and may be dismissed) by the Minister of the appropriate government department. For example, the members of the Electricity Council are appointed by the Minister for Energy. The corporation is the central authority for the industry and is answerable to the Minister, and through him, to Parliament, for its efficiency.

The internal organisation of the corporations varies. Sometimes, as with the electricity industry, authority is delegated to regional boards which are responsible for the day-to-day running of the industry.

Similarly the National Coal Board exercises control through seventeen areas, each under the control of an area director. The latter is responsible for supervising the work of the collieries within the area. On the other hand, control of the gas industry is centralised through the British Gas Corporation.

When the steel industry was nationalised in 1967 the major steel companies were also formed into regional groups. However, in March 1970, the industry was reorganised into six product divisions.

Although Ministers do not interfere in the day-to-day working of nationalised industries, these large-scale organisations are subject to a substantial measure of government control. Each corporation is required to prepare an annual report and submit it to the Minister, who may be questioned on it in Parliament.

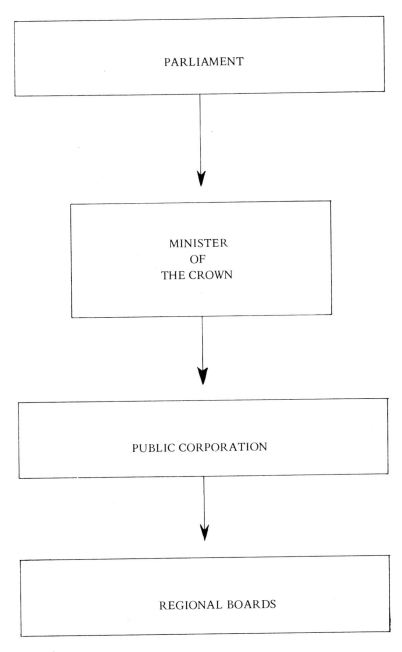

Fig. 16 Organisation of a Nationalised Industry

In order to represent consumers' interests councils have been established for the coal, electricity, gas and transport industries; and for the Post Office. Each consumer council comprises members appointed by the Minister. Nominations to the Minister are put forward by local authorities, trade associations and other bodies judged to be representative of consumers.

The work of a council is two-fold, namely, to deal with complaints and suggestions from consumers; and to advise the Minister of consumers' views.

Although the councils are statutory bodies, their influence has been minimal, mainly because the corporations are not obliged to reply to their representations with reasons or justifications. In other words, the councils' powers are virtually confined to offering opinions. The weakness of many councils has been demonstrated by the way in which local, unofficial pressure groups (for example, on rail closures and season ticket fares) have sprung up without regard to the existing statutory bodies.

Capital, prices and profits
When the government took over the industries mentioned above the former shareholders were compensated for the loss of their shares by the issue of an appropriate amount of nationalised industry stock. (Owners who did not wish to retain these kinds of securities were able to sell them on The Stock Exchange.) The stock carried the government's guarantee and earned a fixed rate of interest. This means that holders of the stock receive interest whether the industry makes a profit or loss. Shareholders in a public company receive dividends only when the company makes a profit, but the ordinary shareholders' dividend is not fixed and when profits are good, they may receive a high return on their investment.

A nationalised industry has power to raise capital by issue of stock and by borrowing money from the commercial banks. These borrowings are covered by government guarantee. In practice, much of the corporations' capital comes from their own commercial profits and from loans from the National Loans Fund. (This Fund, which is financed by the Exchequer, was set up in 1968 as a central loan-making agency to finance the whole of the public sector. The two principal borrowers are the nationalised industries and local authorities).

The nationalised industries are under a statutory obligation to pay their way. Their financial performance is measured in terms of *surplus* or *deficit,* after providing for all the items properly charged to revenue. The government expects them to cover these accounting costs in full, thus avoiding deficits. Thus prices must be such as will prevent a loss 'taking one year with another' and also enable the industries to meet the targets set for them by the government.

Financial targets or objectives have been agreed with most of the industries to serve both as an incentive to management and as a yardstick of performance. The targets have normally been agreed as a percentage rate of return on assets and have reflected social obligations, historic development and potential growth of the particular industry.

If a nationalised industry makes a profit, it cannot distribute a dividend because there are no shareholders. Instead it can do one or more of several things.

(a) Decrease the prices charged to consumers and so eliminate the surplus of income over expenditure.

(b) Raise the wages paid to employees in the industry. This will increase costs and help to eliminate any profit.

(c) Use the surplus to finance capital development.

Losses made by public corporations have to be financed by government grants.

Differences between a public corporation and a public company

	Company	Corporation
OWNERSHIP	Owned by shareholders who elect directors to manage the company.	Controlling authority for a state-owned industry. Members appointed by minister of appropriate government department
CONTROL	Ultimate control resides in voting power of shareholders. Accounts must be presented annually to shareholders.	Annual report submitted to the responsible minister who may be questioned on it in Parliament.
RAISING OF CAPITAL	Appeal to investors. Success depends on how the latter judge its shares.	Power to raise capital and borrow money with government guarantee.
DISPOSAL OF PROFITS	Profits distributed among shareholders in proportion to type and number of shares held.	No shareholders. Profit retained as capital or disposed of by reducing prices or used for paying higher wages.

2 Municipal undertakings

Local authorities provide and administer a number of essential services such as education, health and welfare, fire services and recreation facilities. In addition, local authorities are also involved in trading enterprises although nationalisation has taken from them their most profitable business activities, namely, gas and electricity supplies. Until the passing of the Transport Act 1968, many were responsible for local passenger transport services but the Act designated Passenger Transport Areas to integrate bus and rail services. A professional executive takes over all corporation bus services in an area. However, some important trading enterprises still function. For example, Hull operates its own telephone service and in Birmingham there is a Municipal Bank. Other local authority enterprises include the operation of baths and swimming pools, abattoirs and markets, restaurants and sports facilities, and particularly in seaside towns, the provision of entertainment and other facilities for visitors.

Organisation and control

Control of municipal undertakings is exercised through a trading committee composed of councillors who delegate authority for the day-to-day running to salaried municipal officials (Fig. 17). The latter are answerable to the committee for all matters affecting the undertaking.

Capital and profits

The initial capital for a municipal undertaking is often provided by borrowing. The local authority has to apply to the Department of the Environment to raise a loan for a particular purpose. If the project is approved, the money may be raised by an issue of stock; by application to the National Loans Fund; by issuing mortgages; and by issuing bonds, usually for one year.

Profits made by municipal undertakings may be used to relieve the rates. (This source of income of a local authority comes from rates levied at so much in the £ on the rateable value of property within its area; see page 270.) However, if the enterprise runs at a loss, the latter is borne by the ratepayers.

Advantages of public undertakings

The arguments in favour of the production of goods and services by state and municipal enterprises are as follows:

1 Nationalisation enables the working of an industry to be planned as a whole. Before transport was nationalised, the competing railway companies often constructed two or even three railway lines between

the same two places. In the eighteenth and nineteenth centuries canals were made with different depths, widths and bridge heights (consequently only a very small barge can travel right across the country). This haphazard development of means of transport resulted in a great waste of resources. Thus, it is argued, a nationalised industry which is the sole supplier of a product can avoid wasteful duplication of railway lines, gas mains, electricity cables and so on.

2 Privately owned undertakings operate in order to earn a profit for their shareholders. However, a nationalised industry without shareholders can take account of other objectives in the form of social costs and benefits. For example, trains may be run on certain lines for the

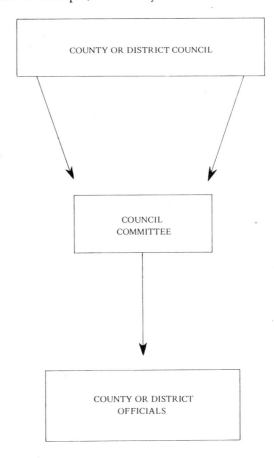

Fig. 17 Organisation of Municipal Enterprise

convenience of people living in the area, although the service may run at a loss. Coal mines may be worked at a loss but be kept open in order to provide employment in certain areas. Similarly, a local authority may subsidise swimming facilities on the ground that a high charge for admission may deprive poorer members of the community of the use of this facility.

3 Certain industries such as coal, steel and transport are basic industries, that is, many other industries depend upon them. It may be argued that if the basic industries were privately owned, the owners might exploit their key position by regulating the supply and prices of their products in order to earn excess profits.

4 Successful municipal trading enterprises may lead to a reduction in the rates. Low rates in a district may attract new industries to it and so increase its prosperity.

Criticisms of public undertakings

The opponents of state control claim the system has many disadvantages.

1 The immense size of nationalised industries creates problems of management and control. In turn, efforts to control these giant enterprises lead to 'red-tape,' form-filling and impersonal labour relationships.

2 People work hardest when they work for themselves, that is, when their own capital is at risk. In a nationalised industry, the men in control are salaried employees and they may show less managerial drive than exists in a private business.

3 Privately owned businesses compete with each other to sell goods and services. Consequently they endeavour to keep costs and prices as low as possible in order to do better than rival firms. A nationalised industry has a legal monopoly so that similar undertakings cannot be set up in competition. Lack of competition may lead to inefficiency and higher prices than would be the case under private enterprise.

4 Nationalised industries may be heavily subsidised so that they become a drain upon the taxpayers. The latter have not the same opportunities for criticism as have shareholders in a limited company.

3 Mixed enterprise

A mixed enterprise is an undertaking in which public authorities and private interests combine to provide capital.

Such undertakings are well established in other countries, notably France, Italy and West Germany but in the past there was comparatively little mixed enterprise in the United Kingdom. Today, however, the position is changing.

Mixed enterprise takes two principal forms: (a) participation by the government and (b) participation by public corporations.

Participation by the government

An important example of this kind of mixed enterprise in the United Kingdom is the British Petroleum Company, one of the world's largest and most successful oil companies. In the early years of this century, the government acquired a majority holding of the shares in order to ensure oil supplies for the Navy, at a time when the Admiralty switched from the use of coal to oil. The government still maintains a substantial share holding in the company.

Although the government appoints two directors of British Petroleum, the relationship of the latter with the government is no different from that of the other oil companies. The Treasury does not attempt to guide the company and British Petroleum operates in the same way as any other oil company with worldwide interests.

Two further examples are the British Sugar Corporation and the firm of Short Brothers and Harland. The British Sugar Corporation was formed in 1936 by the amalgamation of the existing fifteen British producers of beet sugar in order to develop more effectively the output of beet sugar in Britain. The majority shareholdings belongs to the fifteen companies and the government holds 11.25 per cent.

Short Brothers and Harland are an aircraft firm in which the government acquired a majority shareholding during the Second World War (1939-45).

Several further examples of the government investing money in private enterprise resulted from the activities of the Industrial Reorganisation Corporation. The Corporation was set up in 1967 to promote mergers between firms in order to secure the benefits of larger producing units. The IRC was given the power to provide an inducement in the form of public money, which was offered in exchange for ordinary shares or loan stock. In this way a number of shipbuilding firms became mixed enterprises. Another example is that of International Computers (Holdings) which was formed by a merger of the two principal British manufacturers of computers. The aim was to produce a larger organisation capable of meeting American competition. The inducement offered was a grant towards the research and development costs of the new company, and the acquisition of part of its capital.

The IRC was abolished in 1971 but four years later a National

Enterprise Board was set up. Its functions are to build on and enlarge the activities previously discharged by the Industrial Reorganization Corporation.

Purposes

There are a number of reasons for government participation in an enterprise. They are:

(*a*) The need to prevent heavy regional unemployment resulting from the failure of a privately owned enterprise.

(*b*) The desire to acquire potential control of a firm or industry.

(*c*) The decision to develop new technology involving risks too high for private enterprise to accept without help.

(*d*) The need to reorganise a firm or industry.

(*e*) The means of injecting new capital into firms needing it, without the necessity of compulsory purchase.

Participation by public corporations

The nationalised industries are involved in mixed enterprise to a much greater extent than the central government. Some examples are as follows.

The National Coal Board has interests in businesses engaged in the distribution of solid fuel and coal products; the manufacture and supply of bricks and other building materials.

British Airways holds interests in several airlines which serve as feeders to its main route services. It has also invested in a number of hotel companies at home and abroad.

British Gas Corporation holds a 50 per cent share of a company formed to bring liquid methane from Algeria to England.

British Steel Corporation has holdings in mixed enterprises engaged in a wide variety of industrial processes. These include engineering, the operation of ore-carrying ships, bridge construction and the design and construction of buildings. The undertakings are not confined to companies registered in the United Kingdom but include those established in overseas countries.

Purpose

The principal motive for public corporations engaging in mixed enterprise has been to associate with firms engaged in activities which are helpful to the main function of the nationalised industry. The examples listed above illustrate this purpose.

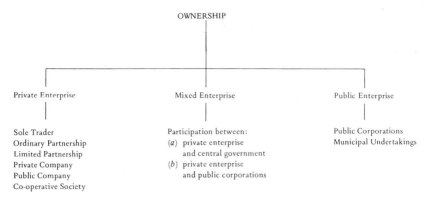

Fig. 18 Classification of Firms by Ownership

QUESTIONS

Write *short* answers to the following:

1 Name five nationalised industries in Britain.
2 Name the organisation which runs a nationalised industry and give three examples.
3 Who is responsible for the management of a nationalised industry?
4 Who bears the risks of a state undertaking?
5 How were the former shareholders compensated when an industry was nationalised?
6 What advantage does a state undertaking possess over private enterprise in the raising of capital?
7 What are the ways in which a state undertaking can make use of any profit?
8 Name as many examples as you can of trading enterprises run by local authorities.
9 How are municipal undertakings controlled?
10 What is a rate?
11 How can nationalisation prevent wastage of resources?
12 Why would a privately owned enterprise be unable to provide a service on social grounds?
13 List four possible drawbacks of state enterprise.
14 Mixed enterprise takes two main forms. What are they?
15 What was the purpose of the IRC?
16 Name the organisation which took over the role of the IRC in 1975.
17 List the reasons for government participation in an enterprise.
18 Why do public corporations engage in mixed enterprise?

Write answers to the following:

1 Write an account of the organization and control of any one nationalised industry. (AEB)

2 What are the main differences between private enterprise and public enterprise? (JMB)

3 'The ultimate aim of production is the making of profit'. How far is this statement correct with reference to (a) private enterprise, and (b) public enterprise? (JMB)

4 What are the characteristics of organisation which distinguish a nationalised industry from a joint-stock company? (Oxford and Cambridge)

5 What are the distinctive features of such public services as gas, water and electricity? Why are they more suitable to be run as public services than either newspapers or entertainments? (Cambridge)

6 Nationalised industries are financed differently from private enterprise industries. Describe the ways in which each is financed, indicating clearly the differences. (Cambridge)

7 In what ways do the nationalised industries differ from the other types of business units? (Cambridge)

8 What is meant by a nationalised industry? Give an account of recent developments in any *one* nationalised industry. (Oxford)

9 What are the distinguishing characteristics of a public corporation (or nationalised industry) as a business enterprise? (Oxford and Cambridge)

10 What are the main arguments for and against the ownership and operation of an industry by the State rather than by private enterprise? (U/L)

11 Distinguish between private and public enterprise and compare the advantages of each as forms of business organisation. (U/L West Africa)

12 'One of the reasons for scrapping capital goods is that they become out of date and need to be replaced by more efficient and more up-to-date capital goods.' How is this financed (a) in private enterprise and (b) in public enterprise? (U/L West Africa)

PRACTICAL WORK

1 Find out the names of regional boards of nationalised industries which supply goods and services in your area.

2 Look up in a daily newspaper the Stock Exchange prices of nationalised industry stock.

3 Discover examples of municipal enterprise in your area. What is the name of the council committee which controls them?
4 Make a study of a selected nationalised industry paying particular regard to (a) its origins and subsequent development, and (b) recent developments and future plans.

8

The scale of production

The firm and the industry

A *firm* may be defined as any business unit (e.g. sole trader, partnership, or company) and several firms producing similar commodities or services form an *industry*. If the entire output of an industry is produced by a single firm (as is the case with a nationalised industry) then the firm and the industry are one and the same.

There are different types and sizes of firms. At one extreme is the sole proprietor's small business with limited capital and at the other, the large public company with thousands of shareholders and many millions of pounds of capital.

Industries may be large or small and may comprise both small and large firms.

What factors determine the size of (*a*) the firm and (*b*) the industry?

The size of the firm

An important motive for setting up a business is the making of profit. Profit is the excess of sales revenue over total costs and an entrepreneur will try, therefore, to reduce costs to the lowest possible level.

It is often found that increasing the size of the firm results in a number of valuable economies and these savings in average costs are called *internal economies* of large-scale production. The word 'internal' is used because the economies are obtained within the firm's own organisation. They are as follows.

In the first place, a large firm can benefit from the application of the principle of the division of labour (see Chapter 5). The average costs of producing every item are lower when the factors of production are specialised. For example, people are more productive when less time is wasted changing from one task to another. They learn to work faster, and thus the cost of employing them, per unit of output, is lower.

Secondly, savings may be achieved both in the buying of raw

materials and in the selling of the finished product. A big firm can place large, bulk orders and obtain sizeable trade discounts for doing so whereas the requirements of a small firm are insufficient to take advantage of this saving. Instead the small firm will buy from a merchant who breaks bulk, sells in smaller quantities and takes a profit for his service.

Similarly, the large firm enjoys an advantage in regard to selling costs. These comprise, for example, advertising charges and salesmen's earnings. Although the total selling costs of a large firm will be higher than those of a small firm, the *cost per unit of output* will usually be lower. For example the selling costs of a large firm might be £250000 per annum while those of a small business might amount to only £10000 per annum. If the large firm sells 2 million items each year while the small firm sells 50 000 units, the selling cost per unit in the large firm (8p) is very much less than in the small firm (20p).

Thirdly, large firms can usually borrow money more cheaply. Generally, banks consider large firms to be the safer borrowers and consequently the rate of interest charged on loans will be lower than that offered to the small firm.

Fourthly, the large firm has a great advantage over the small one in the matter of research. A large firm can spend large sums on laboratories and the employment of scientists and engineers – yet this expense will be only a small part of total costs. Any discoveries made by its employees become the property of the firm. In industries where the average size of the firm is not large, there may be a research association which works for the advantage of the industry as a whole, but the individual firm will assess its value less highly than research carried out entirely for its own benefit.

Limits to the growth of a firm

If, by increasing the size of a firm, certain economies are obtained, why do not firms expand indefinitely?

Expansion is limited by a number of factors.

In the first place, expansion is limited eventually by lack of the factors of production. As a firm grows, more managers will have to be engaged, more workers hired and more capital raised. But if the people needed are employed elsewhere, they will have to be offered higher rewards than they are earning at the time. Consequently costs of production will start to rise.

Secondly, if there is no change in demand a larger output can be sold only by lowering price in order to stimulate sales. Thus a combination of increasing costs (see above) and falling price means that eventually a point will be reached where a further increase in output will add more to costs than it does to revenue. At this point, additional expansion will not be worthwhile.

Thirdly, as a firm grows in size, management becomes increasingly complex. The establishment of a complex management structure in a growing firm means that administrative costs increase until beyond a certain size further growth causes average costs to start rising. When this happens, *diseconomies of scale* are in operation.

Fourthly, the growth of the firm is limited by the size of the market. The scale of production is dependent on demand for the commodity and mass production can be undertaken only for standardised products in wide demand (e.g. cars, washing machines and houses). The market may be restricted by a number of factors. For example:

(*a*) where demand is for an individually designed product as in 'made-to-measure' tailoring;

(*b*) where demand is for a service requiring the 'personal touch' as in dentistry, hairdressing or house decorating;

(*c*) where demand is localised, as is the case with a local newspaper.

In addition, a market may be small because its area is limited by transport costs and time. Thus in the case of services sold by solicitors, accountants, doctors and others, both time and transport costs limit the extent to which either the consumer will journey to the supplier or vice versa.

Fifthly, a firm may not expand beyond a certain size simply because the owner prefers not to do so. This reluctance may be influenced by two factors.

(*a*) Business risks increase as the scale of operations increases. The larger the output the heavier will be the loss from a wrong business decision and a reluctance to bear greater risks may limit the growth of the firm.

(*b*) Expansion may necessitate raising additional capital and this often means sacrificing a measure of personal control of the business. For example, the sole proprietor may be obliged to offer a partnership in order to persuade someone with capital to invest in the business. Thus expansion may be limited because of the owner's reluctance to give up a measure of personal control.

The survival of small firms

Whereas large firms can take advantage of important economies of scale, it is clear that in certain circumstances, the most efficient unit of

production is small. Thus the size of the business unit tends to be small
  (a) where there is only a limited demand, e.g. for model gowns
  (b) where personal attention to the buyers' requirements is particu-
     larly important.

Table 5   The Size of Firms in Manufacturing Industry

Numbers Employed	11 - 24	25 - 499	500 - 1499	1500+
Number of Establishments	60 900	26 000	2 100	708
Percentage of total employment	7	38	22	33

Source: *Britain, an official handbook*

Summary
A firm will expand to its optimum size, that is the size at which costs of
production per unit of output are at a minimum. At that size there will
be no motive for further expansion, for at any other size the firm would
be less efficient.

Combination of firms
In addition to growth in size due to what may be termed 'natural
expansion' that is, increasing output or adding to the range of its
products, a firm may grow larger by amalgamation with other firms.
    Growth by amalgamation is called *integration* and it occurs when two
or more firms combine to form one new firm. Integration may be either
horizontal or *vertical*.
    Vertical integration brings under one control different stages of
production. It occurs when there is a combination of firms at different
stages in the manufacture or sale of a product. For example, manufacturers may (a) integrate backwards in order to take over the source of
their supplies or (b) integrate forwards in order to take over the outlets
for their products. An example of the latter is the large number of
petrol stations owned by oil companies. An example of integration
backwards is the development of rubber plantations by tyre manufacturers.
    The principal reason for integrating backwards is to ensure an
adequate supply of raw materials. By directly controlling these supplies,
a manufacturer protects himself against the damaging effect of a rise in

raw material prices. In addition, he avoids the danger that they may come under the control of a competitor.

Horizontal integration brings under one control firms engaged in the same stage of production. For example, two commercial banks may amalgamate or a number of similar retail shops may combine.

Both vertical and horizontal combinations enable firms to benefit from the advantages of large-scale production outlined earlier in this chapter.

Methods of combining firms

1 In an amalgamation or *merger*, the method of establishment is for one company to absorb another by a takeover bid. For example, Company X may offer cash or its shares to the shareholders of Company Y. If 51 per cent or more accept the offer then Company Y will disappear and Company X takes control. Thus in a merger, one or more firms may lose their identity completely and work henceforward under the name of the takeover firm.

2 *Holding companies* are public companies formed primarily to hold and exercise a controlling interest (51 per cent or more of the voting power) in other firms. The holding company has control over its subsidiaries, which, however, can continue to trade under their own names. Examples of very large holding companies in the UK are Imperial Chemical Industries Ltd (ICI), Imperial Tobacco Company Ltd., and Sears (Holdings) Ltd.

The size of the industry

As has already been noted, the economies possible to a single firm from an increase in size are called *internal economies* of scale. A firm is also able to achieve economies in its relations with other firms and these savings are called *external economies* of scale. The latter are reductions in average costs which become available to all firms in an industry or an area as the number of firms increases.

External economies may result from the following factors.

1 *A supply of skilled labour* When an industry develops in an area, a pool of labour skills relevant to the industry is created. Thus a new firm would be drawn to the area because the skills it required to hire were already in existence there. The alternative would be to train new workers – an expensive undertaking.

An additional attraction to a new firm of an area of established industry is the provision by educational institutions of training courses related to the industry. For example, textiles courses form an important part of Further Education curricula in Manchester and Bradford. Specialised training facilities assist in building up a reservoir of skilled labour for the local industry. A new firm setting up away from the established centre of the industry would have to finance and inaugurate its own training facilities.

2 Regional division of labour   When firms are located close together it becomes possible for individual firms to specialise in single processes. In the Yorkshire woollen industry, for example, some firms will specialise in particular processes, such as spinning, weaving, dyeing and making the finished product. The industry as a whole enjoys the benefits of specialisation. Total output is increased and the average cost of production is reduced.

3 Development of subsidiary industries   When an industry is highly localised, subsidiary industries grow up to cater for the needs of the major industry. For example, wool-textile machinery is made in the West Riding. A woollen manufacturer does not, therefore, have to concern himself with making his own machines and he can devote all his energies to manufacturing. Further examples of ancillary services are repair and maintenance firms, firms making use of waste products and packaging and transport firms. In addition, banks and other financial institutions in the area will develop special facilities for financing the industry concentrated there.

4 Provision of common services   When an industry grows in size, common services are very often developed. These comprise transport, accounting, banking and insurance facilities. Most of these are provided by private firms but others, such as roads, communications and technical education, are provided by the state. In addition, localisation of industry may lead to the establishment in the area of organised markets. The Cotton Exchange at Liverpool and the Wool Exchange at Bradford are examples of such markets.

The economies resulting from concentration of an industry help to explain why it is easier for small firms to become established in an area where there is already a thriving business community rather than in a new centre.

However, these economies do not continue to increase indefinitely as an industry expands. There is an optimum size for the industry, just as there is an optimum size for any firm in an industry. Thus the growth of an industry leads eventually to a point where further expansion will lead to *external diseconomies of scale*. For example, in large concentrated urban areas the movement of materials to and from the industrial centres leads to traffic congestion. Delays cause rising transport costs. Similarly, when industrial sites are much in demand by firms, land costs will rise rapidly.

QUESTIONS

Write *short* answers to the following:
1 Define (*a*) a firm and (*b*) an industry.
2 Why does an entrepreneur seek to keep costs at a minimum?
3 What does the phrase 'internal economies of scale' mean?
4 Name four internal economies.
5 Which factors limit the size of the firm?
6 Give examples of how the market for a good or service may be restricted.
7 Why do some entrepreneurs appear reluctant to increase the size of their firms?
8 Summarise the circumstances in which small firms flourish.
9 What is the optimum size of a firm?
10 What is the meaning of 'integration'?
11 Briefly describe two forms of integration.
12 What is a merger? How is it brought about?
13 In what ways does a merger differ from a holding company?
14 Define the meaning of 'external economies of scale'.
15 Name the factors which encourage a new firm to move to an established centre of the industry.
16 Why does an industry not expand indefinitely?

Write answers to the following:
1 Why is the size of the business unit in retailing sometimes large and sometimes quite small? Give examples to illustrate your answer. (WJEC)
2 What is meant by internal and external economies of scale? Explain (*a*) how a steel works may obtain internal economies, and (*b*) how a West Riding woollen manufacturer may obtain external economies. (U/L)
3 'The large firm is always more efficient than its small competitor.' Discuss, illustrating your answer with examples from industry and commerce. (AEB)
4 Account for the continued survival of small firms in the British economy even when economic circumstances appear to be against them. (JMB)
5 What is meant in manufacturing business, by 'economies of scale'? For what reasons may they arise? (Oxford)

6 What are the advantages of large-scale production? In view of these advantages, why do so many small firms continue to survive? (Oxford)

7 Explain why the average size of a firm is small in some industries and large in others. Give examples of the industries concerned in each case and indicate your measure of 'size'.   (Oxford and Cambridge)

8 Distinguish between vertical and horizontal combines and, with examples, show how these forms of business organization may achieve economies of scale.   (U/L)

9 Outline the factors which influence the size of a business unit. (U/L)

10 Account for the tendency for businesses to be organised into larger and larger units.   (U/L West Africa)

11 For what reasons do firms seek to amalgamate with other firms? (AEB)

12 Why are some markets dominated by large firms? Illustrate your answer with examples and identify *two* factors which might limit the growth of firms in general.   (RSA)

PRACTICAL WORK

1 Draw a bar diagram to show the distribution of different sizes of firms in manufacturing industry, using data from Table 5, p.105.

2 Information regarding the size of firms in the UK is provided by the Census of Production. Consult the latest Census and find out the size distribution of firms in manufacturing industry. Which size of firm predominates? Are these firms responsible for a relatively small or large part of total employment?

3 Collect examples of (a) vertical integration and (b) horizontal integration.

4 Conduct a survey among people you know in order to find out whether or not they have experienced poor service from large firms because of organisational problems.

9
Location of Firms

Factors influencing location

One of the major decisions which the owner of a business has to take concerns the geographical location of the firm. The general aim will be to locate the enterprise where average costs of production per unit of output will be lowest. What are the main factors which influence the choice of a site for the firm?

At one time proximity to *power supplies* and to *raw materials* were important factors. However, modern forms of factory power are supplied by pipeline or cable throughout the country so that access to sources of power is no longer a significant influence on location. Similarly developments and improvements in transport systems have facilitated the movement of raw materials and nearness to the latter is not such an important consideration as it was at one time.

One of the major costs of production is that of *transport* – the transport of raw materials to the factory and the transport of the finished product to the consumer. The costs of transporting raw materials can be minimised by locating as near to their source as possible or alternatively, the costs of distribution can be reduced by locating as near to the market as possible. There are, therefore, two possible courses of action to follow (Fig. 19), and the actual course adopted will depend very largely on the nature of the industry.

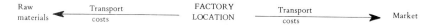

Fig. 19 Influences on the Location of a Firm

In some industries, materials lose weight during the process of manufacture; in others, the product gains bulk. The steel industry is an example of a 'weight-losing' industry and several tons of raw materials are lost in the process of manufacturing one ton of steel. It is cheaper, therefore, to transport the finished product to the market than it is to transport the raw materials. Thus firms using 'weight-losing' materials will tend to be located near to a supply of raw materials. On the other hand, if the finished product is bulky or weight is gained during manufacture (as is the case with brick-making and brewing), the market will exert the strongest pull.

Thus location near to large centres of population appeals particularly to firms whose transport costs in distributing finished goods to consumers are higher than the costs of bringing raw materials into the factory.

External economies

Once an industry becomes localised the area acquires advantages which attract new firms. These acquired advantages result in external economies of scale which exert a major influence on location. The attractions to a new firm of an area of established industry were referred to in Chapter 8. In summary they are as follows:

(a) a supply of skilled labour
(b) regional division of labour
(c) development of subsidiary industries
(d) provision of common services.

The acquired advantages of an area not only strengthen the pull on new firms entering the industry, but help to keep the industry there when any natural advantages once possessed by the area have ceased to exist.

The cotton industry is an illustration of this principle. Originally, Lancashire had a number of natural attractions for this industry. In the first place, fast-flowing streams provided water power and soft-water supplies. Secondly, a humid atmosphere prevented frequent breakages of the thread. Thirdly, coal measures in South Lancashire were available when steam power was used to drive machines. Finally, Liverpool was well situated for the import of raw materials and the export of finished goods. Today, these factors are of little importance: electricity and other sources of power have replaced steam; soft water and a humid atmosphere can be produced artificially; Manchester competes with Liverpool as a cotton port. However, Lancashire continues to be the centre of the cotton industry because of the advantages acquired in the course of its development.

Government policy

Industries tend to become localised in particular areas because, within those areas, certain advantages are available which allow firms in the industry to produce at the lowest costs. Unfortunately localisation makes a district dependent on the prosperity or otherwise of the basic industry. If the principal industry declines or suffers a setback in a trade depression, the whole area is affected and unemployment is concentrated in it. This disadvantage of localisation was apparent during the great depression of the 1930s when a number of areas in which one industry predominated developed rates of unemployment very much in excess of the national average. In these areas the majority of the work-force was employed by the main industry or its subsidiary industries. If the main industry could not sell its products, or get orders for more goods, then the work-force was dismissed from employment. There were in those areas no other industries which could employ the workers. The distressed areas – South Wales, Clydeside, Lancashire, the North-East and the North-West were designated Depressed Areas, later renamed Special Areas. In 1945 the Special Areas were termed Development Areas and then Assisted Areas. Now they are described as the Areas for Expansion.

The first legislation on the problem was the Special Areas Act 1934 and the principal aim of this and subsequent Acts was to introduce a greater variety of industry into the depressed areas.

Since those early attempts to influence the distribution of industry, the government has exercised a growing influence on the location of firms and today, government policy is probably the most important determinant of industrial location. An account of the methods used to influence location is given in Chapter 13. In summary, government policy aims

(a) to encourage new firms to set up in the Areas for Expansion in order to provide a wider range of industry. Some compensation for the extra costs incurred by virtue of an inferior location is provided by a system of government grants and other benefits;

(b) to deny permission to build new factories in areas which already have more jobs available than the local supply of workers.

For and against planned location of industry
Would firms that have been encouraged to set up in the Areas for Expansion have gone elsewhere if they had been left to decide for themselves?

Some firms have claimed that higher costs have been incurred through setting up factories in the Areas rather than on more favourable sites. It seems doubtful, therefore, whether factories would have been set up in the Areas without pressure from the government.

Higher costs reduce the competitiveness of firms and place them at a disadvantage to major competitors in more favourable locations.

Thus attempts to disperse firms may result in higher production costs through taking from them advantages derived from external economies of scale. Against these drawbacks must be set the fact that there are sound social reasons for planning the location of industry.

Concentrated and dispersed industries

Whereas many industries are highly concentrated in a few localities, others are dispersed throughout the country. Retailing and wholesaling, building, insurance, banking, vehicle repair, transport and catering are examples of industries which show no tendency to concentrate. Why are certain industries dispersed?

The major factor influencing either dispersal or concentration of firms is one which has already been discussed, namely, transport costs.

Generally, the difficulties of transport are reflected in the costs of transport. If goods can be loaded and moved with ease the costs of carriage are usually low, but if goods are heavy and bulky the costs of transporting them are higher. Thus, when finished products are bulkier than the raw materials used firms tend to be situated near to the consumer, and as consumers are dispersed throughout the country so are the firms.

A second factor determining dispersal of firms is whether or not a direct personal service is offered to the consumer. In retailing, for example, the service consists of providing suitable quantities of goods that consumers want and at convenient times. Similarly, the personal nature of the service provided by doctors, dentists, teachers, etc., requires these professions to be located close to wherever consumers are found. Hence firms providing direct services of a personal nature are dispersed throughout the country generally, according to the density of the population.

Distribution of industry and of population

There is a clear relationship in Great Britain between the location of industry and the distribution of the population. The latter is concentrated in a few main districts rather than being distributed evenly; and this concentration is in urban and not rural areas.

Urbanisation of the population

In the days before the Industrial Revolution the United Kingdom was predominantly an agricultural country and population tended to be much more widely dispersed than it is today. The development of industry on the coalfields drew workers to these areas and despite the fact that firms are no longer dependent upon steam as a source of power, the location of the basic industries continues to be on the coalfields.

Urban communities grew rapidly in the nineteenth century. Working hours were long, and transport largely undeveloped so that workers were obliged to live as close to their work as possible. Towns mushroomed in the industrial areas and workers migrated to them from the country. Whereas in 1801 nearly four-fifths of the total population lived in rural surroundings, by 1851 over one-third were living in towns of over 20000 inhabitants.

At the beginning of the twentieth century, the trend to urbanisation of the population had left only a quarter of the people of Great Britain in rural areas (an almost complete reversal of the position 100 years earlier). A consequence of this trend was the creation of conurbations, that is, areas where the suburbs of one town link up with the suburbs of another and there are no substantial stretches of countryside between them (see Table 6). These conurbations tend to suffer from overcrowding, lack of open spaces and traffic congestion.

Table 6   Conurbations

Conurbations	Population (thousands)				
	1921	1931	1951	1961	1971
Greater London	7488	8216	8348	8183	7393
South-East Lancashire	2361	2427	2423	2428	2387
West Midlands	1773	1933	2237	2347	2368
Central Clydeside	1638	1690	1760	1802	1728
West Yorkshire	1614	1655	1693	1704	1725
Merseyside	1263	1347	1382	1384	1264
Tyneside	816	827	836	855	805

Source: *Annual Abstract of Statistics*

The development of a town attracts not only people seeking employment in factories but also those non-industrial workers who find employment in satisfying the wants of those engaged in manufacture. Such employments include entertainments, insurance, banking, retailing and so on. Consequently the connection between the distribution of industry and the geographical distribution of the population becomes even more clearly outlined.

114

According to the 1971 Census Report some 77 per cent of the population of the United Kingdom live in urban areas.

Until the beginning of World War II (1939-45) the proportion of the population living in towns was slowly rising – a trend which had commenced with the Industrial Revolution. Since 1939 the trend towards town life has been reversed and the proportion of the total population in rural areas has increased. The change is due to such factors as the mobility afforded by increased car ownership and the desire for pleasanter surroundings away from the large towns. Most of the conurbations shown in Table 6 have experienced a decline in their population or a slowing down in the rate of increase. For example, the centre of London has now become a place in which to work rather than to live. Nevertheless the fact remains that the disparity in the population between urban and rural areas remains very marked.

The drift to the south
During the twentieth century, there has been a substantial shift in the geographical distribution of the population from the north to the south of England.

In the nineteenth century the importance of coal as a source of industrial power drew industry and workers to the Midlands, some northern and western areas of England, southern Wales and central Scotland. As the century progressed, the acquired advantages of the localisation of industry reinforced the natural advantages of the coalfield areas. Hence new firms were attracted by the external economies available and also because large centres of population provided potential customers.

London was the only major centre of population not situated on a coalfield. As the capital of the country, the centre of government and the law, and with financial and commercial connections, it had a strong attraction for many of the developing industrial firms, which set up their head offices in the City.

During the period 1918-39 the drift of population to the industrial areas of the North was countered by the decline in importance of coal as a factor influencing the location of firms. New industries such as motor vehicle manufacture, light engineering and rayon cloth manufacture were freed from a coalfield location by the availability of electric power on a national scale. As a result, sites in the south and east of England became very attractive. Thus a firm setting up near London had about one-fifth of its potential customers close at hand. If part of production was sold abroad, then the Port of London could deal with exports. Additionally, the climate was more favourable and the grime and deteriorating housing of the older industrial areas was less in evidence. The result was that people tended to migrate to the Midlands and the South of England where the new industries were being set up.

The trend of the 'drift to the south' has continued on a much larger scale since 1945. Table 7 shows the way in which the population is distributed between the economic planning regions. More than one-third of them (over 17 million) live in the South-East Region.

The southward movement of the population suggests that people have moved to where employment opportunities and prospects in the newer and thriving parts of the economy are best. Migration has taken place from the regions with outdated industrial structures and fewer job opportunities (see Table 7). Thus employment opportunities (created by changes in the location of industry) affect the distribution population of the country as a whole.

Table 7   Regional Distribution of UK Population

Region	Population (thousands)		Average annual net migration (thousands)
	1961	1971	1961-71
North England	3250	3292	− 10.8
Yorkshire and Humberside	4635	4794	− 7.0
North-West England	6567	6726	− 11.4
East Midlands	3100	3386	+ 7.1
West Midlands	4758	5105	− 1.3
East Anglia	1470	1666	+ 12.1
South-East England	16271	17133	− 3.7
South-West England	3411	3768	+ 22.4
Wales	2644	2724	− 0.4
Scotland	5179	5228	− 32.5
Northern Ireland	1427	1525	− 7.1

Source: *Britain, an official handbook*
The National Plan (Cmnd 2764)

QUESTIONS

Write *short* answers to the following:

1 Why is proximity to power supplies no longer a major determinant of industrial location?

116

2 Why is proximity to raw materials a relatively less important factor in location of a firm today?

3 Why is the steel industry located close to supplies of raw materials?

4 Why are brick-making firms located close to markets?

5 Name the advantages acquired by an area through localisation of industry.

6 Explain how acquired advantages can keep an industry located in an area when its natural advantages have ceased to exist.

7 How can the dependence of a district on a principal industry be a disadvantage?

8 How can government policy on location of industry affect a firm's costs?

9 What has been the principal aim of legislation to help areas of higher-than-average unemployment?

10 Name two factors which determine whether or not the firms in an industry are dispersed.

11 Briefly compare population distribution in the UK before the Industrial Revolution with today.

12 Why did urban communities grow rapidly in the nineteenth century?

13 What is a 'conurbation'?

14 Why has there been some reversal since 1939 of the trend to town life?

15 Why was there some 'drift to the north' of the population during the nineteenth century?

16 Why has there been a 'drift to the south' in population during the twentieth century?

Write answers to the following:

1 Explain why the steel industry is highly localised in Britain whereas the manufacture of furniture is widely dispersed. (WJEC)

2 Why are certain parts of the UK called 'Development Areas'? What kinds of help does the Government give to manufacturers who decide to establish factories in these areas? (AEB)

3 What factors ought to be taken into account by a newly formed manufacturing company when deciding where its factory ought to be located? How have British governments attempted in recent years to influence the location of industry? (AEB)

4 By what means can the Government influence the location of industry? (Oxford)

5 Explain why it is that some industries are highly localised while others are scattered throughout the country.   (Oxford)

6 'The assembly of motor vehicles is mainly concentrated in certain areas, whereas bakeries are generally more widely distributed.' Explain this statement giving reasons for these differences in locations.   (U/L)

7 How does the government influence the location of industry? Explain the advantages of this (a) to employees, and (b) to employers.   (U/L)

8 Describe the present-day geographical distribution of the population of the United Kingdom.   (U/L)

9 Discuss the main changes in the geographical distribution of the British population during the 20th century.   (SCE)

10 Why is the density of population so much greater in some areas of Britain than in others?   (Oxford and Cambridge)

11 Explain with examples, why some industries are concentrated in certain areas whilst others are more widely spread.   (U/L West Africa)

12 Discuss the economic forces that determine the location of productive units in a country. Give examples.   (RSA)

13 Assess the role of transport costs in influencing the location of any *one* industry.   (LCC)

PRACTICAL WORK

1 Select two local industrial firms in your area and find out
(a) the factors determining the original location of each firm;
(b) how far each firm is tied to its present location and for what reasons.

2 The map on page 257 shows the Economic Planning Regions of England and Wales. Find out the latest statistics showing the percentage of total population in each region.

3 Study the prospectus of a technical college in your area. Are any of the courses offered linked with the development of local skills?

10
Distribution

The aim of production is to satisfy consumers' wants. The production process is incomplete, therefore, until the point when commodities actually reach the persons who want them. Goods are distributed through the wholesale and retail trades.

Wholesaling

The wholesale trade serves as a connecting link between (a) the producer of raw materials and the manufacturer, and (b) the manufacturer and the retailer.

Thus the wholesale trade provides services to the following:

1 The producers of raw materials

The bulk of raw materials are imported and the wholesaler purchases supplies as they arrive in this country. In addition he deals with home produced raw materials and his aim is to find markets for both.

Organised markets called commodity exchanges provide meeting places where importers sell raw materials to wholesalers. Examples are the Wool Exchange, the Metal Exchange and the London Commodity Exchange in the City of London. Often an exchange is sited near the docks where the commodity is warehoused. Business is carried on according to a definite set of rules, although the actual procedure depends on whether the commodity is capable of being graded. Where grading is possible, as with wheat and cotton, the commodity need not actually be on view in the market, but some commodities, like wool and tea, vary in quality, and an opportunity must be given to buyers to inspect samples before the sale.

Commodity markets are conducted by brokers who act as agents for buyers and sellers. Commodities which can be easily graded are sold by private treaty; those which cannot be accurately graded and have, therefore, to be sampled and tested, are sold by auction.

Transactions on an exchange may be either for immediate ('spot') delivery or future delivery at one, two or three months ahead. In this way the seller is guaranteed a sale, while the buyer is sure of his future supplies of raw materials. Generally, only commodities which can be graded into standardised qualities can be bought and sold by means of forward contracts. Such commodities can be bought or sold without being seen because buyers and sellers know exactly what the grades mean.

Futures and hedging

Forward contracts are also known as 'futures' and dealings in futures take place in raw materials such as cocoa, coffee, sugar and rubber.

In a futures market there are people called *speculators* who are keenly interested in changes in prices and who try to take advantage of price fluctuations in order to make a profit for themselves. Speculators rarely buy or sell the actual commodity, but instead buy or sell futures contracts. The existence of such speculators makes it possible for those such as manufacturers and importers who store commodities, to 'insure' against risks of loss caused by changes in price. For example, if an importer who holds commodities for long periods fears a future fall in price, he can sell futures now to a speculator and so assure himself of receiving the present price. By doing so he insures himself against loss caused by a fall in price. On the other hand, the buyer of the futures is speculating against such a fall in price, for he hopes to be able to sell at a higher price at the agreed date. In a similar way, if a coffee manufacturer thinks the spot price of coffee is likely to rise in the next few months, he will buy futures (if they are quoted at a lower price than he expects to prevail in the future) as a 'hedge' against a rise in the price. If in fact the spot price rises higher than the price of the futures contract, the manufacturer receives the difference between the spot price and the price of his futures contract. Thus he is compensated for the *loss* on the raw material due to its rise in price by the *gain* on the futures contract. Alternatively if the price of coffee falls, the manufacturer buys on the spot market and pays the difference to the seller of the futures. Thus the *loss* on the futures contract, due to not accepting delivery, is compensated by the *gain* on the raw material due to its fall in price.

Functions of commodity exchanges

Commodity exchanges serve the following purposes.

(*a*) To facilitate the marketing of raw materials by provision of a central meeting place for the convenience of buyers and sellers.

(*b*) To enable buyers to ensure future supplies of raw materials.

(c) To enable producers to sell crops in advance at an assured price.

(d) To enable buyers to cover themselves against fluctuations in price by hedging. This function applies only when graded commodities make a futures market possible.

2 The manufacturer

(a) The wholesaler provides supplies of raw material obtained from home and overseas.

(b) The wholesaler saves the manufacturer a great deal of time and work by making bulk purchases from him and distributing goods to retailers.

This arrangement means that the manufacturer is saved the trouble and expense of dispatching a large number of very small parcels to retailers. The use of the wholesaler saves the manufacturer packing costs, clerical work and transport charges.

Manufacturers prefer to dispose of their output as quickly as possible, since many do not possess storage facilities for large quantities of goods. The wholesaler relieves the manufacturer of storage difficulties by storing finished products in a warehouse until they are required.

The wholesaler collects orders from a large number of retailers and, in the course of his work, he gains a knowledge of the state of the market. He is able, therefore, to inform the manufacturer of any changes in the demand for his products.

Generally, the manufacturer is not prepared to give credit to his customers. He requires large sums of cash every week in order to pay his employees' wages. Consequently he prefers to sell goods for cash. If goods were sold straight to retailers, a long period of credit would be necessary to allow some goods to be sold before payment is made. The wholesaler pays the manufacturer for goods as soon as they are received. In this way the wholesaler saves the manufacturer from having his capital 'tied up' in stock for long periods.

3 The retailer

(a) The wholesaler makes bulk purchases from manufacturers and sells to retailers in smaller quantities. The retailer may, therefore, draw upon the wholesaler's stocks at convenient times and he is saved the expense of maintaining large stocks and storage facilities at his premises. He can maintain a small stock of many individual items and so display an attractive range of goods.

(b) The wholesaler stocks the products of a large number of manufacturers and the retailer is provided with a wide range of choice. He is saved the time and expense of visiting, or ordering from a large number of manufacturers.

(c) Many retailers operate on only a small amount of capital and the wholesaler helps to finance a stock of goods by allowing a long period of credit. Thus a retailer can expect to sell goods before paying for them. If stocks were purchased direct from manufacturers, larger orders would be necessary and a very short period of credit would be allowed by the manufacturer. Under such conditions a retailer would require a greater amount of capital.

(d) As the connecting link between manufacturer and retailer, the wholesaler is in a position to give valuable advice to the retailer. For instance he will provide through his representatives, catalogues and price lists, details of new fashion trends, new products etc. He may also supply the retailer with window display material.

(e) At one time wholesalers used to weigh and re-pack such commodities as sugar for the convenience of retailers. Most goods are pre-packed by the manufacturer these days and small packets in larger packages are sent out to wholesalers. However, some wholesalers may undertake the preparation of the commodity for sale to retailers. Thus a wholesale tea merchant may purchase many kinds of tea, blend them, and pack the tea ready for sale. Some wholesale grocers perform a task in processing food by grinding coffee and smoking bacon.

Wholesale warehouses
Wholesale warehouses are needed to store commodities for the following reasons.

(a) *Most goods are produced ahead of demand* and warehouses are required for storage during the interim period. Warehousing enables the manufacturer to concentrate on making goods and to sell in bulk to wholesalers without coping with the problems of storage or retailing.

(b) *Many commodities are seasonal.* Raw materials arrive at British ports only at certain times during the year. For example, cotton is imported during the summer months and warehoused until required by manufacturers throughout the year. In the case of agricultural products, harvests take place at different times in different parts of the world. Warehousing ensures that food supplies are available to consumers throughout the year.

(c) *The avoidance of large fluctuations in prices.* The holding of stocks by wholesalers means that a sudden increase in demand by consumers can be met by retailers, quickly replenishing their stocks. Without large 'buffer' stocks in warehouses, a sudden increase in demand would lead to scarcity and a rapid rise in price. Similarly if demand falls, the wholesaler's policy of carefully limiting releases from his warehouse moderates the fall in price.

Voluntary groups

The small retailer is faced with ever-increasing competition from multiple stores and supermarkets. These large retailers purchase in such large quantities that they can cut out the wholesaler and buy direct from manufacturers. Consequently wholesalers as well as small retailers have suffered from the growth of large shops. They have a mutual interest in helping one another, and many wholesalers have invited small shops to link together in *voluntary chains* and *groups*.

A group consists of one wholesaler and a number of retailers whereas a voluntary chain consists of several wholesalers and a much larger number of retailers. The names of voluntary chains include VG, Mace and Spar. The organisation of a chain and a group is broadly similar. Retailers guarantee to make a large proportion of their purchases with a particular wholesaler who enjoys the certainty of a fixed quantity of business. The wholesaler saves the expense of sending out representatives to obtain orders and keep in touch with these retailers. In addition, delivery costs and clerical costs are also reduced. In return he offers retailers goods at reduced prices and provides other services such as group advertising on television and in national and local newspapers. Retailers in voluntary chains and groups enjoy the advantages of bulk buying which enables them to compete with large stores.

Self-service wholesaling

In the 1960's a few wholesalers began a *cash and carry* service for retailers and this form of wholesaling has grown rapidly.

The essence of cash and carry or self-service wholesaling is the elimination of credit, deliveries, loading expenses, sales representatives and invoicing. These savings in the wholesaler's costs enable him to reduce prices so that the small retailer can compete effectively with the supermarkets. The retailer may make as many visits a week to the cash and carry warehouse as he likes, so that he can use it as a storage warehouse. Consequently the amount of capital invested in stock is reduced.

Direct dealing

Although most manufactured products reach the retailer through a wholesaler, there are a number of examples where the manufacturer deals direct with the retailer or even the consumer.

Direct dealing occurs in the following instances.

(a) *Large-scale retailers.* Multiple shops and department stores often deal direct with the manufacturers. Their sales are so big that their orders are as large as those of a wholesale firm.

(b) *Manufacturers of branded goods.* Many makers of branded goods distribute their products direct to retailers in order to ensure that their products reach as many shops as possible. An independent wholesaler may not promote the sale of an article as strongly as the manufacturer would like. Hence manufacturers of branded goods prefer, where possible, to distribute direct to retailers. Sometimes products (such as radio and television) are marketed through a limited number of dealers appointed as 'sole agents' within specified areas. Such agencies are particularly appropriate where servicing and a repair service are important.

(c) *Where technical knowledge is of importance.* Manufacturers of office equipment, such as accounting machines, employ representatives with expert knowledge who deal directly with the consumer. The makers of equipment or machinery may undertake after-sales service, that is, they may offer a servicing and repair service.

In spite of the exceptions noted above, wholesaling is an essential part of the work of production. When the wholesaler is cut out, someone else has to do his work. For example, large shops which deal direct with manufacturers have to provide warehouses for their large stocks of goods.

Retailing

Functions of the retailer

All shops seek to offer certain basic services. They are as follows.

1 *A shopkeeper provides the goods that his customers want.* The retailer studies the needs and tastes of his customers and assembles a selection of merchandise to meet those requirements. If the exact requirement is not available a customer will be dissatisfied and may well go elsewhere. The retailer tries, therefore, to carry a varied stock, that is small quantities of many articles, in order to enable customers to exercise their choice.

2 *A shopkeeper provides goods at the time when his customers want them.* The retailer opens his shop for most of the day and waits for customers to come to buy when it suits them. The retailer may open early in the morning for the convenience of early morning shift workers and he may stay open late one evening a week in order to attract the custom of those who work during the day.

3 A shopkeeper provides goods that are suitable in quantity to customers' requirements. The word 'retail' means to cut up or cut off, and the breaking down of large quantities into single items is the prime service given by the retailer. He buys cases of goods ('wholes') from the wholesaler and splits them up into sizes that will suit his customers.

At one time, the retailer weighed, measured and packed goods but a great deal of this work is now done by the manufacturer, who pre-packs articles.

In addition to the three major functions outlined above, a shopkeeper may provide any or all of the following services for his customers.

(*a*) Delivery of goods.

(*b*) The collection of orders by calling at the homes of customers.

(*c*) The ordering of goods not in stock.

(*d*) Advice on purchases. He is the specialist who can help the shopper to judge the value, quality and performance of an article. He will also introduce the customer to the newest and most up-to-date goods.

(*e*) The repair of goods, and some retailers such as clothes outfitters will alter ready-made goods.

(*f*) The provision of credit to those of his customers whom he thinks he can trust.

(*g*) The exchange of goods returned as unsuitable by a customer.

The main kinds of shops are:

> Small shops
> Department stores
> Multiple or chain stores

All these are engaged in retail trade.

Small shops

Small shops (that is shops with no branches) do about half of all the retail business in this country, in spite of fierce competition from their bigger rivals. Small shops sell foodstuffs, clothing and footwear, furniture and household goods, tobacco, books, papers and countless other items as well.

Why is the small shop so popular with shoppers?

1 Many small shop-owners live 'on the premises', and their customers are neighbours. The shop may have the atmosphere of a local club where Christian names are used and personal affairs are discussed. Many people prefer this friendly relationship to the much more impersonal atmosphere of big shops.

2 Personal acquaintance with his customers enables the shop-keeper

125

to provide informal credit. Purchases made during the week may be booked down and paid for at the end of the week.

3 Many small shops are situated away from the main shopping centres. In other words they are within walking distance of homes, offices and factories. It is often handy to be able to obtain one or two items without having to take a journey into town.

4 The small shop-keeper enjoys greater freedom for opening times. Big shops (which employ large numbers of assistants) are restricted in this respect by trade union regulations and the requirements of the Shops Act. The small shopkeeper does not usually employ assistants and so he is not subject to the same legal restrictions on hours of opening. The small shopkeeper is willing to work long hours and often keeps his shop open when big shops are closed. Now that many housewives go out to work, a shop that stays open in the evening or at weekends is a great convenience.

5 Some shop-owners are able to match the 'cut prices' offered by the bigger shops by joining voluntary chains, and by purchasing stock from cash and carry warehouses (see page 123).

Department stores

A department store is a collection of shops under one roof and the aim is to provide in one building everything a customer might require.

Department stores seek to attract customers by the provision of thickly carpeted floors and expensive decorations and fittings. Within their walls are travel agencies, restaurants, hairdressing salons and other facilities which attract shoppers.

Advantages

1 A delivery service which allows customers to send orders by post or telephone.

2 Credit Accounts may be opened which enable customers to buy without having to pay cash on the spot.

3 Shoppers can wander round the store at leisure without being pressed to purchase by assistants.

From the owners' point of view this kind of shop provides opportunities for big sales and profits, economies from bulk buying and the benefits of employing experts in buying and selling.

On the other hand, department stores suffer a number of drawbacks.

Disadvantages

1 The cost of the luxury facilities provided may cause prices to be higher than in some shops.

2 In order to be economical a store needs to attract customers in large numbers. Only large towns or cities which serve as shopping centres for wide areas can support department stores. Consequently stores have to be positioned where rents are high. The store relies also upon quick and cheap transport facilities to bring shoppers from a wide area to shop.

3 Compared with the small shop the atmosphere in a department store is impersonal and formal. Some people may prefer not to shop there for this reason.

4 A store with a large number of departments presents management difficulties. Non-selling activities tend to increase rapidly in such stores and only about one-quarter of employees may be actually engaged in selling.

5 A large number of credit sales involves a great deal of book-keeping and this cost adds to the many high overhead expenses (light, rent, rates, etc.).

Multiple or chain stores
A multiple is a shop that has been multiplied until there is a chain stretching throughout a large area of the country. Some chains have over 2000 shops in their organisation, and the size of the trade gives to the multiple shop strong advantages over smaller rivals.

Multiples (such as Woolworth and Sainsbury) are well known in High Streets throughout the country, unlike the small shop which is only known locally.

Advantages
1 Bulk buying means buying more cheaply and lower prices can be charged to customers. A chain which orders 100 000 cases of goods pays less per case than a shop ordering only 25. Consequently prices to customers can be lowered. Some firms such as Boots actually manufacture many of their own goods for sale. In this way the chain earns the maker's and wholesaler's profits in addition to the retailer's margin. Usually a chain's own brand of goods is offered in its shops at a lower price than an independent manufacturer's product.

2 Nationwide branches of the same organisation mean that (a) stocks which are not selling well in one area may be transferred to another where demand is still high, and (b) all branches in the chain are not likely to suffer at the same time from a period of bad trade. For example, heavy unemployment in one part of the country may well reduce retail sales in the area, but branches in other regions can still be trading normally. Thus losses at a few branches can be carried while the chain as a whole is profitable. The multiple chain is in a very strong competitive

position, therefore, compared with the small shopkeeper who would be forced out of business if trading losses occurred.

Disadvantages

1 The major problem is that of controlling the activities of a large number of branches. The branch manager may be strictly controlled by head office so that he does not have the freedom of action enjoyed by an independent retailer.

2 Usually, no credit is given so that complicated book-keeping can be avoided. Some customers who cannot always pay cash may, therefore, be lost.

3 The atmosphere of these shops is more impersonal than that of the small 'shop around the corner'. Consequently, some customers may prefer to shop locally rather than at the chain store in the High Street.

Middlemen

Retailers and wholesalers are often described as 'middlemen'. The term can be used to describe anyone who comes between the producer and the consumer.

In the home trade the number of middlemen engaged in the distribution of a product depends on the particular character of the trade concerned. In some trades a single wholesaler provides the link between producer and retailer; in others, there may be two or more middlemen. For example in trades where there are large numbers of retailers with relatively small total sales (such as groceries and provisions, tobacco and cigarettes) it may be impossible for large-scale wholesalers to meet their needs. Thus smaller wholesalers buy from regional wholesalers and supply retailers in their local areas.

In foreign trade, the number of middlemen tends to be greater than in the home trade because there are more specialist functions to be performed. Many of these middlemen never own or handle the goods in which they deal. Import merchants, export merchants and brokers are examples of middlemen engaged in foreign trade. Import merchants, for example, arrange warehousing for consignments of goods from abroad and their subsequent sale on a commodity exchange. The work of selling is carried out by brokers who act as agents for buyers and sellers. Buyers include manufacturers and wholesalers who wish to buy supplies of raw material, and the sellers are the producers or growers of the commodity.

Middlemen are frequently blamed for the difference that may exist between the factory price and the price paid by consumers. It is certainly true that each middleman who deals with the goods has to make a profit, so he sells them at a higher price than the price he paid for them.

However, the retailer is not compelled to buy stock from a wholesaler; neither is a manufacturer required to sell to the wholesaler rather than direct to retailers. Thus the fact that many retailers and manufacturers deal voluntarily with wholesalers rather than directly with one another indicates that the wholesaler provides valuable services to both of them.

The greater the amount of specialisation that is introduced into distribution, the greater will be the number of middlemen employed between producer and retailer. Greater division of labour in distribution should mean more efficient distribution, just as in industry greater division of labour achieves more efficient output. Consequently when middlemen are specialists performing a necessary service, their work reduces the cost of distribution rather than increasing it.

Commercial activities
Wholesalers, retailers, importers and exporters are traders engaged in assisting the movement of raw materials in industry and the distribution of finished goods from industry to consumers. They are known as commercial workers. *Commerce* is concerned with the buying and selling of goods at any stage in their progress from raw materials to finished goods. In addition, commercial activities include the various services provided to finance, store, insure, transport and publicise goods during production. The divisions of commerce are shown in Figure 20.

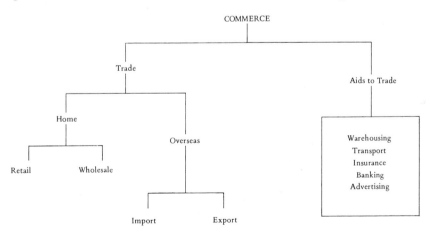

Fig. 20 The Divisions of Commerce

129

Warehousing provides storage facilities for goods until they are required. Many goods have a seasonal demand. For example, summer clothes made during the winter months must be stored until consumers wish to buy; Christmas trade goods are made early in the year and must be stored until needed.

Transport by road, rail, sea and air distributes raw materials and finished goods to where they are required at home or abroad.

Insurance provides compensation for damage to, or loss of, goods and raw materials. Hence traders are relieved of some of the risks – fire, theft, etc. – to which goods (both in the course of transport and in store) are liable.

Banks assist traders by providing (a) a variety of means of payment for goods, and (b) financial assistance in the form of loans and overdrafts.

Advertising provides consumers with information about goods available for sale and seeks to promote sales by persuading people to buy.

Warehousing, transport, insurance, banking and advertising are sometimes called the *aids to trade* because they help to make buying and selling safer and simpler.

QUESTIONS

Write *short* answers to the following.
1 Explain briefly why wholesaling and retailing form part of the production process.
2 Write down three examples of commodity exchanges.
3 What determines whether a commodity is sold (a) by private treaty or (b) by auction?
4 What is the meaning of 'spot' delivery?
5 What is a speculator?
6 How does speculation assist traders in commodities?
7 Define 'hedging'.
8 What are the functions of commodity exchanges?
9 Write down the services performed by the wholesaler for (a) the manufacturer and (b) the retailer.
10 Why are wholesale warehouses needed?
11 What is the difference between a voluntary group and a voluntary chain?
12 Why were voluntary groups and chains formed?
13 How does the cash and carry system reduce a wholesaler's costs?

14 How does the cash and carry system reduce the retailer's investment in stock?

15 Give two examples of direct dealing.

16 (a) What is 'retailing'? (b) What are the functions of the retailer?

17 List some services provided by retailers for their customers.

18 How does the small shopkeeper survive in the face of competition from bigger shops?

19 Why do people enjoy shopping in department stores?

20 Briefly contrast the department store with a chain store.

21 Why is a chain of shops in a better competitive position than the small shopkeeper?

22 What is a 'middleman'?

23 Do middlemen cause prices to be higher than would otherwise be the case?

Write answers to the following:

1 What part does the middleman play in the flow of goods from the manufacturer to the final consumer? Choose examples to illustrate your answer.   (U/L)

2 Describe clearly the organisation of *two* of the following indicating their main characteristics: 'one-man' businesses; multiple (chain) stores; supermarkets; 'cash and carry' stores.   (Cambridge)

3 What difficulties does the small shopkeeper face in Britain today? Has he any advantages?   (Oxford and Cambridge)

4 Are the distinctions of function between manufacturer, wholesaler, and retailer tending to disappear? Illustrate your answer with examples.   (Oxford and Cambridge)

5 What are the functions of organised British commodity markets? What role does trading in futures play in these markets?   (Oxford and Cambridge)

6 'Distribution is part of the process of production'. Explain this statement and indicate the functions of the wholesaler and the retailer in this process.   (U/L West Africa)

7 Why is the size of the business unit in the distributive trades (wholesaling and retailing) sometimes quite large, and sometimes quite small? Choose examples to illustrate your answer.   (U/L)

8 Imagine you are a wholesaler. Write a reasoned reply to a critic who maintains that wholesalers are unproductive.   (U/L)

9 Classify retail businesses into a few main types. Indicate the advantage of each type.   (U/L)

10 By considering their respective advantages, explain the circum-

stances in which (a) a large department store, and (b) a chain of stores, are likely to be successful. (U/L)

11 What are the differences between (a) retail markets, (b) wholesale markets, and (c) commodity markets? Explain how these markets facilitate the flow of goods from the producers to the final consumer. (U/L)

12 What are the functions of a wholesaler? How does the existence of wholesalers benefit consumers? (U/L West Africa)

13 Indicate clearly the meaning of (a) manufacturers, (b) wholesalers, (c) retailers, and (d) consumers. Using suitable examples describe the relationship between them. (U/L West Africa)

14 Warehousing, advertising, insurance and transport are all important forms of business activity. Account for the significance of these services in economic activity. (U/L)

15 Define production and discuss the contribution made to the productive process by those engaged in the distributive trades. (LCC)

PRACTICAL WORK

1 London is the main centre for organised commodity markets. Make use of a library to find out (a) the names of the principal markets and (b) the types of commodities dealt in.

2 Make a survey of the number of voluntary groups or chains operating in the area where you live.

3 Imagine that you wish to become a retailer in your locality. Discuss the following considerations with your fellow students and write down the conclusions. (a) Why might you (and many other people) wish to open a shop? (b) What considerations should you bear in mind before opening a shop?

PART FOUR
Resources

For the production of goods and services it is necessary to have available four resources, namely, land, labour, capital and enterprise. In Part four of this book these resources (or factors of production) are examined and discussed.

11

Labour

The supply of labour available to a community is the total number of people of working age. The factors which determine the size of this labour force are:

(*a*) the size of the total population
(*b*) the age distribution of the population
(*c*) the sex distribution of the population.

Total population
The size of the total population sets an upper limit to the total number of people of working age in a country.

In the United Kingdom, the primary source of population statistics is the population census. The first official census was carried out in 1801 and, with the exception of 1941, it has been repeated every 10 years since. The total population figures for the United Kingdom for a selection of years from 1841 to 1971 are given in Table 8.

Table 8   Population of the United Kingdom (millions)
1841 - 1971

1841	20.1
1901	38.2
1951	50.2
1971	55.5

Source: *Census 1971*

Although the census figures show that every 10 years there has been an increase in the population by something like 2 million, the rate of increase is much lower in this century than it was during the nineteenth century (see Table 9).

Table 9   Inter-censal Rate of Increase of UK
Population 1841 - 1971

Date	Rate of increase (per cent per year)
1841 - 51	1.00
1851 - 61	0.97
1861 - 71	1.13
1871 - 81	1.23
1881 - 91	1.00
1891 - 1901	1.10
1901 - 11	0.96
1911 - 21	0.44
1921 - 31	0.45
1931 - 39	0.45 (estimate)
1939 - 51	0.43 (estimate)
1951 - 61	0.48
1961 - 71	0.49

Source: *Census 1971*

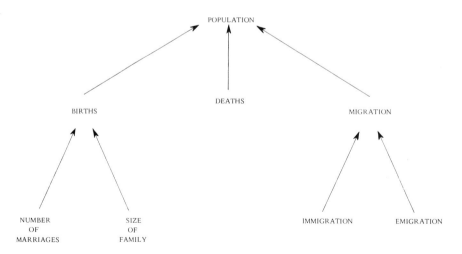

Fig. 21 The Factors affecting Population

An increase or decrease of population during any period depends upon,

(a) the number of births
(b) the number of deaths
(c) migration (see Fig. 21).

Records of births or deaths are kept by the Office of Population Censuses and Surveys (OPCS). The numbers of births and deaths in the country are measured by the birth rate and the death rate.

The *birth rate* is the number of live births per thousand of the population per year. For example, if in a particular year there were 750 000 live births in a population of 50 million, then the birth rate is calculated as:

$$\frac{750\,000}{50\,000\,000} \times 1000 = 15$$

Thus the birth rate is 15 per thousand. Similarly the *death rate* is the number of deaths per year per thousand of the population.

The difference between the birth rate and the death rate is called the rate of natural increase or decrease of the population. Fig. 22 shows the rate of natural increase in population in the UK since 1871.

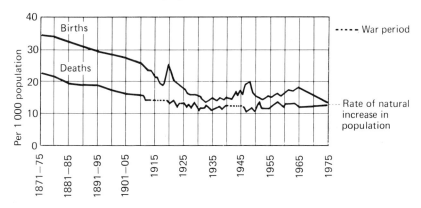

Fig. 22 Rate of Natural Increase in Population

Migration represents the net balance between the numbers of persons leaving the country (emigration) and those entering the country (immigration). Table 10 shows the net gain or loss by migration in the population of the UK.

Table 10 Net gain or loss by migration in the
population of the UK

Period	Migration (thousands) (Net immigration+ Net emigration −)
1901 - 11	− 820
1911 - 21	− 919
1921 - 31	− 672
1931 - 51	+ 435
1951 - 61	+ 57
1961 - 71	− 475

Source: *Annual Abstract of Statistics*

Fig. 22 shows that during the last hundred years or so the general trend in the United Kingdom has been for both the birth rate and the death rate to decline.

A major cause of the fall in the death rate has been the progress of medical science. Diseases such as cholera and typhus which in the past produced epidemics resulting in a large number of deaths were virtually eliminated by the end of the nineteenth century.

Another factor has been the rising standard of living. Greater wealth has made possible the building of more hospitals, the provision of better housing and the shortening of the working week. In addition, improvements in methods of transport made available cheaper food from abroad. The overall result has been a higher standard of health and hygiene.

The chief cause of the fall in the birth rate from the 1870s to the 1940s was the decrease in the size of the family. In the Victorian era the average number of children per family was between five and six but by 1930 it was just over two.

It seems that the reduction in the size of families has been due to planned limitation on the part of parents. But birth control only made possible the limitation of the number of children. The reasons why parents wanted smaller families are rooted in the social and economic changes of the period.

In the first place, before the Factory and Education Acts children became wage-earners at a very early age, but legislation gradually raised the age of entering employment so that by 1918 no child under fourteen could go to work. Children were no longer a source of income and the maintenance of a large number reduced the standard of living of the family.

A second factor was the emancipation of women. Bringing up a large family prevented women pursuing careers of their own and consequently there was a tendency to have fewer children.

Thirdly, the rising standard of living resulted in a number of attractions (such as foreign travel, cars and holidays) being available, particularly for those who preferred them to the expense of bringing up children.

The birth rate rose during the period 1941 - 1947; it declined then until 1955 when it rose again until 1964, since when it has fallen.

Age distribution of the population

By age distribution is meant the division of the population into different age groups. The most useful grouping for purposes of calculating the labour supply is the following:

Group 1   Young persons under 16 years of age
Group 2   People of working age, namely, 16 to 64 years
Group 3   Older persons aged 65 years and over

Group 1 is composed of young people below the official school-leaving age. The latter was raised from 15 to 16 years in 1972.

Group 2 comprises people of working age, that is, 16-64 years for men and 16-59 years for women. The latter may retire at 60 whereas the official working life of men extends to 65.

Group 3 is made up of those who will generally have retired from work, namely, men aged 65 and over and women aged 60 and over.

Table 11   Age Distribution of the Population of the UK

Age Group	1901	1911	1931	1951	1961	1971
Population (millions)						
Under 15	12.4	13.0	11.1	11.3	12.3	13.4
15 - 64	24.0	26.9	31.4	33.4	34.1	34.8
Over 65	1.8	2.2	3.4	5.5	6.1	7.3
Percentage of	1901	1911	1931	1951	1961	1971
Total Population						
Under 15	32.4	30.0	24.2	22.5	23.4	24.0
15 - 64	62.8	63.9	68.4	66.5	64.9	63.0
Over 65	4.8	5.2	7.4	11.0	11.7	13.0

Note: Although the official school leaving age was raised from 15 to 16 in 1972, official statistics continue to use the groupings 'under 15' and '15-64'.

Source: *Annual Abstract of Statistics*

137

An important feature of the age distribution of the population is the relationship between the population of working age and the numbers it has to support in the two dependent groups. (The latter consume goods and services but do not contribute to their production.) This relationship is expressed in the *dependency ratio* which measures the numbers of children under 15 years and people of retirement age together per 1000 people of working age. The ratio has climbed steeply from 502 'dependants' per 1000 in 1951 to 595 in 1971. It follows that for some years those in the working age group have had to produce more goods and services in order to maintain the total population at the current standard of living.

Changes in age distribution
A change in the age composition of the population has been caused by the tendency for the birth and death rates to decline (see Fig. 22). Between 1901 and 1971 the number of people over retirement age increased by 301 per cent, while the total population increased by only 45 per cent in the period. The broad effect has been to produce an increasingly ageing population.

There are a number of major economic consequences of an ageing population.

In the first place, the cost of retirement pensions is likely to increase and this extra cost will have to be paid for in taxation by the working population.

Another factor is that the maintenance of full employment becomes more difficult. This is due to a number of reasons. In the first place, the demand of the younger section of the population will decline relative to the demand of the older members of the community. Unemployment due to changes in demand may, therefore, increase. Secondly, industries which are expanding usually recruit additional workers from school, further education college or university while the declining industries reduce their labour force by not replacing workers who have retired. Consequently older workers may not have to move from one area to another and learn new jobs. However, an ageing population means that the number of new entrants to industry will decline whereas the proportion of elderly workers increases. It follows that expanding industries will have to meet their increased labour requirements by recruiting older workers from the declining industries. Older people are, generally, much less willing to move and rather less able to learn a new job than younger persons, which could cause unemployment to increase.

Thirdly, because demand for many types of goods and services is peculiar to certain age groups, any change in the numbers in each age group will alter the pattern of demand. Thus an increase in the 65 years and over age group means that there will be a rising demand for old people's homes, welfare services and medical care. (Similarly a rise in the birth rate means an increasing demand for primary and secondary school places, educational materials, baby foods, prams, teenage fashions and so on.)

Sex distribution of the population

Women outnumber men in the total population. In 1971 there were nearly 106 females to every 100 males in the United Kingdom. However, if one looks at those under the age of 45 one finds that the ratio of males to females is about equal, whereas after the age of 45 females exceed males so that by the age of 70 there are nearly twice as many females as males.

The sex distribution of the population has an important effect on the labour supply. If the number of females in the population exceeds the number of males, then the labour supply is likely to decrease because, generally, women retire from work at 60 whereas men work for another five years. Anything which reduces the number of males in the population is likely to lead to this effect. For example, in wartime, casualties are higher among men and consequently, there is a rise in the proportion of women in the population. Another factor reducing the proportion of men is emigration (more men than women tend to emigrate).

The working population

The working population is not the same as the total number of people of working age in the country. The latter is the *potential* supply of labour whereas the working population is the number who actually seek employment.

The Department of Employment defines the working population as those over 16 years of age 'who work for pay or gain or register themselves as available for such work.' Included within this definition are:

(a) everyone who is employed including those over the official retirement age (65 for men, 60 for women) and those who are working part-time;

(b) employers and self-employed persons;

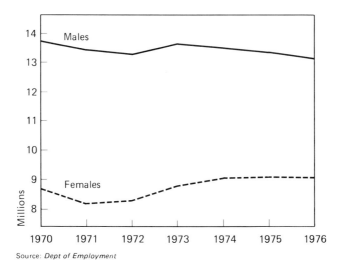

Source: *Dept of Employment*

Fig. 23 Employees in Employment

(c) members of the armed forces;
(d) people registered at employment offices as unemployed and available for work.

Excluded by this definition are:

(a) children under 16 and students who continue their education full-time beyond the age of 16 years;
(b) housewives who do not go out to work;
(c) people who do not need to work because they enjoy private incomes;
(d) retired persons including those such as policemen who retire before the official retiring age;
(e) those who are unemployable because of some physical or mental disability.

Factors determining the growth and size of the working population

The growth and size of the working population of a country are determined by the age and sex distribution of the population; the degree of industrial development; and social organisation.

The influences of age and sex distribution on the proportion of the population which is of working age have been noted on pages 137- 9. Industrial development and social custom are other important factors to consider.

In a poor, agricultural economy, the efforts of the entire family from the youngest to the oldest may be needed to scratch even a bare existence from the soil, whereas in an industrialised community the application of mass production techniques may necessitate the employment of only part of the total population. In addition, men and women in a poor country may have to continue at work so long as they are physically capable of doing so whereas, for example, in the UK which is a relatively rich country, at the present time the working population consists chiefly of those within the 16 to 64 age group – those under 16 being at school and those aged 65 and over being entitled to a retirement pension. Although the labour force is reduced by keeping children at school, this loss may be more than made up by the improved efficiency of the working population resulting from a high standard of education and training.

Whereas in a primitive economy people of both sexes may have to work in order to make a living, in an industralised economy fewer women are expected to work. However, in this country during the present century the extent to which married women obtain employment has altered. Before World War I (1914-18) it was not fashionable for girls from middle-class families to go out to work. However, the events of two World Wars during which women had to perform many of the jobs done formerly by men, changed this attitude considerably, so that the supply of female labour has increased. Today more than one-half of the female working population consists of married women, and since 1921 the proportion of all married women at work has increased from one in ten to nearly fifty per cent.

Occupational distribution of the working population

Having arrived at an understanding of the term 'working population', it is important to consider its distribution among the different occupations. The Department of Employment lists over 30 000 occupations in its Standard Industrial Classification but broad groupings are shown in Table 12.

Table 12   Occupational Distribution of the Working Population
of the United Kingdom June 1975 (thousands)

Agriculture, forestry, fishing	401
Mining, quarrying	352
Manufacturing:	
Food, drink, tobacco	726
Chemical and allied industries	470
Metal manufacture	501
Engineering and allied industries	3383

141

Textiles, leather and clothing	974
Other manufacturing	1435
Total manufacturing	7489
Construction	1313
Gas, electricity and water	353
Transport and communications	1518
Distributive trades	2763
Financial, professional, business and scientific services	4659
Catering, hotels etc.	826
Miscellaneous services	1376
National government service	650
Local government service	1005

Primary employment: all extractive occupations, the products of which are food-stuffs and raw materials.

Secondary employment: those engaged in the production of manufactured goods and also in building and construction.

Tertiary employment: the labour force engaged in services to aid industry or for the direct benefit of consumers, including public utilities (gas, electricity and water), transport and communications, distribution trades, banking and financial services, professional and scientific activities, catering, and all the services of central and local government.

Source: *Annual Abstract of Statistics*

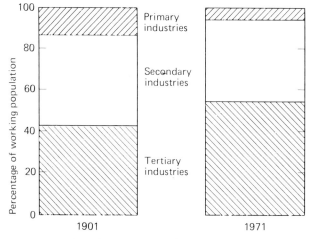

Fig. 24 The Changing Distribution of Employment

Changes in occupational distribution

During this century there have been major changes in the occupational distribution of workers in the United Kingdom as can be seen in Fig. 24.

In the first place, there has been a decline in the numbers employed in the primary or extractive industries particularly in agriculture and coal-mining. There are a number of reasons for these changes. For example, although coal is still an important source of power, greater mechanisation and shrinking markets due to competition from natural gas, oil and nuclear power have resulted in a reduction in the work force. Similarly, whereas seventy years ago, agricultural methods were labour-intensive, i.e. requiring a large amount of man-power, today the industry relies on expensive capital equipment and a smaller proportion of labour.

Table 13   Distribution of Employment

	Percentages	
	1961	*1976*
Primary (extractive)	6	3
Secondary (manufacturing and construction)	46	41
Tertiary (services and public utilities)	48	56

Secondly, since the 1960s there has been a steady drift downwards in employment in the secondary or manufacturing industries (see Table 13) and within this group there have been changes in the importance of different industries as employers of labour. Older industries such as shipbuilding and textiles have declined while the newer, lighter industries such as chemicals, engineering and vehicles have expanded. The main reason for these shifts has been technological change. For example, a large share of world passenger traffic has been taken from shipping by the development of air transport and the quantity of freight carried by air is increasing. At the same time other countries have developed their own shipbuilding industries in direct competition with the industry in this country. The textile industry has declined and chemicals have expanded due to increasing use of man-made fibres and plastics. A further example of technological change is the growth of the communications industry which has provided many additional jobs. Other growing occupations are concerned with electronics and the use of computers.

The decline of the older industries based on coalfields and the expansion of newer industries close to the markets formed by centres of population has resulted in a drift of the working population to the Midlands and South-East of England (see Chapter 9).

Thirdly, the tertiary or service industries have been the most rapidly expanding group. The main reasons have been the redistribution of wealth and the increased leisure brought about by technological changes. Consequently there has been a growth in demand for a wide range of financial and personal services. These include insurance, banking, tourism, advertising and education. There has also been a growth in the numbers employed in the distributive trades.

There has been some change in the nature of employment within this category. At the beginning of the century much of the employment in 'services' comprised those in domestic service. Social changes have reduced the numbers in this work.

Women in employment
About forty per cent of the working population is made up of women and more than half of all women workers are married.

The Sex Discrimination Act 1976, in general, forbids discrimination against women in opportunities for employment.

According to the census of employment 1973 the largest numbers of women were found, as Fig. 25 shows, in the service industry groups. In four service industry groups women outnumbered men. These were the professional and scientific services, which include teachers, nurses and social workers; the 'miscellaneous' group, which includes workers in hotels, restaurants and public houses, laundries and hairdressing, and which had the highest proportion of part-time workers in the whole census; the distributive trades; and insurance, banking and similar services. In only one of the manufacturing industry groups (clothing and footwear), was there a preponderance of women over men employees.

The industry groups which, as Fig. 25 shows, employ the fewest women in proportion to men are construction, shipbuilding and marine engineering, coal and petroleum products manufacture, and the whole extractive industries sector. In the last there is a practical difficulty in that women are prohibited by law from working underground in mining.

The range of variation in the extent of women's employment between different parts of the country is not very great. The proportion of women to all employees varies from 36.4 per cent in Wales to 40.4 per cent in Scotland.

	No. of women employed ('000s)	Women as percentage of all employees 0 10 20 30 40 50 60 70 80
Agriculture, forestry & fishing	114.6	
Mining & quarrying	13.9	
Construction	93.9	
Manufacturing industries		
Food, drink & tobacco	294.6	
Coal & petroleum products	4.4	
Chemicals & allied industries	123.0	
Metal manufacture	58.3	
Mechanical engineering	150.0	
Instrument engineering	57.5	
Electrical engineering	317.6	
Shipbuilding & marine engineering	11.8	
Vehicles	96.8	
Other metal products	166.2	
Textiles	256.1	
Leather, leather goods & fur	19.1	
Clothing & footwear	314.6	
Bricks, pottery, glass, cement etc.	64.7	
Timber, furniture etc.	55.3	
Paper, printing & publishing	185.4	
Other manufacturing industries	127.1	
Total, manufacturing industries	2,302.5	
Services		
Gas, electricity & water	59.7	
Transport & communications	256.3	
Distributive trades	1,486.4	
Insurance, banking, finance & business services	540.0	
Professional & scientific services	2,115.3	
Miscellaneous services	1,171.0	
Public administration & defence	550.7	
Total, services	6,179.4	
Grand total for all industries and services	8,704.3	

Source: Census of employment (*Department of Employment Gazette*, May 1974)

Fig. 25 Women in Employment

Optimum population

This is a term used in economics to describe that number of people which, when combined with the other resources of land and capital, yields the maximum output of goods and services per head of the population.

Thus mere numbers alone do not indicate whether or not a country is over- or under-populated. Production requires the employment of a range of resources, of which labour is only one, and these have to be combined in a certain proportion in order to obtain the maximum output.

A country is said to be under-populated if a larger population would lead to an increase in output per head. Thus under-population may exist even in a well-populated region if there is insufficient labour to make the best use of other resources.

A country is said to be over-populated if a smaller population would lead to an increase in output per head. In other words, there are more people than can make the best use of the available resources. Thus a country poor in natural resources and lacking capital might be economically over-populated, although in point of numbers its population was small.

QUESTIONS

Write *short* answers to the following:

1 What factors determine the supply of labour in a country?
2 What is the primary source of information on population in the UK?
3 Name three determinants of changes in total population.
4 Define the birth rate.
5 If in a given year there were 800000 deaths in a population of 40 million, what was the death rate?
6 How is the rate of natural increase or decrease of a population calculated?
7 What is meant by 'age distribution' of the population?
8 Name three population groupings which are useful for calculating the labour supply.
9 What is the 'dependency ratio'?
10 State briefly the economic consequences of an ageing population.
11 What is the 'sex distribution' of the population?
12 Which groups of persons are (*a*) included in, (*b*) excluded from, the working population as defined by the Department of Employment?
13 State the factors affecting the growth and size of the working population.
14 What does 'occupational distribution' of the population mean?
15 Describe briefly the industrial distribution of women's occupations.

Write answers to the following:

1 What is meant by the working population in the United Kingdom? What may cause the size of it to change, assuming the total population of the country does not change? (WJEC)

2 For what reasons may the size of a country's population change? (SUJB)

3 'The population of Britain is gradually ageing.' What does this statement mean? Explain the causes of this trend, and suggest the economic consequences which it is likely to have. (SUJB)

4 Define (a) birth rate and (b) death rate. How have relative changes in each during this century influenced the age-distribution of the population of the United Kingdom? What effects has this had on the labour market? (U/L)

5 What would be the main economic effects on the UK of (a) a significant increase in population, and (b) a significant decrease in population? (Cambridge)

6 Describe and account for the changes that have occurred in the occupational distribution of the population of the United Kingdom during this century. (U/L)

7 What is meant by the 'age-distribution of population'? Discuss the characteristics of the age-distribution of the population of the United Kingdom. (U/L)

8 What do you understand by the occupational distribution of the British working population? How has this changed since 1945? (Oxford and Cambridge)

9 How have population trends in the United Kingdom changed in the last twenty years in size, sex and age distribution? (AEB)

PRACTICAL WORK

1 Try to find out why the birth rate (a) rose 1941-47, (b) declined 1947-55, (c) rose 1955-64 and (d) declined after 1964.

2 Find out the current official estimates of the future growth of the UK population.

3 *Essay on Population* (1798) by the Rev. T. R. Malthus was the first attempt to give serious attention to the population problem. Find out the substance of Malthus' argument and consider whether his views have relevance today.

4 Look up Table 10 on page 136 showing the net loss or gain by migration in the UK population. Find out (a) why the UK lost population by migration until 1931, and (b) why, after then, the trend was reversed.

5 Refer to Table 12 on pages 141-2 showing the occupational distribution of the working population. Use the *Monthly Digest of Statistics* to find out which industries are expanding their labour force and which are contracting.

6 Find out (a) the ratio of male births to female births, and (b) the number of males and the number of females in the UK population. What conclusion do you draw from the comparison? Can you suggest reasons for what you have discovered?

12
Wages

Wage rates and earnings

In the previous chapter it was stated that the total number of people of working age forms the supply of labour available to a community. This is true if the term 'labour supply' is restricted to mean a particular number of people. However, a more comprehensive definition of the term takes account of the number of hours of work offered by each individual worker. Hence a fuller meaning of the supply of labour is (a) the number of people available for work and (b) the total number of hours of work which they offer.

Probably the most important factor affecting the number of hours which people will work is the wage or salary offered. *Salaries* are usually paid on a monthly basis whereas a *wage* means a payment on a weekly basis. *Earnings* refers to the actual gross amount received by an employee at the end of a week or a month. Thus weekly earnings may be larger than the weekly wage rate because of overtime payments, productivity bonuses, etc. Similarly a basic monthly salary paid, for example, to a salesman may be augmented by commission on sales he has made.

Table 14   Wage Drift
(percentage change on previous year)

Year (1)	Average Hourly Earnings (2)	Average Hourly Wage Rate (3)	Wage Drift (2 minus 3)
1970	16.0	12.4	+3.6
1971	13.7	11.6	+2.1
1972	14.6	18.1	− 3.5
1973	13.6	12.1	+1.5
1974	21.9	20.6	+1.3
1975	28.6	26.5	+2.1

Source: *Department of Employment Gazette*

149

Details of changes in wage rates and changes in earnings are published by the Department of Employment. Table 14 shows that earnings have tended to increase faster than wage rates. The extent to which earnings exceed wage rates is called *wage drift*. It suggests that, due to a shortage of labour, employers have had to offer wage rates higher than those agreed with the trade unions in order to attract workers into their employment. Generally, wage drift occurs as a result of locally negotiated rates of pay in excess of nationally agreed rates. Hence it is not spread evenly throughout all areas of the country. Employers often have to pay 'above the rate' in areas where labour shortages occur.

Differences in earnings in different occupations

Earnings vary between different occupations. For example, barristers, film stars and company directors may earn in a year ten or twenty times the earnings of clerks, office cleaners and labourers. Differences in earnings between occupations are due chiefly to differences in the demand for and the supply of the particular kind of labour.

There are as many markets for labour as there are types of labour. For example, there is a market for typists, another for bakers, yet another for butchers and so on. Occupations differ in their training requirements and in the need for applicants to possess special aptitudes to follow them successfully.

The better-paid occupations might be expected to attract more new entrants than those that are poorly paid. Consequently the supply of labour in better-paid occupations would rise and wages would fall. At the same time because of the reduced supply of labour in the less well-paid jobs, wages would rise in order to attract new recruits. It might be supposed, therefore, that wages in all occupations would tend towards equality, but this does not happen for a number of reasons.

The period of training may be long and quite expensive, as is the case with teachers, doctors, architects and accountants. Attendance at a university for three years or more may be required and the necessity of passing an examination at the end of the course adds a measure of uncertainty. Similarly, a person may spend five years serving an apprenticeship in order to acquire a skill. Only those with sufficient mental capacity, perseverance and character are likely to succeed and the supply of such persons relative to the demand is low. Hence the price of their services is high. On the other hand the supply of labour for unskilled and semi-skilled occupations requiring no particular qualifications other than good health is much larger so that sometimes, supply may exceed demand and wage rates are relatively low.

Where a special talent is necessary for success – as is the case with film stars, pop singers and ballerinas, little can be done to increase supply and persons possessing a unique talent can earn very large sums of money because of the scarcity value. It is not enough, however, to have exceptional gifts in order to earn an exceptionally high income. It is necessary also to have those particular gifts which are most in demand. For example, not many artists have ever made large fortunes, and the ability of a teacher, a social reformer or a politician may be far more poorly rewarded than the ability to entertain and amuse. Thus a pop singer can earn more than the Prime Minister. The most financially successful workers are those who can provide the services for which consumers are willing to pay, not those who, on a moral or aesthetic judgement, are most deserving of reward.

Some occupations offer certain advantages of a non-monetary kind. For example, some kinds of work are more congenial than others and are carried on under pleasanter conditions. In some jobs the employee has a greater degree of independence than in others. A high degree of security of employment may be another attractive feature while some occupations offer other material rewards beside the money wage, such as lunch vouchers, or the use of a company car. On the other hand some jobs, such as mining, are unpleasant; some, such as that of steeplejacks, are dangerous; and others involve various degrees of inconvenience such as shift working, absence from home and working at weekends or public holidays. Generally the greater the non-monetary advantages of a job the greater will be the supply of recruits and hence, the lower the wages. On the other hand the more unpleasant or inconvenient the occupation the fewer there will be who will wish to enter it and hence the higher the financial rewards. It is not, however, always necessary to offer higher wages in order to get unpleasant work done. This type of work often requires little skill and as the supply of unskilled labour often exceeds demand it is poorly paid. Nevertheless in times of full employment many of the more disagreeable jobs become difficult to fill unless higher wages are offered.

Differences in earnings within the same occupation

Rates of pay for people doing similar work may vary due to (a) wage drift and (b) the geographical immobility of labour.

Wage drift raises earnings on a local basis in areas where labour shortages occur. It is, therefore, a means of attracting labour to an area.

However, a higher level of earnings may fail to attract workers because of obstacles hindering their easy movement from one area to another. Some of the restricting influences are as follows.

1 Changing jobs can involve considerable inconvenience. It may mean uprooting a family from accustomed surroundings and old friends to start life afresh in a strange place.

2 A change may be costly. The costs of removal, of selling one house and buying another may be sufficiently high to deter moving to a new area.

3 There is a risk that the relatively high earnings in an area may be only temporary.

As a result of all these factors, differences in earnings exist between workers of the same occupation in different industries and in different areas of the country.

Real earnings and money earnings
The distinction between real and money earnings is important.

Money earnings are the actual sums of money received by an employee in return for his services. Real earnings consist of the amount of goods and services which can be consumed with the money earnings. Money earnings are expressed, therefore, in terms such as '£60 per week' but real earnings relate to the prices of consumer goods. Thus it is possible for money earnings to increase while real earnings are falling, and vice versa. For example, if prices of consumer goods rise at a faster rate than an increase in money earnings, then real earnings will fall. On the other hand if money earnings fall, but prices of consumer goods fall faster, then real earnings would increase. Similarly if money earnings remain stable, real earnings will fall if prices rise; or real earnings will rise if prices fall.

The distinction between real and money earnings means that any comparison between earnings of people in different occupations has to take account of payments in kind or *fringe benefits*. For example, some jobs carry the right to subsidised meals in the firm's dining rooms, to a free uniform or to free travel to and from work. Others provide the use of a car or the privilege of buying certain goods at very low prices. A comparison based solely on money earnings would fail to take account of these 'fringe benefits.'

Any comparison between earnings at different periods of time will necessitate the use of real rather than money earnings. It is not sufficient to know, for example, that in 1900 average weekly earnings were about £1 per week; that in 1939 the figure had risen to £3.50; in 1973 to £41; and in 1975 to £60. In monetary terms, wages had improved by 60 times between 1900 and 1975, but without information of goods or services that could be obtained with the money, the comparison is meaningless.

Methods of payment

An employer may pay his employees on the basis of the *time* they work for him or on the basis of the *quantity of goods* which they produce. The latter system is known as the *piece-rate* system and the former as the *time-rate* system. When a worker is engaged on a time-rate basis the employer requires a certain standard of achievement or performance but if earnings are calculated on a piece-rate basis then the employer expects a certain minimum output.

Time-rate payments take the form of either salaries or wages. They are usually calculated as a certain sum of money per hour. All workers, good and bad, receive equal payment if they work the same number of hours. The employer, therefore, must keep records of the number of hours worked by each employee and usually this is done by workers recording the times of their arrival and departure on a time-clock. A further drawback of this system is that close supervision of workers is often necessary in order to prevent slacking.

Both employer and worker gain some advantages from time-rate payments. When employers and trade unions negotiate rates of pay, they do so on the basis of standard hourly wage rates for particular jobs. This means that the employer can estimate his labour costs very easily and a worker is not required to make an individual bargain with an employer before taking a job – a process which would be time-consuming to both parties.

Time-rates, however, may encourage slackness, and it is necessary to see that the worker does not waste time. In addition, time-rates do not compensate the more efficient worker for his greater industry. Apart from the possibility of promotion, there is no incentive to induce harder work.

In order to provide employees with an incentive to work harder, employers may make the wage dependent on the amount of work done. In its simplest form this system provides the worker with a fixed payment for every unit of work produced. His weekly wages will, therefore, depend upon how many units he can turn out in a week.

Piece-rates can be operated only where each worker's output can be easily measured. If the work is of a continuous nature where quality is important, then payment by piece-rates is not possible. Thus the work of nurses, teachers and shop workers cannot be measured and paid on a piece-rate basis. Neither can bus or train drivers be offered an incentive to accomplish as many journeys in a stated time as possible. However, workers engaged on assembly work, such as in the manufacture of radios and cars, can be paid by the amount they produce.

Piece-rates provide a number of advantages compared with time-rates. The employee has the satisfaction of feeling that his wages are directly related to his effort, whereas, under the time-rate system, good, bad and indifferent workers receive the same reward. The employee is also free from time-keeping and the constant supervision of a foreman. Piece-rates usually bring workers higher earnings. To the employer, a system of piece-rates means the cost of supervising employees will be saved because any slacking will affect workers in the form of lower earnings. Almost certainly, output will be increased and costing is facilitated because the labour costs required to produce a particular number of articles are known in advance.

On the other hand, the piece-rate system tends to encourage rushed work because some employees try to increase their wages at the expense of good workmanship. Thus it will be necessary to employ inspectors to check the quality of the work done.

A second drawback is that continued work at high pressure may prove ultimately harmful to the worker's health and efficiency.

In addition, difficulties may arise in fixing piece-rates. For example, two workers may perform exactly the same task and work equally hard, but with different outputs because they are using machines of different age. Unless adjustments in the basic rates can be made in such cases, friction between employer and employee is likely.

A third method of paying employees is by a *bonus system*. There are a number of these systems and they vary from each other in detail but the basis of most of them is a standard wage for an agreed output plus an additional payment for anything produced beyond the agreed standard. The aim of a bonus system is to reduce some of the drawbacks of straightforward piece-work, such as rushing and neglecting the quality of work. One drawback to a bonus system is that it is more complicated than simple piece-work and, therefore, more difficult for workers to understand.

The determination of wage rates

In the days before large-scale production, workmen negotiated their own wage with their employers. Today the wages and salaries of the majority of workers are settled by a collective bargaining procedure between two groups, namely representatives of the employers (employers' associations) and representatives of the employees (trade unions).

These negotiations settle wages for whole industries or large groups of workers. They lay down basic wage rates and salary scales, overtime rate and holidays. In many cases the agreements are for minimum rates and it is left to the local or plant negotiators to settle details and terms for any earnings in addition to the nationally agreed rates.

Employers' associations

Employers have formed associations in much the same way as that in which employees have formed unions. The Confederation of British Industry (CBI) is a combination of employers' associations and has a membership of about 14 000 individual companies and 300 employers' associations.

Functions of trade unions

The main purpose of a trade union is to enable employees to act as a *group*. Negotiations with employers are carried out by union officials on behalf of the group. One man by himself asking for higher wages or improved working conditions will have little influence; but a large number of men combining together for this purpose will have a much stronger bargaining power.

Trade unions protect the jobs, pay and working conditions of their members. These include wages, hours of work, overtime, apprentice-

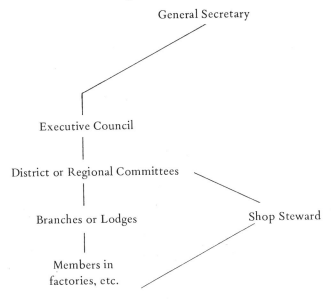

Fig. 26 Trade Union Organisation

155

ship, holidays and redundancies. Questions of health and safety at work are very much the concern of trade unions.

A third function is to offer a range of monetary benefits for their members. Before the development of the welfare state, trade unions were, very often, the only source of financial help to working people in need. The unions provided sickness pay, unemployment pay, accident benefit, pensions, and strike pay. Many of them still provide these services.

Help with education and further training is available for members. There are correspondence courses of various kinds; weekend schools; and classes held by the Workers' Educational Association.

Finally, trade unions try to ensure that their members' interests are considered in a wide area of national life. To this end they play a prominent part in politics. The Labour Party itself developed out of the work of the trade unions in the early years of this century and it is still partly supported financially by trade unions. In addition trade unionists are represented on such bodies as the Monopolies and Mergers Commission, the National Economic Development Council and the National Youth Employment Council. Discussions are held frequently with the government and the Confederation of British Industry.

Types of trade unions

A clear-cut distinction between the different types of trade unions is difficult to make because there is a considerable amount of overlapping. However, the four principal types are shown in Table 15.

Table 15   Types of unions

Category	Examples	Coverage
Craft unions	Amalgamated Society of Locomotive Engineers and Firemen	A single trade or craft
General workers unions	Transport and General Workers Union	Many industries
Industrial unions	Union of Post Office Workers	A single industry
Occupational unions	National Association of Local Government Officers	A single profession or occupation

A *craft union* restricts its membership to workers who follow a particular craft such as plumbing or joinery and its members may be employed in a number of different industries. Sometimes, craft unions form part of an alliance such as the Printing and Kindred Trades Federation, and this may strengthen their bargaining position. However, generally, craft unions have relatively small memberships. They are seldom involved in disputes and are often local in character. They have always concerned themselves more with working conditions, pay, security, and benefits for their members than with politics.

A *general workers' union* covers employees in a variety of industries and speaks for a variety of workers – skilled, unskilled and semi-skilled. They cater especially for unskilled workers who cannot obtain membership of any of the more specialised unions.

An *industrial union* includes in its membership nearly all the workers, skilled and unskilled, employed in a particular industry. This is an advantage for purposes of collective bargaining because employers often prefer to deal with one association rather than negotiate with a large number of separate trade unions. Rivalry exists sometimes between an industrial union and a union representing a skilled section of the industry. For example, the National Union of Railwaymen (NUR) has occasionally clashed with the Associated Society of Locomotive Engineers and Firemen (ASLEF) which represents train drivers and demands higher pay for them on the basis of their skill.

An *occupational union* represents people in a professional occupation. They are often referred to as 'white-collar' workers.

Collective bargaining
Trade union claims for increased pay are usually based upon one or more of the following arguments, namely, comparability; the cost of living; and profitability.

Comparability
This type of wage claim is based upon the fact that other groups of workers have obtained wage increases. As a result the pay differential between them and other groups was upset. Hence the union argues there is a need to secure an increase similar to those obtained by other groups of workers.

Cost of living
A wage claim is made because a rise in the cost of living has reduced the *real* income of union members.

Profitability
The basis of the wage claim is that the increased profits in an industry justify an increase in wages for the workers in that industry.

The stages in the collective bargaining procedure are firstly negotiation and then secondly, settlement of disputes.

Negotiation
The machinery for negotiation in an industry may consist of either (a) a voluntary arrangement between the unions and the employers' association, or (b) a Joint Industrial Council or (c) a Wages Council. (a) and (b) are both schemes involving voluntary negotiation whereas (c) is a scheme of statutory wage regulation.

Joint Industrial Councils exist in many industries such as gas, electricity and furniture. Although they are sponsored by the government, a JIC is not forced upon any industry. A Council is composed of representatives of both employers and workers in the industry and their task is to settle disputes and work out an adequate pay structure.

Wages Councils were set up originally by Parliament to give legal protection to badly paid workers in 'sweated' industries. Today the forty or so Wages Councils can fix terms and conditions of employment, including minimum wages and holidays, in industries where trade union organisation is weak and where inadequate negotiating machinery exists. Wages Councils are composed of equal numbers of employers' and workers' representatives together with additional independent members. They are appointed by the Secretary of State for Employment and cover such industries as clothing, food and drink and textiles together with services such as catering, retail distribution, and hairdressing.

Settlement of disputes
If negotiation fails to produce an agreement between employers and unions, help may be obtained from the *Advisory, Conciliation and Arbitration Service* (ACAS). The latter was set up in 1974 by the government as an independent organisation under the management of a council appointed following consultation with the Trades Union Congress and the Confederation of British Industry. Its main functions are: conciliation in industrial disputes; provision of arbitration services; and provision of advisory and information services for the improvement of collective bargaining. The head office of the Service is in London and regional offices are located throughout Britain.

Although ACAS has prime responsibility for intervention in disputes, the Secretary of State retains powers to appoint a *court of inquiry* or *committee of investigation* into a dispute.

There is also a *Central Arbitration Committee* which is the permanent industrial arbitration body for resolving differences arising in disputes where other means have failed.

Strikes and lockouts

Negotiations between employers and trade unions may sometimes fail. As a result a union may order its members to strike, that is, refuse to work. On the other hand, an employer may refuse to let employees work and this is known as a lockout.

A strike may be official or unofficial. In the latter case, the strike does not have the backing of the union. Very often unofficial strikes are brought about by shop stewards acting on behalf of a relatively small group of workers. Strike pay from the union is not available to members who take part in an unofficial strike.

Blacklegs is the name given to workers who ignore a union's instruction to strike. In order to prevent blacklegging the union may ask members to stand at the factory gates to try to persuade blacklegs from going to work. Although *pickets,* as these persuaders are called, must use only peaceful persuasion, violence often flares up. Work turned out by strike-breaking workers may be 'blacked' by other unions. This means that their members will refuse to handle the work.

As an alternative to striking, union members sometimes 'work-to-rule', that is, they go slow by carrying out every work rule to the last dot and comma.

Strikes may be caused by

(*a*) disputes over wages,

(*b*) disputes over hours or conditions of work,

(*c*) demarcation disputes.

A *demarcation dispute* is a disagreement about which workers have the right to do certain jobs. Usually the work to be done by different tradesmen is obvious enough but difficulty arises when the issue is not clear-cut.

Another reason for strikes is the *closed shop*. This refers to a condition of employment where only members of the appropriate trade union are permitted to work, and employers agree to employ only members of the union. The advantage of this situation is that wage agreements are more easily negotiated when all the workers at the factory belong to one union. However, when union members refuse to work with men who are not trade unionists, then the question of individual freedom arises. Strikes may occur when employers give jobs to men who are not union members, thus failing to close the shop floor to non-members. The union's case for the closed shop is that since unions normally obtain benefits for all workers, all workers should support the union.

QUESTIONS

Write *short* answers to the following:

1 Distinguish between salaries, wages and earnings.
2 What is 'wage drift'?
3 Why does wage drift occur?
4 State briefly why earnings vary between different occupations.
5 State briefly why earnings vary for people doing similar work.
6 What is the difference between real and money earnings?
7 Write down three methods used by employers to pay their employees.
8 How were wages fixed in the days before large-scale production?
9 How are the majority of wages and salaries fixed today?
10 List three functions of a trade union.
11 Write down a classification of trade unions.
12 State briefly the arguments used by trade unions in pressing wage claims.
13 What are the various forms of negotiating machinery for collective bargaining?
14 What are the functions of the ACAS?
15 Define (a) a strike and (b) a lockout.
16 What is a 'blackleg'?
17 Name three common causes of strikes.
18 What is a 'closed shop'?

Write answers to the following:

1 Explain the differences between *real wages* and *money wages*. Why are these differences more apparent during an inflationary period? (U/L)
2 Make a comparison between the methods of wage payment commonly used at the present time in this country. (WJEC)
3 Define each of the following terms and explain *one* point of economic significance about each of them: (a) collective bargaining; (b) industrial unions; (c) a closed shop; (d) demarcation dispute; (e) unofficial strikes. (JMB)

4 What are the relative merits and demerits of time-rates and piece-rates as methods of wage payments? Illustrate your answer by reference to particular occupations. (JMB)

5 How do you account for different wages being earned by people in different occupations and in different regions of the UK? (JMB)

6 You are about to commence work and have to consider joining a trade union. What are (a) the advantages and (b) the disadvantages which you may expect to derive from joining a union? (Cambridge)

7 What are the main functions of a trade union? How does a craft union differ from an industrial union? (Cambridge)

8 Describe the main functions of British trade unions. How can trade unions be classified? (Cambridge)

9 Why are pop singers paid more than dustmen? (Oxford)

10 Why do architects earn more than building labourers? (WJEC)

11 Examine critically the arguments used by Trade Unionists in attempting to justify their wage claims. (AEB)

12 How are wages determined? Account for the differences in earnings of workers with similar skills and training operating in different industries. (RSA)

13 'Wages are the price of labour, and, like any other prices, are determined by supply and demand.' Discuss this contention. (LCC)

14 Distinguish between (a) conciliation, (b) arbitration and (c) collective bargaining as features of industrial relations. (AEB)

PRACTICAL WORK

1 Using the *Annual Abstract of Statistics* find out the percentage change in (a) wage rates and (b) earnings over the last 5 years. Calculate the wage drift shown by these figures (i.e. (b) - (a)).

2 Here is a list of 5 trade unions. (a) Find out the membership figures for each union and (b) state the type of union to which each belongs.

Union	Membership	Type
National Union of Mineworkers		
General and Municipal Workers' Union		
National Union of Teachers		

Union	Membership	Type
Union of Post Office Workers		
Felt Hatters' and Trimmers' Union		

3 Find out why the events listed below are important in Trade Union history: *(a)* 1799–1800 Combination Acts; *(b)* 1834 Tolpuddle Martyrs; *(c)* 1901 Taff Vale Case; *(d)* 1926 General Strike; *(e)* 1964 Rookes *v.* Barnard Case; *(f)* 1972 Industrial Relations Act.

4 Find out why Trade Unions tend to be weak in: *(a)* occupations in which there is a large number of women; *(b)* agriculture; *(c)* hotel work and catering.

5 Obtain a copy of a union handbook. Study it and find out *(a)* the functions of the union; *(b)* the procedure for electing its officers and committees; *(c)* the benefits available to members.

13
Availability of Work

Employment and unemployment

The economic problem of scarce resources and unlimited wants means that the resources available must be used in the most effective ways. The use of resources involves employing all the factors of production – land, labour, capital and enterprise. Thus the terms 'employment' and 'unemployment' apply to all of the factors and not only to labour. However, because of the particular human problems which arise when people are employed, this factor is given special emphasis in economics.

Unemployment is undesirable because

(*a*) it involves a waste of economic resources,

(*b*) it creates personal and social problems,

(*c*) it is an opportunity cost to the community.

Land, labour, capital and enterprise are used to satisfy the wants of the population. If any of these factors is unemployed, the total production of goods and services is lower than it would otherwise be. Thus unemployment involves a waste of economic resources and results in a standard of living lower than it need be.

Personal and social problems arise when people are unemployed. People suffer emotionally, for example, if they can no longer provide for the needs of their families or they realise that their skills are of no further use to the community.

The opportunity cost of unemployment to the community is the value of goods and services which could be produced by unemployed labour when combined with the other factors of production.

Unemployment in the United Kingdom

Every unemployed person is entitled to receive unemployment benefit. In order to claim benefit it is necessary to register at a careers office (under 18) or an employment office (18 and over) on the first day of unemployment. Thus, each employment office and careers office has a constant register of the unemployed and the task of collecting statistics

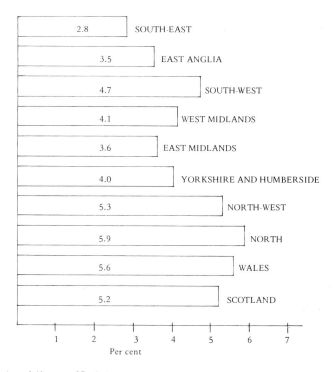

2.8	SOUTH-EAST
3.5	EAST ANGLIA
4.7	SOUTH-WEST
4.1	WEST MIDLANDS
3.6	EAST MIDLANDS
4.0	YORKSHIRE AND HUMBERSIDE
5.3	NORTH-WEST
5.9	NORTH
5.6	WALES
5.2	SCOTLAND

Per cent

Source: *Annual Abstract of Statistics.*

Fig. 27 Regional Unemployment (1975)

of the numbers of people registered as unemployed is simplified.

Some areas of the country have higher percentages of unemployed persons than others. There are two principal reasons for this (Fig. 27).

In the first place, some of the industries which experience the greatest degree of fluctuation in employment tend to be concentrated mainly in one or a limited number of areas. Thus the cotton industry is localised in Lancashire; the woollen industry is concentrated in the West Riding of Yorkshire; and the main centres of vehicle manufacture are at Dagenham, Liverpool, Luton, Oxford and in the West Midlands.

Secondly, the steady decline of the older industries such as coalmining and shipbuilding, which also happened to be highly localised, caused the regions in which they were concentrated to suffer unemployment rates considerably higher than the national average.

Government aid

Government aid to areas where unemployment was high began in the

164

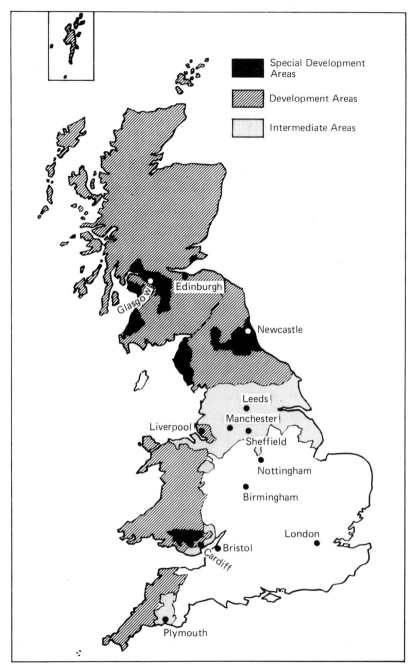

Fig. 28 The Areas for Expansion

1930s and has been expanded considerably over the years. Fig. 28 shows those parts of the country where preferential assistance is offered by the government to encourage industrial development. Broadly speaking, the Areas for Expansion consist of Scotland, Wales, the North of England, Cornwall and part of Devon, and part of Nottinghamshire and Derbyshire. There are three different categories of assisted Areas:

(*a*) Special Development Areas
(*b*) Development Areas
(*c*) Intermediate Areas

All of these areas are suffering from the same sort of problem, namely, a higher than average level of unemployment, though in varying degree. The need for jobs is most acute in the Special Development Areas.

Types of unemployment

The following types of unemployment can be distinguished.

1 Frictional unemployment

Some unemployment is due to economic frictions arising from changes in employers' demands for different types of labour. Thus the skill of certain workers may be made obsolete by changes in the technique of production. In addition, changes in consumers' demands cause expansion in some industries and contraction in others. Consequently at any one time there will be firms wishing to employ additional workers while other firms are being forced to lay off labour. In theory the workers laid off will be engaged by the expanding firms. In practice, however, there are factors which prevent a rapid adjustment and cause unemployment. For example, the new jobs created by the growing demands for the newer goods and services may be of a different type and in different places from the jobs which are being lost. Specialised workers cannot easily be transferred to new work while many workers are hesitant about moving to new areas (see page 152). The overall result is that there may be some unemployment in one industry or in one area, while in some other industry or area labour is scarce.

2 Structural unemployment

This type of unemployment arises through a change in demand which switches production from one kind of work to another. Structural unemployment differs from frictional unemployment in that it occurs through permanent or long-term changes in the structure of the economy. Thus structural unemployment was very severe in this country during the period 1918-39. For example, the growth of the cotton industry in Japan and India cut Lancashire's export trade drastically and the industry declined severely. Other basic industries such as coal-mining and shipbuilding also declined, having lost their major export markets because of increased competition from other manufacturing countries. Coal had also to face increasing competition from oil as a source of fuel and shipbuilding was also affected by the decline in international trade.

Where a fall in demand for the products of certain industries is accomplished by a compensating increase in demand for labour in other industries, such unemployment as arises should be described as frictional. However, where there is no compensating increase in demand, the unemployment is of the structural type. Both types have the same basic cause, namely the immobility of labour.

3 Cyclical unemployment

This form of unemployment arises from the trade cycle and is sometimes referred to as mass unemployment. Since the Industrial Revolution at the end of the eighteenth century, the volume of economic activity (and hence the level of employment) has proceeded in a succession of 'booms' and 'slumps'. A period of good trade has declined into a bad one which in turn was followed by an upswing of renewed activity. Unemployment occurs during the downswing of the trade cycle and is at its worst in the trough of the cycle (Fig. 29).

Cyclical unemployment is characterised by a general deficiency of demand and consequently affects all industries at one and the same time,

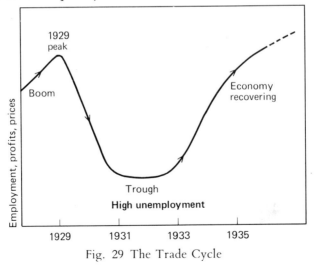

Fig. 29 The Trade Cycle

producing widespread unemployment. Many economists consider that the trade cycle in its severe pre-1939 form should be a thing of the past. However, the economy has proceeded in a series of booms and slumps since 1945 and employment has followed a similar pattern.

4 Seasonal unemployment

In some industries the demand for goods or services fluctuates seasonally. For example, hotels, restaurants and entertainment services in seaside resorts are fully staffed by employees during the summer but many of these workers are laid off during the winter.

A similar problem occurs in some outdoor occupations when bad weather stops production. Examples of these occupations are building construction and deep-sea fishing.

5 Residual unemployment

This classification includes all those people who are unable to work because of physical or mental disabilities. It takes account also of the relatively small number who prefer to live on social security benefit rather than work for an income.

6 Hidden unemployment

This form of unemployment is sometimes known as disguised unemployment. It can take several forms. For example, during a temporary fall in demand an employer may retain on his payroll a greater number of employees than he can provide work for. His motive for doing this is to ensure he does not experience a labour shortage when demand recovers. Alternatively an employer can counteract a fall in demand by introducing short-time working. In neither case will workers be registered as unemployed although there is not, in fact, sufficient work available for them.

This classification of the different types of unemployment shows that apart from cyclical unemployment (an analysis of the trade cycle is outside the scope of this book) most unemployment arises from the fact that either capital or labour is immobile. If these factors of production were completely mobile, few unemployment problems would arise: as some industries declined and were replaced by expanding industries, capital and labour would be reallocated with a minimum of disturbance.

What can be done to increase the mobility of labour and capital and thereby provide a major remedy for unemployment?

Action can be taken along two lines:

(a) labour can be encouraged to move from industries where jobs are scarce to those where jobs are more abundant;

(b) industry can be encouraged to move into areas of high unemployment in order to provide extra jobs.

Government action to improve mobility of labour

There are two kinds of mobility, namely (a) the mobility of labour between occupations and (b) the mobility of labour in the geographical sense.

The hindrances to geographical mobility were explained in Chapter 12. They include the costs of removal and personal and social ties. The barriers to occupational mobility are those factors other than the pay offered which affect the movement of people from one occupation to another. They include lack of the requisite degree of natural ability or aptitude; the cost and length of training which may be required; and the apprenticeship system. The latter is designed to train young people between the ages of 16 and 21. An older person with family responsibilities is hardly able to enter a trade through an apprenticeship because of the relatively low rate of pay allowed to apprentices.

The government seeks to improve the mobility of labour in the following ways.

1 Under the Training Opportunities Scheme (TOPS) government *training centres* have been established throughout the country for the purpose of helping adult workers to re-train, that is, acquire new skills. Intensive courses lasting up to 12 months are provided in a large number of trades, with emphasis on those in which there is a shortage of skilled workers. The centres enable men who missed the opportunity of acquiring a skill by apprenticeship, or who have been made redundant by industrial change, to acquire quickly a new skill which is in demand. The courses are free, and during training the trainees receive allowances to maintain themselves and their dependants. Each centre has its own placing officer who co-operates with the employment office service in obtaining suitable employment for trainees in their new trades.

2 Some re-training is also carried out by the *industrial training boards*. They were set up under the Industrial Training Act of 1964 to provide training courses for certain industries. Each board identifies needs and priorities in its own industry, and develops its activities accordingly. Their work is co-ordinated by the Training Services Agency under the overall control of the Manpower Services Commission.

3 Another scheme aimed at assisting workers to change jobs when their particular skills are no longer required was introduced by the Redundancy Payments Act 1965. Under this legislation, lump sum

redundancy payments are available to people whose jobs cease to exist. The amounts payable are related to a person's age, earnings and the length of time he or she has worked with a particular firm. The scheme is valuable for tiding people over the period when they are searching for a new job or re-training. Under the Employment Protection Act 1976 those given notice of dismissal because of redundancy, if employed for two years or more, are entitled to reasonable time off with pay to look for work or to arrange training for future work.

An earlier attempt to provide an additional 'breathing space' in which workers can either apply for re-training or seek a new job was made in the Contracts of Employment Act 1963. This measure made provision for *minimum periods of notice*. This provision was improved under the Employment Protection Act 1976.

4 *Information concerning opportunities* available in other industries and occupations is available through the public employment service operated by the Manpower Services Commission. The Commission's responsibility is exercised through the Employment Services Agency which operates a country-wide network of employment offices and job centres. Details can be obtained of vacancies which exist locally or in other areas. The register of jobs includes manual work, technical and scientific posts, and professional and executive positions.

Measures aimed at increasing the mobility of labour can be summarised as 'taking workers to the work'. Alternatively 'work can be taken to the workers' by attracting industry into areas where jobs are scarce. In pursuit of this policy the government provides (a) financial incentives and (b) other forms of assistance.

Financial incentives provided by the Government

1 Under the Industry Act 1972, *cash grants* (called regional development grants) are available to subsidise capital expenditure (i.e. the cost of plant, machinery and buildings) incurred by firms in setting up in the Areas for Expansion. These grants are available also to help with improvements and modernisation.

2 *Selective financial assistance* is also available under the Industry Act for projects which are likely to provide, maintain, or safeguard employment in any part of the Areas for Expansion. Assistance may take several forms: (a) loans may be made available on favourable terms; (b) as an alternative to (a) grants may be made towards the interest costs of finance that provides additional employment; (c) removal grants may be paid of up to 80 per cent of certain costs incurred in moving an

undertaking from any part of Britain outside an Area for Expansion to one of these Areas.

3 Modern *factories for sale or rent* on favourable terms are provided by the Department of Industry in the Areas for Expansion. For certain new undertakings rent may be waived in the first five years. Similar ventures are available for *office accommodation*.

4 Under the 1967 Finance Act a *regional employment premium* is payable to firms with manufacturing establishments in the development and special development areas.

5 *Grants and allowances* are available from the Employment Services Agency to assist key workers transferred to an Area for Expansion, and to help unemployed people moving away from home to take up employment.

6 The National Enterprise Board (see page 98) set up under the Industry Act 1975 is intended, among its other functions, to stimulate *investment* in the areas of high unemployment.

Other forms of Government assistance

1 *Industrial Development Certificates* provide a direct influence on the location of industry. Every firm which wishes to set up premises beyond a certain minimum size must obtain a licence to build. It is withheld if the Department of Industry considers the proposal is not consistent with the proper distribution of industry. Thus the purpose of this control is to direct projects towards the areas of greatest employment need. Industrial Development Certificates are not required in the Special Development Areas or the Development Areas, but setting up premises away from these Areas is strictly controlled.

2 *A Contracts Preference Scheme* means that firms in the Special Development and Development Areas can benefit from preference schemes for contracts placed by government departments and nationalised industries.

Regional planning

The development of a regional approach to economic planning helps those areas with special needs, including a high level of unemployment.

For regional planning purposes the country is divided into ten regions (eight for England and one each for Scotland and Wales). Each region has an Economic Planning Council (consisting of representatives from industries, local government and universities) and an Economic Planning Board (consisting of civil servants) which assist in formulating regional plans and advise the government on the regional implications of national economic policies. In addition, some regions have Regional Industrial Development Boards which advise generally on regional industrial opportunities and on selective financial assistance for the development of industry in their regions.

European Regional Development Fund
Britain is entitled to over 25 per cent of the funds allocated to the European Regional Development Fund, set up by the European Community in 1975. Money is available to spend in those regions of the Community suffering from a preponderance of industrial change and structural unemployment.

Full employment
One of the main aims of government policy is the maintenance of 'full employment'. The precise meaning of this phrase is a matter of dispute among economists. An acceptable minimum of unemployment has been variously estimated at 2 to 5 per cent of the working population, but there is no universally agreed figure.

The adoption of a particular percentage as an aim of national policy has certain drawbacks. In the first place, it ignores the fact that on a regional basis there may be serious unemployment in some areas while labour is scarce in others. Secondly, it obscures the difference in unemployment between industries. There may be, for example, heavy unemployment in shipbuilding while in vehicle manufacture there is a labour shortage. In view of these difficulties, it is probably wiser to describe full employment simply as a situation in which the number of unemployed is no greater than the number of vacant jobs.

Full employment does not mean that every worker will always have a job. There are, for example, always likely to be some persons unemployed because of seasonal interruptions to working, as can occur in the building trade.

If government policy has been too successful in that it has created a situation where there are more jobs than workers, then *over-full* employment exists. In this state of affairs a shortage of labour will exist in many industries.

Problems of full employment
The adoption of a policy of full employment creates pressures within the economy which may act adversely upon certain other aims of government policy. In particular *(a)* the maintenance of stable prices and *(b)* the earning of a surplus on the balance of payments may be made more difficult.

Experience has shown that the maintenance of full employment increases the danger of inflation (see page 195). One reason for this is that full employment puts the trade unions in a strong bargaining position. Claims for higher pay are usually more easily secured when unemployment is at a minimum and the extra wage costs are passed on in the form of increased prices for goods and services. In turn, higher prices give rise to fresh wage claims.

If 'over-full' employment exists, the problem is intensified. Shortages of labour will cause employers to offer higher wages in order to attract workers into their employ. Since in these conditions labour can only be drawn from other occupations, wage increases will be offered elsewhere in an attempt to retain labour.

In a country like the United Kingdom, which is so dependent on international trade, inflation has twin dangers. Firstly, it makes export prices rise and so renders sales abroad more difficult. Secondly, higher earnings at home lead to an increase in demand *(a)* for imported goods and *(b)* for home-produced goods which would otherwise have been exported. Hence the achievement of a surplus on the balance of payments is made more difficult (see page 240).

QUESTIONS

Write *short* answers to the following:

1 State briefly why unemployment is undesirable.
2 Why is unemployment heavier in some industries than in others?
3 Give examples of these industries.
4 State two reasons why some regions have heavier unemployment than others.
5 Write down the three categories of Areas for Expansion.
6 How does structural unemployment differ from frictional unemployment?
7 Name a characteristic of cyclical unemployment.
8 Write down examples of industries which are subject to seasonal unemployment.
9 What does 'residual unemployment' mean?
10 What is the meaning of 'hidden unemployment'?
11 What factor is a major cause of unemployment?
12 Outline briefly the ways in which the government seeks to increase the mobility of labour.
13 What financial incentives are provided by the government in order to attract firms to the Areas for Expansion?

14 What are Industrial Development Certificates and what is their purpose?

15 Briefly describe the 'machinery' of regional planning.

16 What is a reasonable definition of 'full employment'?

17 What does 'over-full' employment mean?

18 Name the problems which can result from a policy of full employment.

Write answers to the following:

1 Discuss the main causes of unemployment as far as Britain is concerned. If possible, support your answer by suitable examples. (JMB)

2 Discuss the relationship between unemployment and labour mobility. (JMB)

3 (a) Explain how several kinds of unemployment may exist under 'full employment'. (b) How does the objective of reducing unemployment conflict with other objectives? (JMB)

4 Can unemployment in Britain be cured by encouraging emigration? (Oxford)

5 Define each of the following terms and consider the extent to which each type of unemployment has existed in the UK since 1945: (a) cyclical unemployment, (b) structural unemployment, (c) frictional unemployment, (d) hidden unemployment, (e) regional unemployment. (JMB)

6 Explain how a government can cure unemployment by reducing taxation. Can all forms of unemployment be cured in this way? (Oxford)

7 Why do some areas in Britain suffer more from unemployment than do others? (Oxford)

8 How can unemployment within a country be reduced as a result of restricting imports? (Oxford)

9 Why has the problem of regional unemployment been so difficult to solve? (Oxford and Cambridge)

10 What can the government do to increase employment in those regions of Britain in which unemployment is abnormally high? (Oxford)

PRACTICAL WORK

1 Find out up-to-date figures for (a) the percentage of the total working population out of work and (b) the percentages in the regions.

Comment on these figures. Is the unemployment figure higher than the national average in the region where you live? If so, why?

2 Find out the contribution made by each of the following to the development of a policy of full employment:

(a) the government White Paper on 'Employment Policy' 1944 (Cmd 6527),

(b) 'Full Employment in a Free Society' by Lord Beveridge (1944).

3 Use the library to find out about:

(a) mass unemployment during the period 1921-38 when at no time were less than one million insured workers unemployed,

(b) the growth of government aid to areas of high unemployment. Start with the establishment of Special Areas in the 1930s.

14
Land, Capital and Enterprise

In addition to labour, the resources required for production are land, capital and enterprise.

Land

In economics the term 'land' means:

(a) the earth's surface including the seas and lakes upon it;

(b) the climate associated with it;

(c) the minerals available beneath the earth's surface.

Thus land comprises all kinds of natural resources. Soil, mineral deposits, fisheries, forests and climatic conditions (such as sunshine, wind and rain) are all included in the term. Land provides the site on which production can take place; and the supply of raw materials used in the production of goods.

Land has three important characteristics.

In the first place, the supply of land is relatively fixed and cannot be adjusted as demand varies. It is true, of course, that coastal erosion decreases the supply of land and reclamation from the sea increases supply, but only to a relatively small extent.

On the other hand, the quantity of land for a particular use can sometimes be increased through transfer from a different use. For example, the supply of land for housing can be increased by transferring its use from farming. It is true to say, therefore, that most land has some degree of occupational mobility.

Secondly, each plot of land has a unique set of natural characteristics. Thus one area may be fertile, another plot might be subject to flooding, while a third area may be completely infertile and suitable only for building purposes.

Thirdly, the location of land is fixed. Land cannot be moved from places where it is of little use to places where it could be profitably used. In other words, land is not mobile geographically.

In their original state, natural resources are a gift of nature. They owe nothing to human ingenuity or labour. Thus land, in the economic sense, is unimproved land. In modern industrial society unimproved land is relatively rare. Usually land has been drained or irrigated to produce crops and it may have been used for a variety of purposes, such as, for example, farming and building. Therefore most areas of land contain capital.

Capital

Capital is part of the stock of wealth existing at any given time. It comprises those material resources, other than land, which are used in the production of goods and services. These resources are often called *producers' goods* or *capital goods* and they include factory buildings, industrial plant, power stations, steel, cement and transport facilities.

Producers' goods differ from *consumers' goods* (such as bread, clothes and shoes) in that they are wanted not for the direct satisfaction of consumers' wants but because they assist in the production of other goods.

Whether goods are classed as producer's goods or consumers' goods depends on the use to which they are put. When, for example, oil is used to heat a house it cannot be regarded as a producers' good because it is not being used for productive purposes; but oil used to heat a factory is a producer's good as it is aiding production. In the same way a car is a producer's good to a sales representative who uses it entirely for business purposes, but to someone using a car solely for pleasure, it is a consumer's good.

Capital accumulation

Capital is accumulated by saving money (Fig. 30).

If people save part of their incomes, then:

1 demand for consumers' goods is reduced and some productive resources are freed for the production of capital goods. However, if these resources lie idle no capital creation takes place.

2 Savings are made available for *investment*. In economics the latter term means the production of capital goods. However no one can create capital simply by saving money. Investment will take place only if a businessman thinks that a particular project will be profitable. He will offer savers a rate of interest in return for the use of their money to finance the setting up of a business enterprise.

On the other hand, if people spend their entire incomes on consumer goods, there will be no resources available to make capital goods; and no saving to finance their production.

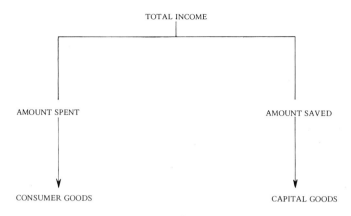

Fig. 30 Capital Formation

It should be noted that if savers use their money to buy existing shares in public companies then new capital has not been created; only the ownership of existing capital has changed. Capital is accumulated when new capital goods are produced.

Any increase in the total stock of capital results in two major benefits.

In the first place, total productive capacity is increased and a greater output of goods and services is made possible. If output rises faster than the population increases, then the standard of living as measured by output per head also increases.

Secondly, if the same or a greater quantity of goods and services can be produced with fewer workers (by the greater use of machines) then it is possible that the working week may be reduced, enabling workers to enjoy more leisure.

Maintenance of capital

Capital goods wear out in time or they become obsolete. Consequently they have to be replaced by new equipment or modern equipment which is more efficient. Thus existing capital has to be made good and before any addition to the total stock of capital is possible a certain proportion of the total output of capital goods has to be devoted to the replacement of capital.

The value of the production of capital goods used every year to replace worn-out and obsolete capital is called *depreciation*. Gross Investment measures the annual total output of capital goods and Net Investment is the addition to the existing stock of capital. Hence:

Gross Investment minus Depreciation = Net Investment.

If a country fails to make good depreciation of its capital, then capital is being consumed. Such a situation can arise in war-time when resources are diverted to military purposes so that worn out and obsolete capital goods are not replaced. In such circumstances the stock of capital goods will be gradually reduced and consequently the production of all kinds of goods will begin to decline.

A summary of the characteristics of capital
1 Capital is wealth used for production.
2 It is created not for the direct satisfaction of wants but for what it will eventually produce.
3 Capital originates from savings.
4 Capital requires continuous maintenance and replacement because it depreciates or wears out. If depreciation takes place at a faster rate than the manufacture of capital equipment, then capital is being consumed.

Mobility of capital
Some items of capital equipment are geographically immobile. It may be theoretically possible to dismantle items such as factory buildings, railways and docks and transfer them to other sites, but the cost of the action is likely to be prohibitive.

Some equipment is also occupationally immobile, that is, it cannot be used easily for alternative purposes. Blast furnaces and railways, for example, have highly specific uses because they have been made for specialised purposes. On the other hand, factory buildings can be adapted to a variety of uses and some capital equipment has a high degree of both geographical and occupational mobility. Thus lorries and vans, desks and typewriters can be used in most industries and are easily moved from one location to another.

Enterprise
Production would be impossible without the organisation of land, labour and capital into some form of undertaking. Someone has to take the initiative and (a) decide on producing a particular commodity or service, (b) select the method of producing it and (c) determine the location of the business which is to produce it. In order to achieve these aims the factors of production must be efficiently employed and organised.

In starting a business, there is always some risk of loss or failure because uncertainty is inherent in all business enterprise. Some of the hazards of business, such as damage to premises by fire, the loss of goods through theft, and injury to employees in the course of their work, can be covered by insurance. In return for a payment known as a premium, an insurance company will agree to pay compensation in the event of a particular loss or group of losses during the agreed period of insurance. However there are many risks incurred in business which cannot be insured against. They are risks which cannot be measured by past experience. Normally an insurance company works out a premium based on the number of times that an event has occurred over a past number of years. If, for example, over a long period of time, fire has destroyed business premises to the value of £500000 a year, such premises can be insured against fire if premiums total £500000 plus a sum to cover the insurance company's expenses and profit. Insurance can be offered only against those risks, the probability of which can be calculated from past experience. If an event is not measurable, then it is uninsurable.

Uninsurable risks must be guarded against by business skill. For example, in deciding what goods or services to produce and in what quantities, knowledge and judgement of the market are necessary. Again, between the taking of a decision to produce and the availability of the product for sale, demand for it may change for all kinds of reasons. Fashions may change, or a 'credit squeeze' may reduce consumers' spending, so that sales are not as high as had been anticipated. A third example of an uninsurable risk is that of a competitor bringing out a better product at a lower price.

The person who (a) organises land, labour and capital for production and (b) bears uninsurable risks is called the *entrepreneur* (i.e. one who runs an enterprise). In the case of the simplest form of business, the entrepreneurial functions are undertaken by the sole proprietor who accepts the entire risks of the business and is solely responsible for its management. Similarly, in a partnership, the entrepreneurial functions are divided between the partners. (In a limited partnership, the limited partners are only responsible for the risks of the business up to the amount they have invested, (see page 73.) As a firm grows larger the ownership may be separated from management and it becomes difficult to say who is the entrepreneur because he does not exist as a single person. Instead enterprise is exercised by a group of people and the functions of the entrepreneur may be divided. Thus in a joint-stock company the shareholders subscribe the capital and therefore bear the risks of the business up to the nominal value of the shares they hold. On the other hand the board of directors undertakes the organisation of production.

Table 16   Entrepreneurial Functions

Business unit	Management	Risks
Sole Proprietor	Owner	Owner
Ordinary Partnership	Partners	Partners
Joint-Stock Company	Directors	Shareholders
Co-operative Society	Management Committee	Members
Municipal Enterprise	Council Committee and officials	Ratepayers
Nationalised Industry	Minister and officials	Taxpayers

Similarly, in municipal undertakings and nationalised industries the risk is undertaken by ratepayers and taxpayers, but the organisation is delegated by Councils and Parliament to paid managers (see Table 16).

Mobility of the entrepreneur
The functions of the entrepreneur are the same in all forms of production. Whatever type of goods or services are produced there will be the twofold need to organise land, labour and capital and to bear uninsurable risks. Thus, the entrepreneur is almost certainly the most mobile of the factors of the production.

In summary it may be said that land, labour and capital are resources which have little economic significance until production begins. Enterprise is the active factor or catalyst which makes the other factors productive.

Factor incomes
Wages or salaries are paid to people for the jobs they do. Similarly the other resources – land, capital and enterprise – receive rewards for their contribution to production. Thus land receives rent, capital is paid interest and enterprise is rewarded by profit.

Rent
In economics, land means unimproved land and rent is the payment made for the use of unimproved land. However, in a community where

land has been cultivated for many generations, where drainage and other improvements have been effected, and where buildings have been erected, it is difficult to discover land in its original state. Very often, the present state of land is the result of ploughing, drainage, fertilisation and other improvements, and it represents the combined effect of the application of labour, capital and enterprise. It is not always possible, therefore, to discover where the reward for the use of land ceases and the reward for the other factors of production begins. Thus the payment made by the hirer of land usually includes an element for interest on capital invested in the land. For example, the rent paid by a farmer to his landlord may include payment for the use of such capital as farm buildings, hedges and ditches, in addition to payment for the use of the land itself.

What determines the site value of land? Why does the rent of an area of land vary in different parts of the country?

In answering these questions, it is important to remember that land is fixed in supply and different plots have particular advantages with regard to fertility and situation.

The strength of demand for land will depend upon its usefulness in a particular production process. Thus sites in the centre of towns will command high rents because the supply of such sites is limited in relation to the demand for them. Commercial enterprises such as banks, shops, cinemas and restaurants bid for these sites because, by reason of their favourable position, custom is likely to be plentiful. People shop in large numbers in the centre of towns and cities and also seek their entertainment there. Such sites are also demanded by non-commercial concerns which need conveniently situated premises for use as hospitals, municipal offices and so on. It is this high level of demand for sites in town centres which gives rise to the high rents in these areas.

Thus the rent of a particular plot of land will be determined by the forces of demand and supply.

Interest
The price paid for the use of capital is interest. It is the amount repaid to a lender of capital over and above the original sum he lends. Thus a person who lends £1000 to someone for a year at 7 per cent will expect to receive £1070 at the end of the year. The additional £70 is interest. The rate of interest is the percentage of the original sum that the additional payment represents, that is, £70 is 7 per cent of £1000.

Functions of Interest
The payment of interest is necessary because the supply of capital (like

all factors of production) is scarce and can be used for alternative purposes. Interest serves the following purposes.

1 It is the inducement offered to the owners of capital to encourage them to part with their money for a period.

2 It directs capital into industries where capital is most urgently required, as indicated by the offer of a high rate of interest.

The Structure of Interest Rates

There are a considerable number of rates of interest. Banks, building societies, finance companies, money-lenders and other lenders offer a variety of interest rates to people who wish to borrow from them. Generally, interest rates are low on short-term low-risk loans and high on long-term, high-risk loans. Thus the rate of interest charged by a money-lender on an unsecured loan will be higher than the rate charged by a bank to a customer who can offer satisfactory security (which the bank can turn into cash if the loan is not repaid). Similarly, the government has generally to offer a higher rate of interest on a long-term loan than on a short-term loan.

Interest is therefore a price paid by borrowers to lenders, and will depend on the supply and demand for loanable money for various purposes. Generally, a large supply of capital relative to the demand means low rates of interest, and a large demand relative to supply means high interest rates.

Profit

Profit is the reward of enterprise. It is the surplus that remains when the total costs incurred by a business in a particular period (e.g. a year) are deducted from the income for that period.

Role of profit in a private enterprise economy

The profit motive provides a stimulus to entrepreneurs to supply goods and services demanded by consumers. Consumers indicate their wants by the way they spend their incomes and, in doing so, they provide indicators for producers. If consumers show an increasing preference for some particular commodity by buying more of it, the increase in demand will cause the price of the goods to rise. Entrepreneurs managing firms producing this commodity will be encouraged to expand supply, with the prospect of a higher selling price, increased sales revenue and higher profits. In turn the increased profits being made by firms in this industry will attract new firms into the industry, which will further increase the supply of goods on to the market. More resources will be attracted into the industry because higher rewards are offered.

On the other hand, where demand has fallen it is likely that price will fall also, as will sales revenue and, therefore, profits. Declining profits will stop output expanding and discourage entrepreneurs from entering the industry. Resources will tend to move away into more rewarding occupations.

QUESTIONS

Write *short* answers to the following:

1 What is the economic meaning of 'land'?
2 Give three important characteristics of land.
3 What is the economic meaning of 'capital'?
4 How are capital goods distinguished from consumer goods?
5 How is capital accumulated?
6 In what ways does a society benefit from capital accumulation?
7 What is the meaning of 'depreciation'?
8 How does gross investment differ from net investment?
9 When does capital consumption take place?
10 Briefly describe the geographical and occupational mobility of capital.
11 Name some business risks which are uninsurable.
12 Why are they uninsurable?
13 What are the functions of the entrepreneur?
14 Who is the entrepreneur in *(a)* a partnership, *(b)* a public company, *(c)* a nationalised industry?
15 Why is the entrepreneur probably the most mobile of the factors of production?
16 Define the economic meaning of rent.
17 Why does a rent payment often include an element of interest on capital?
18 How is the site value of land determined?
19 Briefly state the functions of interest.
20 What role do profits perform in an economy?

Write answers to the following:

1 What is capital? How is it accumulated? (WJEC)
2 'What a farmer calls his profit may really consist of wages, rent and interest as well.' Explain this statement. (WJEC)

3 What does the economist mean by 'profit'? What role is played by profit in the economy? (AEB)

4 What is an *entrepreneur*? Explain how the function of the entrepreneur is undertaken in (a) public enterprise and (b) private enterprise. (U/L)

5 What determines the rent of land? Why is it that the rent of an acre of land in the Home Counties is higher than that of an acre of land in Mid-Wales? (JMB)

6 'Capital' is the most important single factor in the development of an economy.' Explain and discuss this statement. (RSA)

7 Outline the factors that determine the nature and size of the reward that goes to the entrepreneur. (RSA)

8 Distinguish between the risks which must be borne by an entrepreneur and those which he can cover by insurance. (LCC)

9 Why may a country benefit by encouraging saving in order that more resources may be diverted to capital accumulation? (LCC)

10 'Production must exceed consumption if capital is to be accumulated.' Explain this statement. (LCC)

11 How can the payment of interest and profit to those who provide capital for industry be justified on economic grounds? (LCC)

12 Comment on the forces that affect the mobility of the factors of production. (RSA)

13 What does the economist mean by the term 'capital'? How does a country accumulate capital? Distinguish between capital formation and capital consumption. (AEB)

PRACTICAL WORK

1 Saving is the surplus which provides the resources needed to finance investment. Enquire among your family and friends to discover:
  (a) their reasons for saving;
  (b) the forms of saving which they use.

2 An important section of the insurance market is at Lloyd's in London. Find out about the history of Lloyd's and how the market operates today.

Part Four
Money and Banking

In a modern economy based upon specialisation and exchange, the use of some form of money is essential. The value of money is shown by the level of prices, a general rise in the level of prices indicating a fall in the value of money, and vice versa. The supply of money is controlled through the banking system.

15

Money

Barter

Before money was invented, exchange took place by barter, that is, the direct exchange of goods and services for goods and services. But barter is a clumsy, time-wasting and often quarrelsome way of satisfying wants.

Its greatest disadvantage lies in making exchange dependent upon what is called a 'double coincidence of wants'. For example, it is not sufficient for a fisherman with fish to exchange to find someone requiring fish; if he wants corn in exchange for his fish someone must be found who not only wishes to dispose of corn, but who at the same time requires some fish. Even if the fisherman manages to find a suitable farmer, there is the further problem of deciding how many fish have to be exchanged for a particular quantity of corn. A third problem arises when a person has only a large commodity to offer but requires a number of smaller items in exchange. Many goods cannot be easily divided and so, for example, the owner of a horse could not deal with separate sellers of fish hooks, knives and loin cloths because the horse cannot be divided up while still alive.

Development of money

In early times the drawbacks of barter caused people to use a 'go-between' or money, which made buying and selling much simpler. Surplus goods were exchanged for money which, in turn, was exchanged for the goods wanted.

Many seemingly odd things were used before money, as we know it, came into use. Anything in common use and considered to be valuable for its own sake served as money. For example, grain, cattle and salt were widely used.

However, the use of commodities as money has serious drawbacks. Cattle vary in quality; they are not easily carried around for the settling of debts; they are too large for making small purchases; and sooner or later, disease, age and death will reduce their value. In view of these disadvantages, metals – gold and silver – came into use as money. They suffered none of the disadvantages of commodities and both were easily worked into manageable small pieces that would serve for everyday dealings. Coins were the natural next stage.

It is said that the Greeks were the first people to make coins, that is, standard units which could be easily counted. In early societies coins were worth what they weighed and money had an intrinsic value as metal.

The first paper money was the bank note developed in the 17th century by the goldsmith bankers. Its significance lay in the fact that its value depended not on its intrinsic worth as paper but on the credit of the banker who issued it. Once paper money became acceptable there was no need to maintain a coinage of intrinsic value. Gold sovereigns went out of use in 1914 and modern 'silver' coins are minted from an alloy called cupro-nickel. Thus the currency, both notes and coin, is now entirely a token one, i.e. the paper or metal is not worth the value printed or stamped on them.

The final stage in the development of money has been the use of bank deposits as money. Cheques have long since taken the place of notes and coin for the greater proportion of commercial transactions. A cheque is an order from the owner of a bank deposit to his banker to transfer a stated sum to the person named on the cheque. The banker carries out this instruction by reducing the deposit of the drawer and crediting the account of the payee. It should be noted that it is the bank deposit which is money and not the cheque. The latter is merely a written instruction.

Thus the main stages in the development of money have been as follows:

(a) commodities which are generally acceptable

(b) precious metals
(c) predetermined weights of metal in the form of coins
(d) paper money or bank notes
(e) bank deposits transferable by cheque.

Types of money
The supply of money in the United Kingdom comprises the following.

1 Notes and coins
Coins and bank notes are called token money because they have little or no value in themselves. Their only value lies in acting as a means of exchange.

The Bank of England still prints on its notes the promise to pay the bearer on demand the value of the note. Originally this meant that the Bank would give gold in exchange for notes but notes have been inconvertible since 1931.

Bank of England notes are legal tender up to any amount, that is, a creditor cannot refuse notes in settlement of a debt of any size. The Bank's notes of denominations less than £5 are legal tender in Scotland and Northern Ireland. However, coins are limited legal tender in order (a) to protect creditors from being burdened with excessive quantities of coins and (b) to keep coins for their intended use which is to make small payments. The limits are as follows:

bronze coins are legal tender up to 20p;
'silver' coins up to 10p are legal tender up to £5;
50p coins are legal tender up to £10.

Table 17   Currency Circulation (£ million)

Notes and Coins	1973	1974	1975
Bank of England notes	4451	4988	5744
Scottish banknotes	196	226	266
Northern Ireland banknotes	28	30	34
Coins	367	393	429
Total	5042	5637	6473

Source: *Monthly Digest of Statistics*

2 Bank deposits
The major part of the money supply consists of bank deposits or bank money as they are sometimes called. As noted above, cheques are used to

transfer ownership of bank deposits and it is important not to confuse the method of transfer with the deposit it represents. If a drawer has insufficient funds in his current account to meet the cheque, the bank refuses to pay it and returns the cheque to the person who paid it in for collection. Consequently cheques are not legal tender and no one is obliged to accept a cheque. In a similar fashion other means of payment – stamps, postal orders and credit cards are not legal tender and a creditor may refuse them if he wishes. They are not forms of money but simply methods of transferring ownership of money.

Functions of money
Money performs a number of functions in a modern society.

A medium of exchange
Barter is the only alternative to using money and as a system of exchange it would be quite impracticable today. For example, if the baker who supplied the greengrocer with bread had to take payment in lettuces and carrots, he may either not like these foodstuffs or he may have sufficient stocks of them for his requirements. He would, therefore, be obliged to re-sell the produce which would take time and be very inconvenient. To replace these complicated sales by the use of money saves a great deal of trouble. If the baker takes payment in money he can spend it on whatever he wishes and he is not required to accept goods in payment which he may or may not want. The use of money as a medium of exchange overcomes the drawbacks of barter.

A measure of value
One of the disadvantages of barter is the difficulty of measuring the value of goods. For example, a horse might be valued as worth fifty fish or six spears or three sacks of corn. In other words the horse (and any other good or service) has a series of exchange values.

Money acts as a common denominator and permits everything to be priced, that is, valued in terms of money. Comparing prices enables people to see the relative values of different goods and services. Thus (a) consumers can plan their expenditure, and (b) businessmen can keep records of income and costs in order to work out their profit or loss.

A store of value
One disadvantage of using commodities such as cattle or salt as money is that after a time they deteriorate and lose value. They are unsatisfactory as a means of storing wealth. Modern money – coins, notes and bank deposits – allows people to save their surplus income and know that

when they wish to spend it in the future, the money will have kept its value. Obviously, money can only act effectively as a store of value if its own value is stable. If, for example, a person thought that in a year's time his savings would become worthless, he would spend them at once and save nothing. For many years in the United Kingdom the value of money has been falling, but in the short run – for day-to-day purposes – money has sufficient stability of value to serve satisfactorily as a store of value.

A standard of postponed payments
Since the value of money is usually stable over a period of time, the use of money permits postponement of spending from the present to some future occasion.

Much buying and selling today takes place on the basis of credit. For example, consumer goods may be bought on hire purchase; houses may be purchased by means of a mortgage loan; most businesses' dealings permit payment in the future for goods delivered immediately; and employees wait until the end of the week or month for payment for their services.

Thus the use of money makes it possible for spending to be deferred from the present to some future date.

Qualities of money
In order to carry out the functions outlined above, whatever serves as money must possess certain qualities. It must be
(*a*) acceptable
(*b*) durable
(*c*) divisible
(*d*) portable
(*e*) scarce
(*f*) homogeneous.

The commodities used as 'go-betweens' in early times (for example, cowrie shells) were unable to satisfy these requirements. Shells vary in size; they are easily damaged; large payments require much counting and carrying; and they are too easy to find. Other commodities have similar drawbacks.

The precious metals, silver and gold possessed the necessary qualities and so they superseded other things as money. They were (*a*) acceptable to people in many countries; (*b*) easily stored; (*c*) capable of division into small units; (*d*) easy to carry about; (*e*) limited in supply; and when they were coined, (*f*) all the pieces were the same. Even today, gold still serves as the international standard of value.

Advantages of money

1 It provides the most efficient means of satisfying wants. Each consumer has a distinctive set of wants and money enables him to choose which wants he will satisfy and in what order of satisfaction.

2 Money makes specialisation possible. For example, there is no need for a doctor to grow his own food and make his own clothes. He can give all his time to practising medicine because the money received in payment can be easily exchanged for any goods and services required. Further, he can save part of his earnings for future needs. Specialisation results in a greater output of goods and services, and a higher standard of living.

3 Money facilitates loans. Borrowers can use the money to obtain goods and services when they are needed most instead of having to do without them until the cash price has been saved. A newly married couple, for example, would need a lot of money to completely furnish a home at once.

The value of money and index numbers

Goods and services are valued in terms of money. Their prices indicate their relative value. When prices go up, the amount which can be bought with a given sum of money goes down; when prices fall, the amount which can be bought increases. In other words, when prices fall, the value of money rises; and when prices rise, the value of money falls.

An index number is a statistical device used to express price changes as percentages of prices in a base year or at a base date. There are a considerable number of prices levels, for example, retail prices, wholesale prices, export prices, and many others. A separate index number can be calculated to measure changes in each price level, and the method of construction is the same in every case. Very simply, an index number is compiled by selecting a group of commodities, noting their prices in a given year (the base year) and assigning the number 100 to the total. If the prices of the selected commodities rise by, for example, three per cent during the next year, the index number at the end of the year is 103. A fall in price of one per cent would be shown by an index number of 99.

Problems of index numbers

The construction of index numbers presents some very serious problems and, as they cannot be ideally solved, the index numbers themselves are limited in their value and reliability as a measurement of changes in the level of prices.

The first problem lies in the fact that it is impossible to record the price of every single type of good or service. In addition, the price at which a particular good or service is sold may vary from one part of the market to another. A representative selection has to be made, therefore, and a further complication will arise when choices have to be made between various grades or qualities of goods.

Secondly, it is necessary to decide how much significance or relative weight should be given to the items selected. Since consumers' incomes and tastes differ, the pattern of expenditure will differ from one locality to another, from one person to another, from one income group to another, and from one period to another. In practice, the compiler of the index number makes an arbitrary decision by selecting for a particular year (the base year) what he considers to be the pattern of expenditure (known as a 'basket') in a sample of consumers. He allocates a relative weight to each item according to its share of total expenditure. The pattern selected is used to apply weights to the various commodities in succeeding years for which the index number is calculated.

Clearly, the index number will be limited in its significance. There will be many consumers who will weight their expenditure differently by buying different baskets of goods.

A further drawback is that the chosen basket is really only applicable to the base year. Over a period of time the whole pattern of expenditure changes as incomes alter, as the national income changes in size and in the manner of its distribution, as qualities alter, and as new commodities and services come into existence and use.

The third major problem concerns the choice of a base year. Movements in prices will appear to be more or less significant, according to the base year chosen for the prices of items selected. It is important, therefore, to select a base year when prices were relatively stable and so years during periods either of severe inflation or deflation should be avoided.

On account of the many difficulties associated with their construction, little importance can be attached to index numbers for comparing price changes over long periods of time. The further from the base year the more inaccurate is the index number likely to become, for the basket is more liable to change.

Moreover, since patterns of expenditure vary in different localities and different countries, an index number has very limited value in comparing price changes in different places.

Nevertheless, despite its limitations an index number is the best means of measuring short-term changes in the level of prices of the particular group of commodities selected.

The best-known index number is probably the General Index of Retail Prices (or Cost of Living Index as it is sometimes called) published each month by the Department of Employment. The Index measures the month-to-month changes in the prices of a large and representative selection of goods and services. The number of separate commodities and services for which prices are regularly collected is nearly 300 and about 150 000 separate price quotations are obtained each month from shops throughout the United Kingdom. Prices of the same quality of goods are noted at the same time each month and on the same day of the week.

Weighting

Some of the selected items are relatively more important than others and so a system of weighting is used (Table 18). For this purpose, weights are allocated in accordance with the pattern of consumption of an average family as shown by the annual Family Expenditure Survey.

Table 18   How the Retail Prices Index was
weighted in 1976

1	Food	228
2	Alcoholic drink	81
3	Tobacco	46
4	Housing	112
5	Fuel and light	56
6	Durable household goods	75
7	Clothing and footwear	84
8	Transport and vehicles	140
9	Miscellaneous goods	74
10	Services	57
11	Meals outside the home	47
		1000

Note: The total weight of the basket is 1000 units and each item is given a weight according to the proportion of the average household's expenditure it takes up. Thus food accounts for 22.8 per cent of the expenditure of the average index household and a weight of 228 is attached.

The Survey is based on records of the budgeted expenditure of a representative sample of the population. The budgets are analysed to provide information on the pattern of consumer spending. The only households not included are high-income households and pensioner households. From this information is derived the pattern of consumption of the average family. The weighting (the importance given to each type of spending, such as food or transport) is brought up to date each year.

With its monthly check on prices, the Index gives an up-to-date 'running commentary' on the way retail prices are moving. It is used to assess changes in the value of money and changes in the Index form the basis of many wage claims. While acknowledging the usefulness of the Index it must be remembered that it suffers from the general limitations of indices as mentioned earlier.

Changes in the level of prices

Figure 31 illustrates the steady rise in retail prices since 1972. The Index has moved from 100 in 1972 to 196 in December 1976. This means that a collection of goods and services which cost £100 in 1972 had risen in price by 96 per cent by the end of 1976. In other words the value of money has been steadily falling.

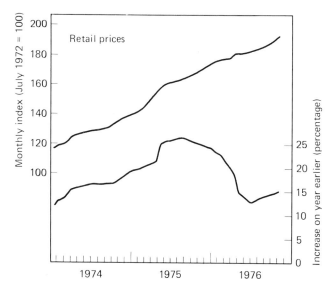

Fig. 31 Retail Prices

A slow rate of increase in prices of 2 or 3 per cent has certain beneficial effects. For example, production is stimulated because entrepreneurs are encouraged to invest. A decision to produce is taken in anticipation of demand and if the selling price of the goods proves to be higher than expected then profit margins will be greater than expected. This will cause producers to increase output to its maximum in the short-run and encourage long-term investment. Rising prices and increasing profits encourage a high level of production and full employment is much easier to maintain. Periods of falling prices have been in the past, associated with decreasing output, a decline in profits and heavy unemployment.

Thus a general rise in the level of retail prices – mild inflation – is acceptable if it can be kept down to a rise of 2 or 3 per cent annually. When prices rise by 15 per cent as they did in the UK in 1976 then the effects are most undesirable.

Meanings of inflation

The rate at which the general level of prices increases can vary. Hence there are several types of inflation.

1 *Creeping inflation* is the term used to describe a rise in the price level at a rate of 2 to 3 per cent per annum. This type of inflation does not do very serious harm and it may, in fact, stimulate investment.

2 *Moderate inflation* describes a rise of 4 to 5 per cent per annum and this rate is high enough to have undesirable effects.

3 *Rapid inflation,* that is, a rise of 6 per cent or over is positively harmful and has undesirable effects on incomes, imports and exports, savings and consumption.

4 *Hyperinflation* is a runaway inflation during which prices rise at phenomenal rates. The value of money declines daily; people lose confidence in the currency; and the monetary system begins to disintegrate. People revert to barter as a medium of exchange because money which is rapidly falling in value is unacceptable as a method of payment. Eventually the currency ceases to function as money and has to be scrapped. A runaway inflation occurred in Germany in 1923. Towards the end of the year paper money was losing a half or more of its value in one hour. Wages were fixed and paid daily. In 1924 the German government withdrew the virtually valueless notes and issued a new currency.

The causes of inflation

The causes of inflation are complicated but can be explained by two kinds of forces affecting the level of prices, namely, demand-pull and cost-push.

Demand-Pull

The prices of goods and services depend on two factors – the quantity of goods and services available, and the amount of purchasing power in the hands of consumers. When the volume of purchasing power increases at a faster rate than the output of goods and services, prices will rise. In other words, demand is pulling up prices.

The increase in purchasing power or the money supply can be caused by a number of factors. For example, consumers might be spending a greater proportion of their income; incomes themselves may have risen; or cheap and easier credit facilities might have been used to finance a spending boom.

Cost-Push

If an inflation is mainly induced by rising costs of production, it can be described as a cost-push inflation.

In conditions of full employment, trade unions are able to gain wage increases which are not related to increases in productivity. Under full employment, demand for labour exceeds the supply and in such conditions demands for higher wages are more likely to be met. As labour costs are often one of the main costs of production, firms may be compelled to raise the prices of their goods and services, in order to cover the addition to the wage bill. However, the price rises will lead to a further round of wage demands as people endeavour to restore the buying power of their incomes. In turn, further price increases will result and the chain of events will continue to repeat itself in an inflationary spiral of prices and incomes.

It should be mentioned that a cost-push inflation may be attributed to increases in costs other than wages. For example, increases in raw material prices may cause costs to rise. However, increases in wage rates unaccompanied by increases in output per man-hour are the best-known cause of rising costs.

Effects of rapid inflation

Rapidly rising prices have effects on incomes, savings, the balance of payments and the National Debt.

People on fixed incomes suffer most. Those living on pensions, debenture holders, and landlords receiving ground rent from leasehold property become progressively worse off as prices rise. Those living on state pensions may be given increases from time to time to offset the cost of living, but all who live on fixed incomes suffer a decline in real income during a period of rising prices.

Rapidly rising prices can have serious effects on the country's balance of payments. Goods become relatively dearer in foreign markets so that exports may decline. On the other hand, goods from abroad become relatively cheaper and more are likely to be imported. Thus inflation may encourage imports at the expense of exports and create an unfavourable balance of payments (see Chapter 19).

Finally, all debtors gain and all creditors lose during a period of inflation. For example, if a borrower undertakes to repay £15 per week for twenty-five years to a building society, then, if prices and incomes rise, the real value of the £15 will decline. As a debtor, the borrower gains; the building society, as the lender, will lose.

The burden of the National Debt is decreased because a smaller proportion of the national income has to be raised by taxation in order to pay the interest charges to lenders. The real cost of paying the interest falls. This occurs because as incomes increase so do the proceeds from taxation, whereas the interest charges on the National Debt remain the same.

Controlling inflation

The consequences of allowing inflation to reach a point where it threatens to destroy the currency are so serious that the government is bound to exercise controls. There are a number of disinflationary policies that may be used by the government for dealing with the inflationary spiral. They are:

(a) fiscal measures – making use of changes in the government's revenue and expenditure in order to influence economic activity (see page 262);

(b) monetary measures – to affect the amount of purchasing power available (see page 207);

(c) a prices and incomes policy.

One solution to ending the spiral of rising incomes and prices is to ensure that incomes rise at no higher rate than productivity. This is the aim of an incomes policy. In carrying out such a policy the government states at the beginning of each year the size of wage increases that can be given without causing an increase in prices, in the light of recent or expected increases in productivity. This figure is used to guide the trade unions and employers in their wage negotiations.

The aim of a prices policy is to secure price stability. This is very difficult to achieve.

A prices and incomes policy can be voluntary, or statutory, that is, the government enforces compliance on trade unions and employers. However, in a free society, where wages are settled by freely conducted collective bargaining, and where trade unions are committed to retaining their freedom to negotiate on behalf of their members, the statutory enforcement of wage levels may not be a practical proposition.

QUESTIONS

Write *short* answers to the following:
1 What is barter?
2 Describe briefly the problems of barter.
3 Outline briefly the stages in the development of money.
4 Which types of money are used in the United Kingdom?
5 Write down four functions of money.
6 What are the qualities of a good monetary media?
7 Describe briefly the advantages of money.
8 What is an index number?
9 Outline the problems involved in constructing an index number.
10 Is an index number of any practical use?
11 What is 'weighting'?
12 Explain briefly how the Index of Retail Prices is calculated.
13 What is the meaning of 'inflation'?
14 How is creeping inflation different from hyperinflation?
15 Who or what are affected by rapid inflation?
16 What are two main causes of inflation?
17 Name the principal methods used to control inflation.

Write answers to the following:
1 Which sections of the community are likely to (a) benefit, (b) suffer from the effects of a sharp rise in the general level of prices? (SUJB)
2 What can the British government do to halt inflation? (Oxford)
3 'To facilitate trade any form of society needs money.' Why? (JMB)
4 How would you construct an index of retail prices and what difficulties would you expect to encounter? (JMB)
5 How can one measure changes in the cost of living? Are the measures available to us in any way biased or otherwise defective? (Oxford)
6 What are index numbers? Give an example of their use. (Oxford)
7 What is meant by the statement: 'Money is a medium of exchange'?

How far do you consider this to be a satisfactory definition of money? (AEB)

8 Does inflation do any harm? (Oxford)

9 How can one measure changes in the cost of living? Is it possible to have an increase in the cost of living and the standard of living at the same time? (Oxford)

10 What are the main causes of changes in the value of money? (Oxford)

11 What is meant by 'the quantity of money'? (Oxford and Cambridge)

12 'Our money comprises notes and coin. These are issued by the Bank of England, and the supply of money is therefore under its control.' Explain why this statement is inadequate. (U/L)

13 What is the main form of money in use in Britain? How is its supply controlled? (Oxford)

14 What is meant by money? Why is money essential to a modern economy? (U/L West Africa)

PRACTICAL WORK

1 Modern money comprises notes, coins and bank deposits. In the past money has taken many other forms, such as, for example, shells, fish, cattle and gold. Find out all you can about the history of money.

2 Find out the meaning of Gresham's Law. Sir Thomas Gresham was Elizabeth I's finance minister. What conditions caused him to formulate his law?

3 Keep a record of the Index of Retail Prices which is published monthly. Plot the Index on a graph. The Index is published in the *Department of Employment Gazette;* in the *Economist;* and in newspapers.

4 Look up the following Indices and note their purpose.
   (a) Index of Wholesale Prices published in the *Economist.*
   (b) Index of Wages published by the Department of Employment.
   (c) Index of Earnings published by the Department of Employment.
   (d) Index of Stock Market Prices published by the *Economist.*

5 Find out the names of the central bank in (a) the United States, (b) France.

6 Using either the *Annual Abstract* or the *Monthly Digest of Statistics* make a graph to plot the following indices for the last 5 years.
   (a) the Index of Retail Prices
   (b) the Index of Average Earnings
   (c) the Index of Industrial Production. What conclusions can be drawn from the graph?

16
Banks

Origin of banking

In this country banking began with the London goldsmiths, who, because of the nature of their business, had facilities for storing valuables. Their first banking function, therefore, was accepting *deposits* of cash from merchants who had no safe place in which to keep their money.

After a time the receipts for deposits began to be used as a *means of payment* by merchants. Eventually the early bankers issued bank notes.

A more advanced stage in the development of banking came when bankers began to *lend money*. The increasing use of bank notes meant that fewer people wished to withdraw their deposits in cash from the bankers, who found it safe, therefore, to lend out at interest some of the money deposited with them.

In this brief outline of the origin of banking, there can be seen the development of the main functions of banks at the present day, namely,

    (*a*) repositories for cash
    (*b*) agents for payment
    (*c*) sources of loans.

Kinds of banks

There are, at present, several main types of banks in this country. They are

    1 commercial banks
    2 the Central Bank
    3 merchant banks
    4 savings banks
    5 National Giro
    6 finance companies.

1 Commercial banks

Banks which undertake most kinds of banking business are generally known as commercial banks or sometimes by their older name of joint-stock banks. In recent years a number of banks have amalgamated so that the following groups now exist:

1	2
Barclays Bank	National Westminster Bank
	Coutts and Co.

3	4
Lloyds Bank	Midland Bank

There are also several smaller banks such as Williams and Glyn's Bank, C. Hoare and Company and the Co-operative Bank.

The three main Scottish banks are (a) Bank of Scotland, (b) Clydesdale and (c) Royal Bank of Scotland.

The commercial banks have three main functions. They provide:
(a) a safe way in which customers can hold their savings,
(b) a means of making payments,
(c) loans to businesses and private persons.

Commercial bank deposits are a convenient way of holding savings. Deposits can be made in either a *current account* or a *deposit account,* or in both. A third type of account, which is called a *savings account,* is designed to encourage small savings.

A person who leaves money in a current account does not receive any interest from the bank and will probably have to pay charges for the work done by the bank conducting the account.

On the other hand he enjoys two advantages:
(a) money can be withdrawn on demand,
(b) payments may be made by cheque.

The holder of a deposit account does not pay charges, and he receives interest from the bank. (Each bank decides its own rates of interest for deposit and savings bank accounts.) He must give notice (usually seven days) of withdrawal and he cannot make payments from a deposit account by cheque. The bank provides him with a record of deposits and withdrawals.

The current account depositor receives a cheque book which is used both to make payments to others and to withdraw cash personally.

Cheques may be open or crossed. A crossed cheque is so called because it has two parallel lines across it; an open cheque does not have them.

The difference between them is that a crossed cheque cannot usually be cashed across the counter (the crossing cancels out the order to pay on demand). An open cheque can be cashed at the branch of the bank it is drawn upon.

Like other businesses the banks operate with the aim of making a profit. Income is earned by investing and lending the money deposited by people with the bank. A bank receives additional income from the charges it makes for some of its services, but the greater part of a bank's earnings arise from lending its deposits.

Out of its income a bank has to pay interest to its depositors, salaries to its staff and various other business expenses. From the net profit remaining, the bank's shareholders receive a dividend.

Clearly, the greater the amount of money lent the higher will be a bank's earnings and profit. On the other hand, a bank must always have sufficient notes and coin in its tills or in reserve, to meet customer's demands for cash. Customers are constantly drawing cash from their accounts to spend and to pay wages and salaries to employees but this money is soon returned by shopkeepers and other traders who receive it. Cash earns nothing for a bank and it is costly to store and transport, so as little as possible is kept.

How does a banker decide, therefore, the amount of cash to keep available?

It must be remembered that although bank deposits are subject to withdrawal in cash, the extensive use of the cheque system to transfer the ownership of bank deposits, means that only a small proportion of a bank's total deposits is actually converted into cash. From long experience the banks found that they needed to keep only a proportion of their total deposits either in notes and coin or in accounts at the Bank of England. The banks can quickly obtain more cash from these accounts should they require it.

Liquid Assets
In order to reinforce its cash reserve, a bank invests a proportion of its deposits in assets which can be quickly turned back into cash. These 'liquid assets' comprise loans made to discount houses on the money market (see Chapter 17) for periods ranging from 'on demand' to 14 days; commercial bills and Treasury bills. The use of commercial bills or bills of exchange is described on page 210. Treasury bills are a means of short-term (usually 91 days) borrowing by the Government. They are, in effect, bills of exchange drawn by the Treasury on itself. Treasury bills are available for purchase every week and they are completely liquid since they can either be resold to other financial institutions or the

Bank of England. The bills are bought in 'parcels' so that a proportion mature every day and a continuous flow of cash is made available if required by the bank. Thus a bank can replenish its cash reserves at any time by turning some of its liquid assets into cash. For example, loans to the discount houses can be called in or fewer bills may be bought than those currently maturing.

Since 1971 the Bank of England has required that certain of these assets (called *eligible reserve assets*) should not be allowed to fall below 12½ per cent of certain deposits. (These are deposits excluding those made for over two years and are called *eligible liabilities*)

The main reserve assets comprise the following:

(*a*) cash balances at the Bank of England

(*b*) money at call in the London money market

(*c*) Treasury bills

(*d*) commercial bills (up to a maximum of 2 per cent of total deposits)

(*e*) British Government securities with one year or less to final maturity.

The following are not included as reserve assets:

(*a*) notes and coins in the tills in the banking system

(*b*) money at short notice.

Although a bank will wish to maximise its earnings by lending as much money as possible, the *reserve assets ratio* provides a very definite limit to its ability to offer loans.

Earnings Assets

A bank's liquid assets earn interest but at rates which are generally less than can be obtained from the other two chief ways of using deposits. In other words, the least liquid assets generally earn the highest interest. They are (*a*) investments and (*b*) advances to customers.

The investments held by a bank are mainly in British Government securities. Holders of these securities receive a fixed sum of interest every year, but their market value on The Stock Exchange may fluctuate. Hence although they are easily convertible into cash, the bank may not wish to sell substantial amounts of securities if the prices are depressed.

Advances are the amounts which a bank lends to its customers. Customers' loans and overdrafts have always been the major source of earnings because they earn a higher rate of interest than the bank's other assets.

When banks lend, they will first satisfy themselves that the borrower can repay a loan; and secondly they will usually require security. The title deeds to land and property, stocks and shares, National Savings Certificates, life assurance policies and guarantees (under which someone promises to repay the bank if the customer fails to do so) may be deposited with the bank as security for a loan. If the customer fails to repay, the bank can, in the last resort, sell the property or surrender the assurance policies and so get its money back.

A large number and wide variety of customers borrow from the commercial banks. Most of the banks' lending is to businesses but substantial amounts are also lent to public authorities – local councils, government departments and nationalised industries – and to private customers.

The illustration of the balance sheet of a commercial bank (Table 19) shows how a bank distributes its assets and compromises between the competing aims of *liquidity* and *profitability*. The item 'Special Deposits' refers to the extra deposits which the Bank of England sometimes requires from the commercial banks. They earn interest at the current Treasury bill rate. Calling special deposits has the effect of reducing the banks' cash and liquid assets, and they have to reduce their total deposits to maintain the minimum reserve assets ratio.

Table 19 Simplified Version of the Balance Sheet of a Commercial Bank

Liabilities	£m	Assets	£m	£m
(Amounts owed by the bank to depositors)		Cash:		
		Till money	3	
Deposits: Current accounts	55	Balance at the Bank of England	2	5
Deposit accounts	35			
		Money at Call and short notice	10	
Savings accounts	10			
		Treasury bills	3	
		Commercial bills	2	15
		Total of liquid assets		20
		Earnings Assets		
		Investments		12
		Advances to Customers		65
		Special Deposits with the Bank of England		3
Total deposits	100	Total assets		100

204

Additional services

In addition to the three main functions outlined above (holding savings, providing a means of making payments, and providing loans), commercial banks offer a number of other services for the convenience of their customers.

1 Executor and trustee departments will administer customers' wills.

2 Travellers' cheques are available to provide a safe way of taking money when travelling at home or abroad.

3 The standing order service provides for the automatic payment of regularly-recurring fixed items such as subscriptions, insurance premiums and the like.

4 Direct debiting provides for the automatic payment of varying amounts at irregular intervals. Under this arrangement, the supplier sends *(a)* an invoice to the buyer and *(b)* a direct debit form to the buyer's bank. The buyer is saved the trouble of remembering due dates of payment and sending off cheques. The direct debit system of money transfer differs from the standing order in that it is the supplier who gives payment instructions, and not the buyer.

5 Arrangements can be made for the purchase or sale of stocks and shares, National Savings Certificates or Premium Bonds.

6 Important documents or small valuables may be placed in safe custody at the bank.

7 The night safe provides a means of safely depositing notes and coins for customers (such as shopkeepers) who do not end the day's business until after the bank has closed.

8 Cash dispensers supply a prepackaged sum of bank notes, at any hour of the day and night to customers who have obtained a cash card from the bank. After the card has been inserted into the machine, the customer taps out a code number on the keyboard and the dispenser delivers a cash pack.

9 Banks will assist with tax matters.

10 Budget or planned expenditure accounts are designed to assist customers with forward budgeting. The customer opens a separate account on which he draws for the purpose of paying regular bills such as rent, rates, season tickets, gas and electricity. The account is fed by a monthly transfer of a fixed amount from the current account. Thus the budget account will sometimes be overdrawn and sometimes in surplus. However, as long as cheques drawn on it are for the purposes included in the scheme, the bank will honour them. The cost of regular items of expenditure is spread evenly over the year.

11 A bank credit card such as a Visacard (Barclaycard) or an Access Card enables holders to make credit purchases at establishments (shops, hotels, garages, etc.) in the scheme. The advantages to the customer are: *(a)* less cash can be carried, *(b)* a number of bills can be settled with one cheque once a month which means a saving on bank charges.

12 An insurance service is available to customers. In effect the bank acts as an insurance broker offering advice and obtaining commission from insurance companies for policies sold to customers.

13 Firms which require cash each week to pay out wages to their employees can make arrangements for it to be available in the form required – notes, silver and copper coins.

14 Foreign currency can be made available.

15 Information regarding foreign markets and the financial status of foreign buyers is available to exporters.

2 The Central Bank

The Bank of England is a 'central bank', that is, it is at the heart of the banking system and plays a major part in administering the government's monetary policy. Unlike the commercial banks, its aim is not to make a profit for its shareholders (in fact the Bank of England was nationalised in 1946 and has no shareholders), and it does not compete with the commercial banks for ordinary banking business. The Bank has a number of branches throughout the country. Ordinary banking is still carried on, but is only a very small part of the Bank's work and only a few private customers are now accepted.

Functions

1 The Bank controls the issue of bank notes in England and Wales. It prints notes and authorises the minting of coins by the Royal Mint. New notes and coins are put into circulation in return for old ones which are removed by the commercial banks as they deteriorate.

In order to prevent an over-issue of notes the Bank Charter Act of 1844 laid down that apart from a *fiduciary* issue of £14 millions, all notes were to be backed by an equivalent amount of gold in the Bank. However, the fiduciary issue (that is, notes backed by securities) has risen steadily until today the whole of the note issue is fiduciary.

Note circulation is highest at the two peak spending periods of the year, that is, in August and towards the end of December.

2 The Bank acts as banker to the government. In the course of this work, it keeps accounts, arranges loans and provides means of payment.

All government revenue (such as the proceeds of taxation) is paid into the Exchequer Account and payments for goods and services received by the government is made out of this Account. The Bank also keeps the accounts of a number of government departments.

Loans are raised in a number of ways.

(a) Ways and Means Advances made by the Bank to the Treasury are comparable to the overdrafts provided to businesses by the commercial banks. This direct form of borrowing forms only a very small proportion of government borrowing.

(b) Short-term loans are raised by selling Treasury bills in the money market (see Chapter 17).

(c) Long-term loans are obtained by selling new issues of government stock in the capital market (see Chapter 17). Repayment dates can be anything between 5 and 30 years and sometimes no date is fixed for their redemption. Registers of stock-holders are kept by the Bank which also pays the interest and arranges transfers and repayments when due.

Thus the management of the National Debt (except that controlled by the National Savings Bank) is entrusted to the Bank.

In addition to the basic banking functions outlined above, the Bank provides a number of additional services to the government. These include:

(a) management of the Exchange Equalisation Account to maintain the value of the pound in the foreign exchange market (see page 249).

(b) Advice on general financial matters such as the level of interest rates or the volume of bank credit. However, the Bank is directly under the control of the Treasury and it is the latter which is responsible to Parliament for whatever decisions are taken.

(c) Maintenance of relations with international monetary authorities (such as the International Monetary Fund) and with the central banks of other countries.

3 The Bank acts as banker to the commercial banks by holding a proportion of their cash reserves. This enables the banks to settle any indebtedness to each other created by the daily clearing of cheques, by transfers between their accounts at the Bank of England.

4 The Bank acts as lender of the last resort to the Money Market. This function is explained in the next chapter.

5 The Bank is responsible for the management of the government's monetary policy.

Monetary policy means varying the price and supply of money. It is more flexible than fiscal policy since changes can be made at any time. In addition, the effects are less obvious and hence the introduction of a 'credit squeeze' is less unpopular than higher taxes.

Monetary measures are designed to reduce total spending by raising the cost of borrowing and limiting the availability of loans. The money supply comprises mainly bank deposits and so monetary controls are intended to regulate this major form of money. Controls are applied by the Bank of England acting on the instructions of the Treasury. They comprise open market operations; the use of special deposits; and directives. A restriction of the money supply by these methods will aim to deter investment and consumption by making finance more expensive and difficult to obtain.

Open market operations consist of selling or buying of government securities by the Bank on The Stock Exchange. If the Bank sells securities, buyers pay by means of cheques drawn on the commercial banks. The balances of the commercial banks at the Bank will, therefore, be reduced, and if the reserve assets ratio is to be maintained, then bank advances must be reduced.

Funding is an aspect of open market operations. It means lengthening the age structure of the National Debt by issuing less short-term debt (i.e. the sale of Treasury bills through the discount houses) and more long-term or funded debt. In this way the Bank of England can alter the banks' opportunities to purchase liquid assets, because Treasury bills are easily converted into cash. Thus if the Bank wishes to decrease the money supply, the sale of Treasury bills is restricted by converting the desired amount of short-term debt into funded debt. Consequently the banks must seek alternative liquid assets or reduce deposits. A drawback to the effectiveness of this process is that the banks may maintain their liquidity by increasing their holdings of commercial bills. These bills are bought from the discount houses and are just as liquid as Treasury bills.

The drawback can be overcome to some extent by using *special deposits* as a form of control.

The Bank of England can call for special deposits equivalent to a given percentage of the commercial banks' total deposits. These special deposits do not count as part of the liquid assets and so, in order to raise them, the banks have to call in part of their advances.

Open market operations and calls for special deposits are insufficient in themselves to achieve full control over bank advances. For example, instead of reducing their advances, the banks may prefer to sell their investments. Therefore, the Bank may supplement its action by issuing *directives* to the banks to restrict loans.

Until the introduction of a monetary policy reform in 1971 the *Bank*

Rate was used to influence rates of interest and hence, the cost of borrowing. Technically, Bank Rate was the minimum rate at which the Bank of England was prepared to re-discount bills of exchange brought to it by members of the London money market. However, the chief importance of Bank Rate lay in its function as the sheet anchor of interest rates throughout the country. Changes in Bank Rate influenced other rates of interest. When Bank Rate was raised, borrowing became more expensive and demand for loans was reduced, thereby reducing purchasing power.

In 1972 Bank Rate was superseded by a new rate called the 'minimum lending rate' to the money market. The role of Bank Rate (which was the oldest instrument of monetary policy employed by the Bank of England) had been severely modified by the government's new policy on competition and credit control introduced in September 1971, and since then Bank Rate had been less an instrument of policy and more a technical lending rate of last resort in the money market. Thus the abolition of Bank Rate in 1972 and the introduction of a minimum lending rate marked the completion of a reform of monetary policy.

Whereas Bank Rate functioned as (a) an instrument of monetary policy and (b) an interest rate, the new minimum lending rate acts only as the latter.

At the same time as he announced the abolition of Bank Rate, the Chancellor of the Exchequer said it would be resurrected when it was needed.

Bank Rate has fallen into disuse in the past. In 1932 it was argued that Bank Rate was not an effective instrument of monetary policy because a low rate did not necessarily encourage lending in the severe depression of that time. Consequently Bank Rate remained unchanged at 2 per cent (except for a brief period on the declaration of war in 1939) until its revival as a monetary instrument in 1951.

In this chapter the central bank's controls have been described from the standpoint of combating inflation by contraction of the money supply. The controls can, however, be used equally well to expand the supply of money. Thus if the government wishes to stimulate trade it can instruct the Bank to reduce the cost of borrowing by increasing the availability of loans through releasing special deposits, and buying securities in the open market; and by issuing directives encouraging adoption of a generous lending policy.

3 Merchant banks
The merchant banks are found almost exclusively in London. They are

specialised banks which work almost entirely for trade and industry.

Most merchant bankers originated as prosperous merchants who began to perform various financial services for small traders. Gradually the financial side of the business grew more important until eventually they gave up trade and concentrated on banking.

One of the main functions of the merchant banks is the provision of credit for financing foreign trade. An acceptance credit is arranged by an importer in London with one of the merchant banks. The credit is opened in favour of the exporter abroad who, when the goods have been supplied, draws a *bill of exchange* for the amount due to him.

The bill is an order addressed by the seller to the buyer, or to the merchant bank acting for him, to pay a certain sum of money on a certain date – usually three months distant. This bill is sent by air mail to London where it is 'accepted' by the bank. The bill then becomes a document which can be sold or discounted at a good price in the London money market. The cash, less the discount, can be secured immediately by the seller (see page 216).

The accepted bill of exchange commands this ready market largely on the strength of the name of the merchant bank. When the bill comes to maturity, the accepting bank pays over the amount stated on the bill to whoever presents it and will expect to receive the necessary funds from the exporter who drew the bill, a few days before maturity.

A second function of the merchant banks is to act as issuing houses for companies making issues of shares or loan stocks. An issuing house will advise on the type of security to be offered, the method and time of issue, and the terms of the offer. It will also negotiate with the Council of The Stock Exchange for a quotation and assist in the preparation of the prospectus.

As well as arranging issues, the merchant banks also underwrite them (i.e. in return for a commission, undertake to buy the shares unless they can be sold to the public) and arrange for payment of dividends as they fall due.

In addition to these functions, the merchant banks also engage in the following activities:

(a) management of investments for pension funds, charities and unit trusts;
(b) dealing in foreign exchange;
(c) financing mergers and take-overs;
(d) provision of specialist advice in arranging loans to industry.

Many merchant banks also perform the more usual banking facilities such as servicing current accounts, but only on a limited scale.

4 Savings banks

As their name suggests, these banks were formed with the aim of encouraging saving, especially by people with small incomes.

The oldest are the *Trustee Savings Banks* many of which were founded quite early in the nineteenth century. Unlike the commercial banks, trustee savings banks are not profit-making banks. They are under the management of voluntary local boards of trustees.

The Post Office Savings Bank was set up by an Act of Parliament passed in 1891. The name was changed to the *National Savings Bank* when the Post Office became a public corporation in 1969.

Both types of savings bank accept deposits which are recorded in a customer's savings bank book. Deposits can be withdrawn in cash very easily, small sums on demand, and larger ones at short notice.

The recording of deposits and withdrawals in a bank book enables the customer to see at a glance just how much he has on deposit at the bank.

Interest is paid on these deposits and a certain amount of interest is exempt from personal tax. In addition to ordinary accounts customers may open investment accounts which offer a higher rate of interest.

Both interest and capital are guaranteed by the government, and money deposited in the savings banks is handed over to the National Debt Commissioners, who use it to invest in government securities.

The Trustee Savings Banks provide a current account service.

The National Savings Bank does not offer a cheque service but sums of £1 or more may be withdrawn by crossed warrant payable through a bank. Several days' notice is required for the issue of the warrant by the National Savings Bank.

Both kinds of banks will undertake standing order payments, that is, regular payments of a fixed amount from depositors' accounts.

The savings banks have played an important part in the National Savings Movement through which millions of small savers have lent money to the government in times of both war and peace.

5 National Giro

The National Giro was opened by the Post Office in the autumn of 1968. A Giro service is one in which all accounts are held at a single centre. Instead, therefore, of using cheques which pass from drawer to payee (who probably have accounts at different banks) payments between account holders can be made by sending transfer instructions to the centre. Drawer and payee are informed by the National Giro Centre that the transfer has been made.

Three main facilities are provided for Giro account holders:

(*a*) bills may be paid by transfers from one account to another;

(*b*) small sums can be withdrawn on demand at either of two post offices nominated by the account holder. For large sums, or for withdrawals at another post office, notice of a few days is required.

(*c*) Deposits can be made at all post offices except for the very smallest ones.

In addition, account holders are entitled to the following:

(i) standing orders for regular payments of fixed amounts to other Giro account holders;

(ii) girocheques to pay people who do not have a Giro account and cannot be paid, therefore, by direct transfer;

(iii) statements showing deposits, payments and the balance remaining on the account.

National Giro does not claim to compete with the commercial banks in providing a wide variety of services. It concentrates on providing current accounts. Overdraft facilities are not available but Giro account holders may apply for personal loans.

6 Finance Companies

Finance companies obtain their funds partly by accepting deposits at fairly high rates of interest and by borrowing from the banks. Funds are used to provide loans (mainly in the form of hire purchase and personal loans) to businesses and to private borrowers. Finance companies also undertake financing of house purchase.

The Companies Act 1967 included a provision under which companies could apply to the Department of Trade for a certificate stating they were banks. Fairly strict conditions have to be met before the Department will issue a certificate.

A number of finance companies applied for certificates and a small proportion of the total number of finance companies can now legally claim to be banks. Probably the main motive for a finance company wishing to turn itself into a bank is status.

Special deposits which may be required by the Bank of England from time to time apply to all banks and finance companies.

QUESTIONS

Write *short* answers to the following:

1 Write down the three main functions of the commercial banks.

2 An account upon which interest is paid is called ———— ; an

account on which cheques may be drawn is called ———— .
3 Write down the names of two kinds of cheques.
4 How does a bank earn income?
5 What is a Treasury bill?
6 What are eligible liabilities?
7 List a bank's liquid assets.
8 What is the reserve assets ratio?
9 Which assets are not included in the list of reserve assets?
10 List a bank's earnings assets.
11 Name forms of advances available from a commercial bank.
12 List five services available to customers of a commercial bank.
13 Name three functions of the Bank of England.
14 Write down two functions of merchant banks.
15 Write down the names of two Savings Banks.
16 How does payment through National Giro differ from payment through a bank?
17 How does a finance company use its funds?

Write answers to the following:
1 Describe clearly the services which a commercial bank would be able to offer a customer who wished to:
   (a) make regular monthly payments to his tailor
   (b) spend a holiday in France
   (c) borrow money from the bank. (SUJB)
2 What are the main features that distinguish the Bank of England from a commercial (joint stock) bank? (Cambridge)
3 How do banks make profits? In what ways do they compete with one another and with other financial institutions? (Oxford and Cambridge)
4 Explain the meaning of the following terms used in the banking business: (a) Bank overdraft, (b) Crossed cheques, (c) Night safe, (d) Deposit account, (e) The Bank Rate. (JMB)
5 'Without banks economic activity today would be impossible.' Show what part banks play in modern economic activity and why they are so important. (JMB)
6 Describe a typical balance sheet of a Commercial Bank, and explain how the distribution of its assets is a compromise between the competing ends of liquidity and profitability. (JMB)
7 Describe the functions of the commercial banks. (SUJB)
8 Give a concise description of the work of the Bank of England. (SUJB)

9 What are the main services which banks provide for their customers? How are these services paid for? (U/L)

10 Examine the structure of a joint stock bank's assets, explaining each item fully. (WJEC)

11 'Building societies conduct some banking business.' Why do not the commercial banks undertake building society business? Discuss. (Oxford and Cambridge)

12 Distinguish clearly between the following:
   (a) deposit account and current account;
   (b) a cheque and a bank note;
   (c) a bank loan and a bank overdraft. (U/L)

13 What are the main limitations on the ability of a commercial bank to create credit? (SCE)

14 Describe how the Central Bank may increase (a) legal tender in circulation and (b) the volume of bank credit. (U/L West Africa)

15 Explain the difference between
   (a) a Central Bank,
   (b) Commercial Banks,
   (c) Savings Banks.
   What is their usual inter-relationship? (U/L)

16 How do merchant banks differ from commercial banks? Discuss the function of both in the framework of the English banking system. (RSA)

17 'Whatever the nature of his business, a trader, or manufacturer will make use of his bank's services.' Discuss this statement. (LCC)

18 The information below relates to a combined balance sheet of the London clearing banks.

Liabilities		Assets	
Eligible liabilities	£1 000 000	Eligible reserve assets	£125 000
		Other assets	£875 000

(a) Calculate the reserve assets ratio.
(b) Assume that the banking system acquired additional reserve assets of £10 000. What is the maximum possible increase in total deposits? (AEB)

PRACTICAL WORK

1 Find out how to open an account (a) with the National Savings Bank, and (b) with a commercial bank.

2 Make use of reference books in a library to write an account of each of the following.
   (a) the development of banking in England
   (b) the history of the Bank of England since its formation in 1694
   (c) the origin and growth of a merchant bank, e.g. Rothschilds, Baring Brothers, Hambros.
3 Obtain a recent copy of a commercial bank's balance sheet. Calculate the reserve assets ratio.

17

Markets in Money and Capital

There are a number of important financial markets in the City of London (Fig. 32). They are
- (a) the money market dealing in short-term loans
- (b) the discount market dealing in commercial bills and Treasury bills
- (c) the capital market dealing in long-term loans
- (d) the stock market dealing in existing capital
- (e) the foreign exchange market dealing in foreign currencies.

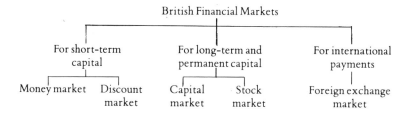

Fig. 32 Britain's Financial Markets

Only one of these markets has a particular building in which business is conducted, namely, the securities market at The Stock Exchange. The others comprise networks of institutions.

There is a close connection between the money market and the discount market because bills form the most important item of short-term lending. Thus for study purposes it is convenient to group these two markets together.

The money and discount markets
The money market in the City of London is essentially a market for short-term loans and is composed of the *discount houses*, the *merchant banks*

216

or *acceptance houses,* the *banks* (both British and foreign) and the *Bank of England.*

The twelve London discount houses occupy a central position in the money market and their business is the discounting of Treasury and commercial bills.

Merchant banks acting as acceptance houses assist the process of discounting by acting as guarantors for bills of exchange. A bill is drawn by the exporter and sent to the importer for his written acceptance and signature. However, the importer may not be a well-known person of financial standing and a discount house might not be prepared to take the risk of advancing cash on his written acceptance. The difficulty is overcome by the acceptance houses. In return for a fee they are prepared to accept bills which would otherwise not be negotiable because the original acceptor's name was not known to the discount house. In effect, an acceptance house guarantees payment of the bill. The acceptance houses have agents in the chief commercial centres of the world and they possess, therefore, expert knowledge of the standing of foreign importers.

The money employed by the discount houses is borrowed mainly from the banks and for very short periods of time. The banks keep part of their assets in 'money at call and short notice' and these loans are made mostly to the discount houses. The discount houses make a profit by borrowing at a certain rate of interest and charging a slightly higher rate for short-term loans (of approximately three months' duration) to the government or to traders.

In addition to providing loans the banks also buy bills from the discount houses in parcels composed of bills varying in their maturity dates. Generally, the banks like to have quantities of bills becoming due every day. They prefer bills to be not more than two months from maturity when they acquire them.

When the discount houses are short of funds because the banks will not renew the daily loans, they can borrow from the Bank of England. In fact, the discount houses are the only City institutions which may borrow directly from the Bank. The rate of interest charged by the Bank is known as the minimum lending rate. The Bank fulfils, there-fore, the function of being the 'lender of the last resort' to the discount market. When the discount houses are 'forced into the Bank' the latter lends against the security of bills. Borrowing in this manner is more expensive because of the higher rate of interest charged by the Bank.

In addition to guaranteeing loans to the discount houses, the Bank of England acts as agent for the issue of Treasury bills. Tenders are invited for the weekly offering and the discount houses and other institutions make their bids. The discount houses guarantee to buy up all those issued if other institutions do not want them. Thus they guarantee to lend to the government the money it needs in the short term.

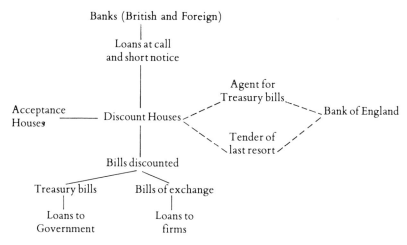

Fig. 33   The Money and Discount Markets

Summary of the working of the money market (Fig. 33)

1   The banks keep a ready supply of liquid funds on hand to enable them to meet demands from their customers for cash.

2   Loans to the discount houses form one important liquid asset. Money at call can be recalled immediately and money at short notice can be recoverable if necessary after seven days. Thus the discount houses provide the means whereby each bank can adjust its liquidity.

3   Discount houses use borrowed money to provide short term loans, *(a)* to traders by discounting bills of exchange, *(b)* to the government by discounting Treasury bills.

4   Merchant banks assist the system of discounting by acting as guarantors for bills of exchange.

5   The Bank of England *(a)* guarantees to lend to the discount houses if the latter are short of funds, *(b)* arranges the issue of Treasury bills.

1   Provision of a short-term loan market which enables bank balances to earn interest while ensuring there is always sufficient cash to meet the banks' daily requirements.

2   Provision of a market in bills of exchange *(a)* where any bill can be

218

discounted at the appropriate rate, thus providing an important service to international traders; (b) where banks which are sometimes in need of big parcels of bills can satisfy their exact requirements.

3 Provision of a link between the Bank of England and the commercial banks. There is a tradition that the banks do not ask for direct assistance from the central bank when they are in need of additional cash. If their cash reserves fall below the desired level, they restore the position by calling in loans from the money market. If all the banks are doing the same thing, the money market will be short of funds and will have to replenish its resources by getting assistance from the Bank of England.

The capital market

The money market supplies traders and the government with short-term finance. Industrial firms on the other hand, generally obtain their short-term or circulating capital from the commercial banks. This capital is used to work the business. A stock of raw materials will be bought and after manufacture, products are sold to customers who pay cash which can, in turn, be used to buy more stock. This kind of capital circulates and is constantly changing. On account of their need to maintain a proportion of their assets in liquid form, the banks are reluctant to provide long-term capital for industry. Long-term capital is used to buy fixed assets such as premises, machinery, fixtures and fittings which are essential to production and will be retained in the business over a long period of time. Generally, therefore, industry has to look to sources other than the banks for long-term capital.

The capital market consists of a number of institutions which collect the savings of private individuals and reinvest them in various enterprises. This is the market which deals in loans longer than the typical ninety-one day loans dealt with by the money market. All medium- and long-term loans are raised on the capital market. Thus funds are made available for business firms, local authorities and governments requiring capital for a period of years. The main institutions in the capital market are described below.

Insurance companies receive premiums on life assurance policies which may be in existence for many years. Thus they have available large sums of money for investment in long-term securities. The insurance companies are large buyers of existing stocks and shares, take up new issues of shares and invest about fifty per cent of their investments in government securities.

Investment trusts are joint-stock companies which engage in the buying and selling of other companies' shares. They invest capital in shares and gilt-edged securities on which they will be paid dividends and interest, and obtain any appreciation of their value. The net yields from these investments are distributed as dividends to their own share-holders.

Unit trusts engage in similar activities to investment trusts. They are not, however, public companies but trusts run by an independent group of managers. Their total investment is split into a large number of units of low nominal value. A large proportion of the funds are used to buy existing securities, but investment may also be made in new capital, particularly 'rights' issues.

Finance corporations exist to lend money to industry. Banks and insurance companies subscribe to their funds and each corporation tends to have a specialist function (see page 80).

Finance companies borrow money from banks and the public and provide funds for hire purchase agreements which are used to finance the purchase of both consumer and capital goods.

The *National Savings* and *Trustee Savings Banks* collect the savings of a large number of depositors. The savings are invested in government and local authority securities.

Pension funds operated by companies, local authorities and the government for their employees are invested in stocks and shares. The purpose is to earn an income on the fund, thus providing the pensions required.

Building societies supply long-term loans to people wishing to buy houses or other property. The most common repayment term is twenty to twenty-five years. Security for the loans lies in the deeds to the property. The funds of the societies are obtained from money invested in them by the general public.

The new issues market
This is part of the capital market and deals with new public issues of stocks and shares. The various methods by which a new issue of shares can be placed were described in Chapter 6. The part played by the merchant banks as issuing houses was explained on page 210.

The stock market
Some details of the working of The Stock Exchange were given in Chapter 6. The Exchange is a market for old securities, and not a source of new supply to the capital market.

Functions
1 The Stock Exchange provides a market for the purchase and sale of stocks and shares. If there was no Stock Exchange, investors would have

to claim their money back from companies. No business could function under such conditions because assets such as premises or machinery might have to be sold quickly in order to raise money to refund shareholders.

2 It assists in raising new capital for industry. The Exchange itself does not issue shares to the public (it is, as has been noted, a market for secondhand shares). But by granting a quotation or permission to deal in new shares, the Exchange makes it much easier for companies to obtain buyers for new shares. Many investors would not buy new shares unless they had obtained a quotation on an Exchange and could, therefore, be turned easily into cash.

3 It mobilises savings for investment. In addition to direct investors (that is, those who buy and sell through brokers) there are many indirect investors. These are people whose savings are invested on The Stock Exchange by the institutions which hold them. For example, the National Savings Bank, the Trustee Savings Banks, and insurance companies are institutional investors. This great flow of savings comprises the supply of loanable funds which are needed by industry to buy land, buildings, machinery and equipment; and by the government to build roads, schools, docks, hospitals and so on.

4 It provides a basis for the valuation of shares. The Daily List enables valuations to be made for assessing capital transfer tax payable on a deceased person's shareholding, or for assessing capital gains tax.

5 It safeguards the interests of investors. A company which applies for a quotation must comply with the Exchange requirements regarding publication of information considered essential for investors. In addition, business on the Exchange is conducted only by the members and according to rules drawn up by the Council of the Exchange. An investor who is faced with financial loss because a member of the Exchange cannot pay, for any reason, is compensated by the Exchange.

6 It facilitates borrowing by the government and local authorities. Investors know that they can, whenever they wish, turn government and local authority stock into cash by selling on the Exchange.

The foreign exchange market
An exchange rate is the price of one currency in terms of another. The foreign exchange market provides international traders, tourists and others requiring foreign currencies or needing to dispose of them with the money they need.

The London foreign exchange market has no fixed formal meeting place. Nearly all business within the City of London is conducted over the telephone and by telephone, telex and cable with overseas financial centres. The dealers number nearly 200 and comprise the banks authorised as foreign exchange dealers by the Bank of England. In addition there are about ten firms of foreign exchange brokers, who act as intermediaries between the banks.

The London market works within the framework of exchange controls laid down by the government. Before the outbreak of war in 1939, exchange rates were determined by the forces of demand and supply. In many countries there were no restrictions on persons or firms who wished to move assets from one country to another and from one currency to another. Since the end of war (1945) exchange control over the purchase and sale of both gold and foreign currencies has existed. Control is administered by the Bank of England as agent for the Treasury.

There are many geographical centres of foreign exchange trading in addition to London. Markets in New York and Switzerland have always competed strongly with London and after 1958, when the major European currencies were declared convertible, markets in other West European countries developed rapidly. Outside Europe and the United States, the most important foreign exchange markets are in Canada and Japan.

In spite of the many geographical centres of foreign exchange trading there is in reality, one worldwide market for currency. Banks authorised to deal in the various major centres buy and sell currencies with each other operating through telephone and telex links.

Since it is possible to buy and sell in so many different centres at the same time using virtually instantaneous means of communication, rates of exchange are kept in alignment with each other throughout the world. The process which brings this about, namely the buying and selling of currencies in the most advantageous market, is called *arbitrage*. Free movement of funds permits the arbitrage process to quickly correct any temporary local variations which arise in exchange rates.

QUESTIONS

Write *short* answers to the following:
1 Name five important financial markets in the City of London.
2 Which market is located in a particular building?
3 What is the close connection between the money and discount markets?
4 Which institutions make up the money market?

5 How do discount houses make a profit?
6 What part do the banks play in the money market?
7 How is the Bank of England 'lender of the last resort'?
8 What part do acceptance houses play in the money market?
9 List the functions of the money and discount markets.
10 How do industrial firms obtain short-term finance?
11 What is the difference between circulating and fixed capital?
12 Which institutions make up the capital market?
13 How do investment trusts and unit trusts differ?
14 What is the difference between finance corporations and finance companies?
15 Outline the various methods of placing a new issue of shares.
16 What role does an issuing house play in the process?
17 How does The Stock Exchange assist in raising new capital for industry?
18 What is an exchange rate?
19 Which institutions make up the London foreign exchange market?
20 What is arbitrage?

Write answers to the following:
1 'The capital market serves the needs of industry and commerce, governments and local authorities.' Outline the main elements within the capital market which undertake these functions. (U/L)
2 What are the relationships between (a) the Bank of England and the Money Market, and (b) the Joint Stock Banks and the Money Market? How are these relationships advantageous to the banking system? (U/L)
3 Describe briefly and explain the functions of any *three* of the following financial markets:
    (a) the Money Market
    (b) the Capital Market
    (c) the Stock Exchange
    (d) the Foreign Exchange Market   (JMB)
4 Answer *three* of the following questions:
    (a) What are discount houses?
    (b) What is the new issue market?
    (c) What is funding and why is it used?
    (d) What do brokers and jobbers do?
    (e) What functions does an acceptance house perform?   (Oxford and Cambridge)

5 Name the chief types of businesses which make up the money market, indicating the work done by each. (U/L)
6 What are the functions of The Stock Exchange? (U/L)
7 Outline the operations of the market for new capital. (RSA)
8 Explain the function of the London Money Market and comment on its economic significance for the economy. (RSA)

PRACTICAL WORK

1 Since the late 1950s a number of 'new' money markets have developed. They include markets in (a) short-term deposits with local authorities and finance houses, (b) Eurodollars, (c) inter-bank loans and (d) inter-company deposits. Find out what you can about each of these markets.
2 Find out the meaning of these Stock Exchange terms: (a) bull, (b) bear, (c) stag, (d) blue chips, (e) gilt-edged.
3 A prospectus for the issue of shares or loan stock is often printed in an abridged form in national newspapers. Find one and note (a) the name of the issuing house, (b) the terms of the issue, (c) the reasons for the issue, (d) the amount of existing shares and loan capital, (e) the published profits.
4 Look up in the financial pages of a national newspaper (a) the exchange rate of the pound against the dollar, (b) the London gold price, (c) the Bank of England minimum lending rate.

Part Six
The Interdependent World

Land, labour and the other resources used in production are distributed unevenly throughout the world. Minerals, for example, such as coal, iron and gold are found only in certain areas. Similarly, the climatic conditions essential for the growth of particular commodities (such as cane sugar, rice and tropical fruit) are found only in certain regions of the world. Thus countries are dependent upon each other for supplying their deficiencies in foods, raw materials and other products. But countries cannot buy the products they need from each other without selling in return. Thus they are dependent upon each other for markets.

18

International trade

Trading between countries differs from trade within a country in a number of ways.

1 Language
Different countries have different languages and this can be a barrier to trade. Traders who sell abroad may have to employ language specialists and incur additional expense through the necessity of having special forms, labels, instructions, etc., printed.

2 Currency
Each country has a different currency, that is a different type of money which is acceptable only within its own frontiers. In Britain the currency is the pound sterling, in France the franc, while in the United States dollars are used. If a British importer buys goods from a French manufacturer then payment must be made in francs which have to be purchased in the foreign exchange market. Such a procedure is more

costly and time-consuming than payment in the home trade. Furthermore, foreign exchange rates vary and an adverse movement in the conversion rate may involve a trader in a loss.

3 Payment

Payment may be longer delayed and less certain than that for home sales. An exporter has to obtain payment from a debtor who may live on the other side of the world and about whom he may know very little. He will be reluctant to ship the goods without being reasonably certain of payment, while the importer will not wish to pay without some guarantee that he will receive the goods. In the home trade, a manufacturer may often get cash on delivery or rapid settlement of his bill from a wholesaler.

4 Distance

The risks involved in transporting goods increase with the distance and the number of times the goods are handled. Hence there is greater likelihood of loss, damage or delay when sending goods to countries abroad.

5 Customs duties and import quotas

Certain goods may be subject to heavy duties or tariffs, making it almost impossible for exports to compete in price with home production. In addition, exports may be limited by quotas imposed by importing countries.

Even if an exporter considers he can compete (in spite of customs duties) he has to ensure that the correct duty is paid. Duties vary according to the way that goods are classified and strict penalties apply to false declarations. Hence a correct understanding of the classifications list is essential.

Finally, an exporter runs the risk that duties and quotas may be charged suddenly so that his market in a particular country may shrink or even vanish overnight.

6 Competition

At home, a manufacturer may be sheltered from foreign competition by duties or quotas imposed by his own government. Hence competition may be restricted to other home manufacturers. However, in overseas markets, the manufacturer may have to face competition from producers in that market and from other foreign exporters.

7 Local conditions

An exporter has to consider the customs and habits of the countries to which he sells goods. For example, foreigners may like their goods in different dimensions and in different kinds of packages from those found suitable in the home market. Similarly, attention must be given to the methods of trading adopted in foreign markets. For example, at home, the manufacturer may leave the provision of spare parts and an after-sales service to others, but if no such facilities are available abroad he must organise them himself.

Thus trading abroad involves considerably greater risks and difficult-ies than the home trade.

International division of labour
In Part Three of this book it was seen that division of labour within a country results in an increase in total output of goods and services. Just as division of labour within a firm can be extended to division of labour within the industry, so division of labour within a country can be extended into the international sphere.

Countries tend to specialise in those commodities which depend for their production on the resources which the country has in relative abundance. Thus countries possessing an abundance of land relative to labour will tend to specialise in agricultural products, and will trade these products for the manufactured goods made by countries having an abundance of labour relative to land. Australia, for example, produces wool and mutton because of large land areas and a suitable climate; Canada produces wheat for similar reasons. Countries specialise, therefore, in the production of certain goods and exchange a part of their total production for goods made in other countries. International trade is the extension of the principle of the division of labour to the international sphere.

Foreign trade would, however, be very limited if countries merely exchanged those commodities which others could not produce. All countries import items that could be home-produced if necessary. For example, Britain imports agricultural products which can be produced very well at home. She does not, however, specialise in the production of foodstuffs because she can produce other things, chiefly manufac-tured goods, more advantageously. Similarly, Britain imports cheap cotton cloth from India although she could produce it herself.

Each country tends to specialise in the production of just a few of the things that it is capable of producing. A country's choice of the forms of production in which to specialise will be determined by its ability to produce certain things more cheaply than other countries. For example, if Britain can offer dairy produce at £2 per unit and manufactured goods at £20 per unit, while Country X can offer dairy produce at £4 per unit and manufactured goods at £120 it will be more advantageous for Britain to produce manufactured goods and for Country X to specialise in dairy produce. This is known in economics as the *principle of comparative cost*. One object of international trade is to take advantage of the comparative cheapness of commodities in other countries.

Advantages of international trade
The main benefits derived from trade between countries are as follows.

1 Variety
Without international trade, many countries would have to go without some products. For example, countries with a temperate climate would have to do without certain fruits, cotton and rice; others would be unable to use minerals which were unobtainable at home. Thus international trade enables each country to enjoy a greater variety of products.

2 Efficiency
Access to an enlarged international market enables industries to attain greater productivity through economies of scale. Large-scale production results in economies in many industries (see Chapter 8) and selling abroad as well as at home extends the market and so makes increased output possible.

3 Specialisation
Foreign trade enables each country to specialise in the production of those commodities for which it is most fitted by natural conditions – climate, soil, etc. In addition, the peoples of the world differ in talents and abilities. The differences may be in skills which have been acquired by tradition (e.g. wine-making in certain parts of France, Italy and Portugal) or those taught through education and training (e.g. engineering). Thus foreign trade permits a country to concentrate on producing those goods and services for which its resources are most suited and at the same time, to satisfy its other wants by importing.

4 Interdependence
International trade makes the countries of the world interdependent. A country depends upon others (*a*) for supplying its deficiencies in goods and services and (*b*) for markets for its own products. Trade may lead to an exchange of knowledge and culture between countries which, it has been argued, should reduce the possibility of war.

Britain's overseas trade

International trade is important to Britain for a number of reasons.

The population of this country has grown steadily since the time of the Industrial Revolution. Before that time Britain was almost self-supporting in regard to food supplies. The growth of population has resulted in a dependence on foreign supplies of foodstuffs. This country grows less than half of her food supplies and relies on imports to supplement her own agricultural produce.

Foreign trade is important, too, in providing a variety of foodstuffs. This country lacks the climate, both as regards warmth and rainfall, which is necessary for the production of many foodstuffs (such as cane sugar, rice and tropical fruit) and beverages (such as tea, coffee and cocoa). Supplies have to be obtained from other countries.

Secondly, this country is dependent on foreign countries for supplies of raw materials for industry. Minerals such as nickel, zinc, aluminium and copper are imported together with certain chemicals such as sulphur and nitrates, and cotton, rubber and tobacco. Many industries depend, therefore, on foreign supplies of raw materials and it is true to say that a great many workers depend on foreign lands for their employment.

Thirdly, foreign trade is important to Britain because of her geographical position. This country's island position in the North Atlantic has given rise to great advantages in foreign trade. A large merchant navy has been built up which carries goods for other countries as well as for traders at home. Products brought to this country are sold on the London commodity markets, which are used by continental buyers to obtain their supplies. Thus London is an important distributing centre for north-west Europe, and raw materials and foodstuffs are re-exported after purchase by buyers from abroad.

Fourthly, international trade provides employment for people who are not directly engaged in the manufacture of goods. For example, not only are most of Britain's imports and exports carried in British ships, but a good deal of trade in which this country has no direct interest, is undertaken by British shipping companies. In addition, banks and acceptance houses help to finance foreign trade by accepting and discounting bills of exchange; and a great deal of the world's marine insurance is transacted at Lloyd's.

Finally, foreign trade has made Britain an important market for the goods of other countries. Countries such as New Zealand, Canada, South Africa, and India which send raw materials and foodstuffs abroad are as dependent upon the general prosperity of trade as the more industrialised countries such as Japan and Britain. Thus if industries in Britain are idle or not working to full capacity, the demand for imported raw materials will be less. If exporters of raw materials are faced with a decreased demand, their income, which is used to purchase manufactured goods, will be reduced. Hence the importance of Britain as a market for the goods of other countries.

British imports and exports

Commodities

Since international trade takes place primarily because resources are distributed unequally throughout the world, the pattern of Britain's trade demonstrates that this country has a relatively plentiful supply of some factors of production and a deficiency in others.

On the credit side, Britain has a large supply of capital in the form of machinery and factories. There is also a skilled working population and a high proportion of managers, scientists, engineers, economists and other experts in various fields. In addition, this country possesses a large merchant fleet which carries not only British goods but also goods for other countries.

On the debit side, Britain is deficient in agricultural land; a supply of cheap labour; certain minerals such as copper and nickel; certain chemicals; and a climate suitable for the production of foodstuffs such as rice and tropical fruit; beverages such as tea and coffee; and raw materials such as rubber.

This analysis of Britain's resources, as compared with the resources of other countries suggests that *exports* will consist chiefly of manufactured goods, and *imports* will comprise mainly foodstuffs and raw materials. In fact, Table 20 shows that manufactured goods (such as vehicles, machinery, radio, television, and electrical equipment) make up over eighty per cent of the total of exports. On the other hand, food, drink, tobacco, basic materials and mineral fuels make up over forty per cent of total imports (Table 21).

Table 20   Composition of UK Exports 1975

Exports	*Percentage*
Manufactures (metal, machinery, vehicles etc.)	83
Food, beverages and tobacco	7
Miscellaneous exports	10
	100

Table 21   Composition of UK Imports 1975

Import	Percentage
Food, beverages and tobacco	19
Industrial materials, fuels etc.	27
Manufactured goods	52
Miscellaneous imports	2
	100

There has been a most marked change in the composition of imports in recent years. An increasingly large proportion is now made up of manufactured goods. Such imports rose from just under 34 per cent of total imports in 1960 to 40 per cent in 1965, and to 52 per cent in 1975. See Fig. 34. Manufactured imports include both capital goods (such as aircraft and machinery) and consumer goods of the kinds which Britain also exports in large quantities.

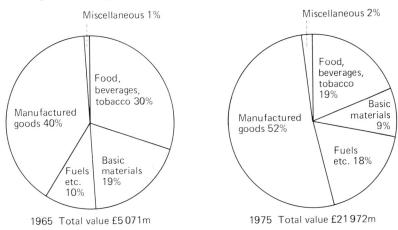

Fig. 34 Changes in Composition of UK Imports

The growth of world trade in recent years has taken place largely in industrial products and the trend for manufactured goods to take a larger share of total imports is one which is common to most industrial countries. It can be expected to continue as rising living standards increase the demand for the widest possible choice of manufactured articles. For this reason imported goods may sometimes be preferred to similar British goods simply because they are different.

Whereas food and unprocessed materials have taken a smaller *share* of total imports, the *volume* has, nevertheless, increased. Thus it is important to note that Britain is not importing fewer foodstuffs and materials, but rather the *proportion* in relation to the total of imports has fallen.

Geographical pattern

Figures 35 and 36 show the main sources of British imports and the principal export markets.

The earlier analysis of resources suggests that Britain's *imports* will be purchased from countries which have tropical climates or a high proportion of agricultural land or reserves of various minerals and chemicals. In fact, British trade with the rest of the Sterling Area (comprising the Commonwealth, excluding Canada, together with a few other countries such as South Africa and the Irish Republic, with which Britain has traditional trading links) was built up on the complementary basis of exchange between Britain's manufactured goods and their primary products.

However, by 1965, the share of British imports from the Sterling area had fallen to around 12 per cent. In 1975 this figure had been further reduced to about 8 per cent. On the other hand, between 1965 and 1975 the share coming from Western Europe increased from 37 per cent to 53 per cent. Over the same period, North America's share of the British market declined from 20 per cent to 12 per cent.

The change in the area *export* pattern is similar. Western Europe has become an increasingly larger market for British exports whereas the Sterling Area has become relatively less important. In fact, Western Europe has now become the largest buyer of British goods and also the largest source of British imports.

This change in the structure of British foreign trade is due, as mentioned earlier, to the growing tendency for trade between manufacturing countries to be much the fastest growing sector of world trade. Trade has become less complementary – between industrial and agricultural countries – and more between the industrial nations themselves. In addition, Britain's entry into the Common Market in 1973 encouraged the Commonwealth countries to seek links elsewhere. At the same time, there has been increasing competition in Commonwealth markets from other countries such as Germany, Japan and the United States.

Services

In addition to trading in goods, countries perform services for one another. Goods are usually referred to as *visible* items because they can be seen and recognised. Services are termed *invisible* items because they

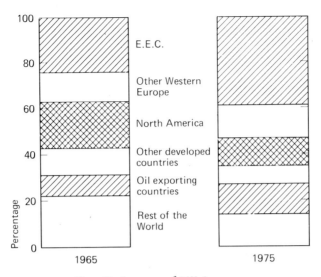

Fig. 35 Sources of UK Imports

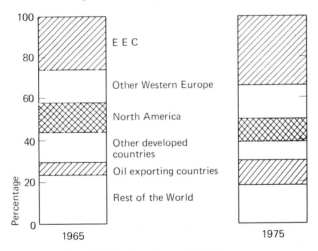

Fig. 36 Destination of UK Exports

cannot be seen or touched. Those services which are sold to people in overseas countries are invisible exports while services bought by people who live in Britain are invisible imports. As with visible items, payment is made abroad for invisible imports and money is received for invisible exports. The nature of invisible exports and imports is summarised below:

233

Payments (Invisible imports)	*Receipts* (Invisible exports)
1 Government Expenditure on government services abroad, e.g. cost of keeping troops abroad, cost of embassies and diplomatic expenses.	Payments by foreign governments for their forces in Britain.
2 Transport Charges made by foreign shipping companies and airlines for carriage of British people and goods.	Earnings of British shipping and airlines through carrying foreign people and goods.
3 Travel Spending of British tourists and business people abroad.	Money spent by overseas visitors in Britain.
4 Interest, profits and dividends Payments made to foreign owners and lenders of capital by firms in Britain.	Income received from overseas investments held by private people and firms and the government in Britain.
5 Private transfers Money sent (e.g. gifts, pensions) by people in Britain to relatives and friends abroad.	Money sent by people abroad to residents in Britain.
6 Government transfers Economic grants to developing countries made directly or through international organisations.	Economic grants received from foreign governments.
7 Other private services Payments made to foreign firms for various financial and other services.	Earnings received from financial and other services to foreign firms.

The item showing receipts from 'other private services' includes the earnings of the City of London from the provision of insurance, banking and other financial services for overseas customers. Under this heading are also included the royalties received from the sale of books and records overseas.

Terms of trade

The rate at which one country's products exchange for those of another is referred to as the terms of trade. If the terms of trade move in a nation's favour, it gets a larger quantity of imports for a given quantity of its exports. This has happened because import prices have fallen relative to export prices. For example, if in a certain year Britain can import ten tons of wheat in exchange for the export of one tractor, and in the following year fifteen tons of wheat can be imported in exchange for one tractor, then the terms of trade have moved in Britain's favour. If, on the other hand, two tractors had to be exported in exchange for ten tons of wheat in the second year, then the terms of trade would have moved unfavourably to Britain.

The terms of trade depend on the world prices of commodities entering into international trade, and fluctuations in the terms of trade are likely to have an effect on the standard of living of a country which, like Britain, has a high level of imports and exports. Thus, when the terms of trade are favourable, a trading nation like Britain can enjoy a higher standard of living. This is achieved not by an increase in the production of goods or services at home but because import prices have fallen and a greater quantity of goods can be imported in exchange for the same quantity of exports.

The British terms of trade are calculated by the Department of Trade, using the following formula:

$$\frac{\text{Index of Export Prices}}{\text{Index of Import Prices}} \times 100 = \text{Terms of Trade Index}$$

Consider the following. If the index rises then it will indicate a trend favourable to Britain in world trade. For example, assuming the Index of Export Prices changes to 120 and the Index of Import Prices changes to 60, then, $\frac{120}{60} \times 100 = 200$, which means that Britain's exports are exchanged for twice as many imports as in the base year, when the Index was 100. On the other hand, a fall in the Terms of Trade Index indicates an unfavourable trend because the prices of imports will have risen compared to the prices obtained for British exports (see Table 22).

Table 22 The Terms of Trade: (1970 = 100)

Year	Export prices	Import prices	Terms of trade
1970	100	100	100
1971	106	105	101
1972	111	110	101
1973	126	140	90
1974	163	218	75
1975	199	246	81

Source: *Monthly Digest of Statistics*

QUESTIONS

Write *short* answers to the following:

1 List the differences between home trade and foreign trade.
2 Why does Britain import agricultural products when these can be produced at home?
3 State the principle of comparative cost.
4 List four advantages of international trade.
5 State briefly why international trade is important to Britain.
6 Describe briefly the characteristics of Britain's (a) exports and (b) imports.
7 What change has taken place in recent years in the composition of British imports?
8 What is the main reason for this change?
9 State briefly why Britain's trade with Commonwealth countries has declined.
10 What are (a) visible and (b) invisible items in international trade?
11 Write down three examples of (a) invisible imports and (b) invisible exports.
12 Give a definition of the 'terms of trade'.
13 Briefly explain the relationship between the terms of trade and a country's standard of living.
14 How are the British terms of trade calculated?

Write answers to the following:

1 How does international trade differ from trade within a single country? (WJEC)

2 What are the purposes of international trade? (SUJB)
3 'The export market is of fundamental importance to the United Kingdom.' Explain why this is so and discuss the possible ways a government might act to boost exports. (JMB)
4 In what ways is international trade of importance to the UK? (Cambridge)
5 What are the main goods imported and exported by Britain? Indicate their relative importance in the British economy. (Oxford and Cambridge)
6 What are the main imports and exports of your country? What are the advantages of international trade? (U/L West Africa)
7 (a) Describe the geographical distribution of Britain's visible imports and exports.
(b) Why are both visible and invisible imports and exports so important to this country? (U/L)
8 The UK imports a large proportion of her food and raw materials. Why is this so and in what ways do we pay for these imports? (SUJB)
9 'International trade depends on international division of labour'. Explain this statement, giving examples. (U/L)
10 What is the law of comparative costs? How does it operate? (RSA)
11 Why may a country gain by importing goods which it could produce more cheaply at home? (LCC)
12 Outline the advantages of international trade. (LCC)

PRACTICAL WORK

1 Draw up a list of foodstuffs that come from abroad and which you might eat in the course of a day or look around your home and draw up a list of commodities which have been imported from abroad.
2 Find out the meaning and purpose of the General Agreement on Tariffs and Trade (GATT).
3 Find out the economic aims of the European Economic Community (EEC).
4 Using the dates below calculate the terms of trade for each year:

Year	Import price index	Export price index
I	103	99
II	109	113
III	107	109

5 From the *Annual Abstract of Statistics* you can conveniently identify the countries which supply Britain's imports. Group appropriate countries together (as in Fig. 35) and work out the value of goods imported from these countries as a percentage of the total.

6 From the *Annual Abstract of Statistics* identify the destination of Britain's exports. Group appropriate countries together (as in Fig. 36) and work out the value of goods exported to those countries as a percentage of the total.

19

International Payments

Balance of trade
The Customs authorities provide the Department of Trade with details of goods entering and leaving the country by sea or air. Exports are valued free on board (f.o.b.), which means that payment received by the exporter includes only the carriage charge as far as the ship. Additional transport and insurance costs incurred in getting the goods to their destination are paid by the importer. Imports to Britain are shown as including cost, insurance and freight (c.i.f.). Hence the trade statistics tend to over-value the total amount spent on imports.

From the information supplied by the Customs authorities, the

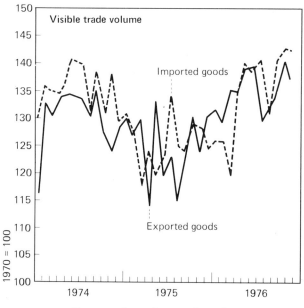

Fig. 37 The Balance of Trade

239

Department produces a monthly statement giving a summary of imports and exports for the preceding month.

The Balance of Trade is the difference between the value of imports and exports of goods (i.e. visible items) for a particular year. When visible exports are higher than visible imports the Balance of Trade is said to be favourable – because sales exceed purchases. On the other hand, when imports exceed exports, the Balance is adverse or unfavourable. Sometimes the latter situation is referred to as the 'trade gap' (Fig. 37).

Balance of payments

The annual statement of all payments made to countries and total receipts from them is known as the Balance of Payments. The full accounts are set out in *United Kingdom Balance of Payments* (known as the Pink Book), which is published annually. The way in which the accounts are presented divides the various transactions into (*a*) Current Account, (*b*) Currency Flow, (*c*) Official Financing.

Current account

The current account comprises money for current dealings as opposed to money for investment. It is made up of two parts, namely visible trade and invisible trade (see Table 23).

Table 23   Current Account 1975

		£ million
A	*Visible trade*	
	1 Exports	18 768
	2 Imports	21 972
		– 3204
	Visible balance (*1* minus *2*)	
B	*Invisibles*	
	Government services and transfers (net)	– 1025
	Other invisibles	
	Private services and transfers (net)	+ 1607
	Interest, profits and dividends	
	Private sector	+ 1494
	Public sector	– 545
	Invisible balance	+ 1531
C	*Current balance (A + B)*	– 1673

It is customary for Britain to have a deficit on the visible balance but this is not such a disastrous situation as might at first be thought.

Table 24 The UK Balance of Payments: Summary 1965–75
£million

	1965	1966	1967	1968	1969	1970	1971	1972	1973	1974	1975
Current account											
Visible trade	−223	−66	−554	667	−156	−25	+280	−702	−2334	−5220	−3204
Invisibles	+197	+167	+256	+395	+616	+758	+804	+856	+1598	+1873	+1531.
Current balance	−26	+101	−298	−272	+460	+733	+1084	+154	−736	−3347	−1673
Current balance	−26	+101	−298	−272	+460	+733	+1084	+154	−736	−3347	−1673
Capital transfers	–	–	–	–	–	–	–	–	−59	−75	–
Investment and other capital flows	−326	−578	−600	−1006	−165	+573	+1817	−714	−39	+1614	+188
Balancing item	−1	−70	+227	−132	+392	−19	+245	−705	+45	+136	+6
Balance for official financing	−353	−547	−671	−1410	+687	+1287	+3146	−1265	−789	−1672	−1479
Allocation of Special Drawing Rights (+)	–	–	–	–	–	+171	+125	+124	–	–	–
Gold subscription to IMF (−)	–	−44	–	–	–	−38	–	–	–	–	–
Official financing											
Net transactions with overseas monetary authorities	+599	+625	+556	+1296	−699	−1295	−1817	+449	–	–	–
Foreign currency borrowing: by HM Government	–	–	–	–	–	–	–	–	–	+644	+423
by public sector under exchange cover schemes	–	–	–	–	+56	–	+82	–	+999	+1107	+387
Official reserves (drawings on +/additions to −)	−246	−34	+115	+114	−44	−125	−1536	+692	−210	−79	+669

Note: Special Drawing Rights refers to a facility available to member countries of the International Monetary Fund (IMF). In some years there is also a gold subscription to the IMF.

Source: *United Kingdom Balance of Payments*

Invariably there is a surplus on invisible earnings so that the current account can be in surplus in spite of a visible trade deficit.

The current balance (i.e. the balance of visible and invisible trade taken together) shows whether the country is making a profit or loss on day-to-day dealings. Thus a surplus over a number of years demonstrates that sufficient foreign currency is being earned to buy imports and to build up reserves of foreign currency.

Capital flows

Apart from the current account, there are other flows of money into or out of the country and these are flows of *capital*. They comprise, for example, money going out of Britain for investment in industry or property and money coming into Britain for similar purposes; loans between the British government and other governments; borrowings abroad by the nationalised industries and local authorities; the credit given for exports and received when buying imports. Other flows are provided by overseas countries, and their private citizens and firms adding to or withdrawing from the bank balances they hold in Britain; and the lending and other dealings in foreign currencies of British banks (see Table 24).

When the total of these capital transactions is added to the current balance, the total never tallies exactly with the amount of foreign currency which the country has in fact gained or lost in the year. (This amount is recorded exactly by the Bank of England). Few of the transactions in the accounts can be recorded precisely – for example, the foreign spending of British people taking holidays abroad, or money spent by tourists in Britain. An additional difficulty is the differences of timing between transactions and payments. For example, exports may be shipped abroad in December 1977 and the payments for them come in in March 1978, so that some payments relating to 1977 will be incorporated in the 1978 figures for the total currency flow. Thus variation in timing from year to year makes consistent recording impossible. The *balancing item*—in effect the total of recording errors and omissions—makes up the difference between the total value of the transactions recorded and the precise accounts kept by the Bank of England. If the balancing item is 'plus', it means that more money has actually come in than the records of transactions have shown. If it is 'minus', the opposite is the case.

Total currency flow

When added together, the *current balance* plus the total of *capital flows* plus the *balancing item* give the *total currency flow* which has come into (plus) or gone out of (minus) the country. In Table 24, the total currency flow is recorded as 'balance for official financing'.

If the flow is a plus figure, it shows the money available for (a) adding to the foreign exchange reserves or (b) repaying loans from overseas. When there is a loss—a minus currency outflow—it has to be covered by (a) drawing on the foreign currency reserves or (b) borrowing from overseas central banks or (c) borrowing from the International Monetary Fund (IMF). The latter is a fund of currencies contributed by the member countries and it provides short-term borrowing facilities for countries in temporary balance of payments difficulties. There are two further ways of covering a loss: foreign investments can be sold to raise funds or bank deposits from abroad can be attracted by high interest rates.

However, each of these methods possesses a disadvantage in that they create future difficulties. Thus loans have to be repaid, generally with interest; the IMF imposes certain conditions on borrowers (with the aim of helping them to solve their problems); the sale of foreign investments reduces future income; while bank deposits are very volatile and can be quickly moved to another country with higher interest rates (hence the term 'hot money').

Official financing
The last two rows of figures in Table 24 show how the government has covered a net loss or used a net gain. The plus and minus signs may appear rather confusing because plus is usually taken as favourable and minus as unfavourable, as is the case in the current account. In fact, the minus sign here means money going 'out' to pay off debts or into the reserves, and is therefore a good indication, whereas a plus means additional government borrowing from abroad or 'borrowing' from the reserves, both of which are unfavourable.

Summary
The two totals in the annual statement which are of most economic importance are:

1 the current balance—showing the country's position in day-to-day dealings with the rest of the world;

2 the total currency flow—showing the country's ability to build up reserves or pay off debt—or inability to do so.

Correction of a deficit on current account
If a country's monthly earnings from visible and invisible exports are insufficient to cover its liabilities for total imports, it is failing to pay its

way. The situation is similar to that of a person who persists in spending more than he earns; borrowing and using up savings will finance the extra expenditure for a time, but sooner or later an effort has to be made to get earnings and spending into balance.

There are two main methods of remedying a deficit on current account. If, as is often the case, inflation at home has raised prices to a level where exports are uncompetitive in world markets and imports are rising because foreign goods have become relatively cheaper, then either (a) prices can be reduced or (b) the exchange value of the currency can be cut.

The first method—*deflation* (using monetary and fiscal measures outlined on page 207 and page 262)—seeks to prevent costs and prices from rising as fast as in other competing countries. By reducing demand through increased taxation and less government expenditure reinforced by reductions in the supply of money and higher interest rates, a deflationary policy aims to reduce imports and through contraction of the home market, to encourage manufacturers to sell abroad and so expand exports. Exports should rise, imports fall, and the deficit should be eliminated.

However, this policy has a serious drawback in that it seems to be impossible to adjust prices without adjusting incomes as well. A lowering of incomes reduces demand which, in turn, is likely to have a much greater impact on production and employment than upon prices. A government which is committed to a policy of full employment is unlikely to pursue deflationary policies which cause unemployment if there are alternatives available.

The second method involves the *devaluation* of the currency in terms of other currencies, either by fixing its exchange value at a lower level or by allowing it to be depreciated by market forces. The great advantage of this method compared with the alternative of deflation, is that the levels of income and prices at home remain unchanged. Hence devaluation does not create unemployment or curtail economic growth.

The immediate effect of devaluation by a country (assuming no change in the value of other currencies) is that its goods become cheaper in terms of other currencies whereas imported goods become dearer in terms of the home currency. For example, in 1967 the pound was devalued by 14.3 per cent in terms of the dollar. Before devaluation the pound exchanged for 2.80 dollars and afterwards it exchanged for 2.40 dollars. Thus a car manufactured in Britain, priced at £1000 and exported to the United States before devaluation cost $2800; after devaluation the car cost $2400. On the other hand, a $4200 car made in the United States sold in Britain at £1500 before devaluation and at £1750 afterwards.

At first sight, the immediate effect of making imports dearer and exports cheaper appears to be a decrease in imports, an expansion in exports and an improvement in the current account balance. However, the net effect will depend upon the *elasticities of demand* for exports and imports. A fall in export prices will only lead to greater earnings of foreign currency if demand is elastic, that is, if the volume of exports increases by a greater percentage than the percentage fall in price as a result of devaluation. In other words, to benefit from devaluation, a country must obtain a greater revenue from exports than before. Similarly, a rise in import prices will only reduce expenditure in home currency on foreign goods if demand for them is elastic. If demand is inelastic, more foreign currency will be spent than formerly.

Elasticities of demand are not, however, the only consideration. Account must also be taken of *inelasticity of supply*. If export industries are already fully employed, if resources cannot easily be attracted out of other industries into the export industries, and if it is difficult to reduce consumption at home in order to supply customers abroad, it will not be possible to meet in full the extra demand created by the devaluation.

Finally, it should be borne in mind that devaluation may provide price advantages in export markets only if other countries do not retaliate by devaluing their currencies to the same extent. If they do, then exchange rates will remain the same. For all these reasons, it is by no means certain that devaluation will eliminate a deficit on current account.

It is sometimes possible to avoid the harmful effects both of deflation and devaluation by imposing *controls aimed at restricting imports*. Controls may take various forms.

Import duties (tariffs) may be levied or, alternatively, *import quotas* may be fixed by the government decreeing the quantities of imports allowed during a certain period. Whereas a duty restricts imports by raising their prices, quotas raise prices by restricting supply. In each case, imports may be reduced below the level which would otherwise prevail. However, the effect of a duty on the level of imports depends on the elasticity of demand; and a quota based on volume leaves the value of imports to be determined by the effect on price. Further, both duties and quotas apply only to visible imports.

A more effective method, from the point of view of reducing expenditure of foreign currency is to fix quotas in terms of expenditure. This form of *exchange control* means that once an allotment of foreign currency has been spent, no more imports will be allowed during the remainder of the allotment period. Rationing of foreign currency restricts both visible and invisible imports.

The effect of trade restrictions is the same as that of devaluation, namely, imports become dearer. Yet on the other hand, the administration of a widespread system of controls may be expensive. For example, a great deal of form-filling is necessary. Further, a policy of trade restrictions is equally open to retaliation by trade competitors.

There are, therefore, weaknesses in, and objections to, each of the methods outlined above. The ideal solution is to *increase exports* and eliminate the deficit without a reduction in imports or in the level of home demand. A great deal of government effort is, in fact, devoted to expanding exports. Unfortunately the response of exports to the various inducements offered cannot be guaranteed. Hence if exports are inadequate, remedies have to be applied to imports.

Balance of payments and the terms of trade

The meaning of the 'terms of trade' was explained in the previous chapter (page 235). When a greater quantity of imports may be bought for a given volume of exports, a country's terms of trade are said to be favourable. On the other hand the latter are judged to be unfavourable when a greater volume of exports is necessary to exchange for a given quantity of imports.

A *favourable* movement in the terms of trade may have an *unfavourable* effect on the balance of payments current account.

If export prices rise, additional foreign currency will be earned only if the volume of exports does not change, or at least falls by less than the percentage change in price. For example, if export prices rise by 10 per cent, causing a favourable movement in the terms of trade, there will be a favourable effect on the balance of payments only if the volume of exports remains constant or falls by less than one-eleventh. In other words, demand abroad must be inelastic if there is to be a favourable effect on the balance of payments.

Similarly, if import prices fall by 10 per cent, causing a favourable movement in the terms of trade, there will be less foreign currency spent on imports only if the volume bought does not expand by more than one-ninth. In other words, demand for imports must be inelastic if there is to be a favourable effect on the balance of payments.

If the demand for exports and imports were elastic, the favourable movements in the terms of trade would worsen the balance of payments, since expenditure abroad would rise and income from abroad would fall.

There is also the income effect to consider. If the terms of trade improve because import prices fall, the result is that other countries' earnings from exports will be reduced. Consequently their ability to purchase imports will be correspondingly reduced. Thus if the prices of Britain's exports rise, less may be sold abroad not only because of the price increase, but also because foreign countries are less able to pay for imports.

On the other hand, an *unfavourable* movement in the terms of trade may have *favourable* effects on the balance of payments.

A fall in export prices will lead to greater earnings of foreign currency if demand is elastic. Whether or not demand is elastic depends upon the nature of the exports and the ease with which they can be substituted for similar goods from other producers in the importing country and in other exporting countries.

Similarly, a rise in import prices, causing an unfavourable movement in the terms of trade, will reduce expenditure on foreign-produced goods if demand for them is elastic.

However, elasticities of demand are not the only consideration. Account must also be taken of elasticities of supply. If a fall in export prices leads to an improvement in the terms of trade, and assuming that demand abroad is elastic, it may not be possible to meet in full the extra demand created by the fall in prices. This could happen if the export industries are already fully employed, if resources cannot easily be attracted into the export industries, and if home consumption cannot be reduced. Thus if the supply of exports is inelastic, a fall in their prices will adversely affect the balance of payments.

Foreign exchange
One of the problems associated with international trade is that each country has its own kind of money which is generally unacceptable in another country. For example, the Spanish peseta is of no use to a British exporter who has sold cars to a Spanish importer unless (a) the exporter wants to buy Spanish goods with the pesetas or (b) he can exchange pesetas for pounds sterling. Alternatively, he may receive payment in sterling, in which case the buyer must obtain pounds with his Spanish currency.

Thus when international trade takes place an exchange of currencies is necessary. In practice, this work is performed by the banks on behalf of their customers. Fig. 38 explains the process. The foreign exchange market consists of most banks together with a small number of firms who specialise as foreign exchange brokers. There is no meeting place for the market since nearly all business is conducted over the telephone and telex. Banks throughout the world conduct business with each other in this way and the market is, therefore, international. Through the foreign exchange market each currency acquires a value in terms of the other currencies which can be bought and sold for it.

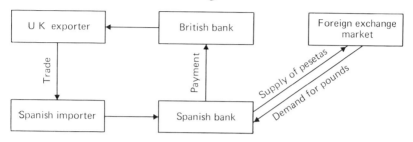

Fig. 38 International Payment

An *exchange rate* is the price of one currency in terms of another. It is determined mainly by the supply of, and demand for, the particular currency. Thus the supply of pounds, for example, depends on the extent to which people, business firms and governments wish to sell pounds in exchange for other currencies. The sellers will include British importers and investors in foreign firms. On the other hand, those who create the demand for pounds will include foreign importers and overseas investors in British Government stocks and the shares of British companies.

The foreign currency earned by British firms through exporting is held by the banks and forms part of the country's foreign currency reserves. If earnings from exports are less than the amount spent on imports, then British banks will sell more pounds to get foreign currency than foreign banks wish to buy for their own importers. The extra pounds will have been bought by the Bank of England in exchange for part of the foreign currency reserves built up in previous years.

If the reserves were in danger of being used up, the Bank of England would have to borrow foreign currency from other central banks. Thus it is essential that the export earnings of British firms are sufficient to provide importers with the currency they need. Hence the importance of the Balance of Payments current account which shows whether or not Britain is paying her way in world trade.

Under free market conditions, the price of a currency is determined by the forces of demand and supply. This is a system of *free* or *floating exchange rates*.

An alternative system is that of *fixed rates*. Under this system, the value of a currency is fixed in terms of the currencies of other countries and any appreciation or depreciation is allowed only within narrow limits. Thus the forces of demand and supply working through the foreign exchange market can affect the actual exchange rate only within narrow limits. (For example, in 1970 the exchange rate of the pound and the US dollar was fixed within the band of 2.38 to 2.42 dollars to the pound.)

The first essential for a country wishing to stabilise the exchange value of its currency is to establish a means for making equal the demand for and the supply of its currency in the foreign exchange market. In Britain this stability is achieved by the Bank of England operating the Exchange Equalisation Account. The latter is a kind of buffer stock of foreign currencies and pounds and is used to stabilise the value of the pound. When the value of the pound falls, the Bank enters the foreign exchange market and buys pounds, using for this purpose its stock of foreign currencies. The increased demand for pounds raises the exchange value of the pound back to the required value. When the value of the pound rises above this level, the Bank sells pounds. Consequently its stock of foreign currencies is replenished and the value of the pound is brought back to the required level.

Although a fixed rate of exchange can vary only within narrow limits, this does provide, nevertheless, an indicator of the strength of a currency in the foreign exchange market. If, for example, pounds are in great demand the market rate will be near the upper limit and there will be a tendency for the foreign currency reserves to increase. If, on the other hand, there are more sellers than buyers of pounds, the rate will be near the lower limit and there will be a tendency for the reserves to fall.

QUESTIONS

Write *short* answers to the following:
1 How are (a) exports and (b) imports valued by the Customs authorities?
2 Define the Balance of Trade.
3 When is the Balance of Trade (a) favourable, (b) adverse?
4 Name the main sections of the Balance of Payments statement.
5 What is the difference between the Balance of Trade and the Balance of Payments?
6 Which kinds of trade make up the current account?
7 What is the importance of the current account?

8 Write down three examples of capital flows.
9 Why is there a balancing item in the Balance of Payments statement?
10 Which items comprise the total currency flow?
11 What uses can be made of a gain from total currency flow?
12 In what ways can a loss on total currency flow be covered?
13 What does the section 'Official Financing' show in the Balance of Payments statement?
14 List the various methods of correcting a deficit on current account.
15 Define devaluation.
16 How do import duties differ from import quotas?
17 Describe briefly how a favourable movement in the terms of trade may have an unfavourable effect on the balance of payments.
18 What is an exchange rate?
19 How is an exchange rate determined under a system of floating rates?
20 What is the Exchange Equalisation Account?

Write answers to the following:
1 How does the United Kingdom acquire reserves of foreign currencies? How might an adverse balance of payments on current account affect these reserves? (U/L)
2 Describe the constituent items of 'invisible trade'. What is the significance of 'invisibles' in the British Balance of Payments? (JMB)
3 'Whereas the balance of payments must balance, the balance of trade need not.' Explain and comment on this statement. (WJEC)
4 What is meant by an 'unfavourable' balance of payments? What steps may a government take to improve the balance? (SUJB)
5 What is meant by a surplus in a country's balance of payments? In what circumstances, if any, should a government seek to promote such a surplus? (Oxford)
6 What is the difference between:
(a) An import duty and an import quota
(b) A visible export and an invisible export
(c) The balance of trade and the balance of payments? (U/L West Africa)
7 What do you understand by 'devaluation'? In what ways can devaluation affect the international trade of the UK? (Cambridge)
8 What are the main items in a country's balance of payments? Explain how a country's ability to lend abroad is dependent on its balance of payments on current account. (Oxford)
9 What is meant by a country's 'terms of trade'? Does an improvement

in the terms of trade necessarily mean there will be an improvement in the balance of payments? (Oxford)

10 What are a country's *terms of trade*? How can they be calculated? What is their significance to a country's balance of payments? (AEB)

11 Describe briefly the likely effects on the British balance of payments of *each* of the following:
   (a) A decline in the overseas earnings of British insurance companies
   (b) An increase in the investment of foreign capital in Britain
   (c) Increased expenditure by British people on holidays abroad
   (d) An increase in the production of food in Britain. (Oxford)

12 The following figures are based on statistics for the United Kingdom in a current year: (+ indicates a surplus; – indicates a deficit)

	£ million
Imports (f.o.b.)	5024
Exports and re-exports (f.o.b.)	4471
Shipping	– 27
Civil Aviation	+26
Travel	– 43
Other services	+239
Interest, profits, dividends	+435
Private transfers	– 20
Government	– 431

   (a) Calculate the *Balance of Trade* for the year.
   (b) Calculate the *Balance of Invisible Items*.
   (c) Calculate the *Balance of Payments on Current Account*. (AEB)

13 Write notes on *three* of the following:
   (a) Sterling Area
   (b) Gold and dollar reserves
   (c) Terms of trade
   (d) Invisible imports and exports
   (e) Devaluation (U/L)

14 The data below is part of the balance of payments accounts, of a country in successive years.

	Year 1 (£ million)	Year 2 (£ million)
Visible exports	3500	4000
Visible imports	4000	5000

Invisible exports	3000	4000
Invisible imports	2400	3700
Capital flows (net)	500 (−)	500 (+)

Calculate:

(a) the percentage change between the two years in the balance of trade.

(b) the current account balance in year 2.

(c) the percentage change between the two years in the total currency flow. (AEB)

PRACTICAL WORK

1 Using reference material in a library find out the meaning and significance of each of the following.
(a) International Monetary Fund (IMF)
(b) Sterling Area
(c) Reserve currencies
(d) The Gold Standard.

2 Discover up-to-date Balance of Payments figures (see Table 24) from the *Annual Abstract of Statistics*. Comment on the trends shown by the statistics.

3 Britain has operated various forms of (a) free and (b) fixed foreign exchange rates since 1945. Find out (a) the dates when new systems were introduced and (b) the reasons for the changes.

4 The exchange value of the pound in terms of other currencies is reported in the financial pages of most national daily newspapers, or in *The Economist*. Keep a record of the pound in relation to the dollar and note the reasons given by journalists for significant changes.

Part Seven
The Government and the Economy

Government intervention in the economic life of Britain has increased enormously during the twentieth century. Nowadays each of the major political parties agrees that a certain amount of government planning is necessary. They differ, however, as to the amount of control the government should undertake.

In the next three chapters, the role of the government in the economy is examined.

20
Economic planning

Meaning of economic planning
In Britain the growth of state influence has resulted in the government becoming involved in economic planning. Formerly, the word 'planning' was associated only with collectivist economies such as those in communist countries, and there remains a fundamental difference in the meaning of the word in relation to (*a*) a private enterprise economy and (*b*) a collectivist economy.

Under a *collectivist* system, the ownership of material resources is closely governed and restricted by the state. The control and use of land, labour and capital are in the hands of a central authority which makes its decisions in accordance with its opinion as to what consumers need. The typical procedure in this kind of centrally planned economy is for the government to fix targets for the various state-owned industries for a number of years ahead. Each industry and firm is allocated the resources which are considered sufficient to permit them to fulfil their target output. Prices are fixed by the central authority. This form of planning is described sometimes as *planning by direction.*

In a *private enterprise* system (which operates through a system of markets and the price mechanism), planning is based on persuasion rather than compulsion. The state does not control the allocation of all resources and so the operation of a plan involves co-operation between business firms and the government. The latter may set production targets—for both private and public enterprise in a selected number of industries, or it may try to set targets for the economy as a whole—but their achievement is dependent upon financial incentives or disincentives—not compulsion. This form of planning is described sometimes as *planning through the market.*

Economic planning in Britain

Planning in the sense of forecasting expenditure on a year-to-year basis has long been practised in both publicly and privately owned industry. Economic planning is, however, a much broader concept. It looks ahead for a period of at least four or five years and is concerned with the use of all resources as distinct from monetary expenditure.

Economic planning in this country takes the form of *national planning* and *regional planning.* Separate machinery exists for each type although neither can be completely separated from the other.

National economic planning

The initial steps were taken with the setting up of the National Economic Development Council (NEDC) in 1962. The Council, which was soon nicknamed 'Neddy', brought together representatives of the government, management and trade unions for discussions on economic planning. Between February 1963 and March 1964 the Council published a number of documents which were largely based on consultations with industry. The first publication dealt with the growth of the United Kingdom economy for the period 1961-6 and was based on the assumption that the economy would grow at an annual rate of four per cent. The Council considered how the needs of industry for capital, labour and raw materials would be affected by this growth rate. These documents were publications of the Council itself and not of the government, and so the government was not committed to action.

In 1964 the NEDC began to create a series of Economic Development Committees (EDCs) for particular industries. The Committees deal with most of the country's major industries and they are often called 'little Neddies'. Each Committee is composed of representatives of management, unions and the government. The work of the Committees is to serve as a source of information on the performance, prospects and plans of individual industries in the formulation of national plans. In addition, they report on progress towards the achievement of plan targets and take action on matters likely to prevent their attainment. The EDCs have no executive power and no powers of compulsion.

Both the NEDC and the Committees are served by the staff of the National Economic Development Office.

In 1964, with the establishment of the Department of Economic Affairs (DEA) the main responsibility for national planning was taken over by the government. (Note: in 1969 the DEA was disbanded and overall planning responsibility was transferred to the Treasury.) During the following year a National Plan was published.

Although it was overtaken subsequently by unforeseen events, the National Plan provides a useful illustration of the purposes and methods of economic planning. The Plan was built around the target of a 25 per cent growth from 1964 to 1970. This target was based upon surveys made by the DEA of individual industries. Forecasts were made of demand and growth targets were fixed for each industry.

As a result mainly of severe balance of payments difficulties, the National Plan proved to be unattainable. Further, the problems before and after devaluation in 1967 produced uncertainties which prevented the publication of a new five-year assessment in 1967 and in 1968.

In 1969, however, a new planning document called *The Task Ahead* was published by the government. It offered a guide to the likely development of the economy until the end of 1972.

The principal aim of the plan was to transfer resources from home consumption into exports, in order to build up a substantial surplus on the balance of payments. Hence major decisions were necessary about the future use of resources. Machinery for consultations between the government and both sides of industry on these major issues already existed in the form of the NEDC and the Economic Development Committees in each industry.

The Task Ahead embodied the main lessons learnt from the failure of the 1965 National Plan. For example, a single growth target was avoided and allowance was made for variations in the rate of growth due to the emergence of unforeseen developments.

Benefits of economic planning
The failure of the 1965 National Plan brought into question the value of

national economic planning in this country. However, the fact that forecasts may go astray is not necessarily a decisive argument against economic planning. It is useful, therefore, to examine the benefits which arise from economic planning even though the targets forecast are not achieved.

1 Information is made available which assists business people in making decisions. The process of economic planning builds up an overall picture of the economy and the statistical information is valuable to firms planning future investment projects. For example, the future demand for steel depends on the volume of output of industries making steel products. The planned targets of the latter industries are of direct concern, therefore, to steel producers.

2 The study of individual industries draws attention to problems which may not have otherwise been foreseen. For example, restrictions on the future growth of an industry caused by raw material or skilled labour shortages may be foreseen and appropriate remedies planned.

3 A plan involving targets for certain industries has merit in setting standards to be pursued. If the standard is not reached, this may indicate not a defect in the forecasting, but a failure in an industry's productivity.

Difficulties of economic planning
The basic difficulty lies in forecasting economic behaviour. Human wants are unlimited and the influences affecting consumers' and producers' decisions are so complex that an accurate estimate of demand for each product is virtually impossible.

Secondly, in a country like Britain which exports and imports on a large scale, the problems of forecasting and control are increased because events in countries abroad are beyond the control of the home government.

Regional economic planning
Some areas of Britain have suffered for a long time from below-average economic expansion and above-average unemployment. The chief cause is contracting employment in certain old-established industries such as coal, cotton and shipbuilding. Hence high local levels of unemployment has remained a persistent problem in Scotland, Wales and parts of England, even when the general level of unemployment is very low (see pages 164–5). Consequently, in these areas there is a wastage of resources and social problems arising from unemployment.

In contrast to these areas of slow economic expansion, there are areas such as the Midlands and South-East England, with a high proportion of newer industries and where demand for labour tends to be relatively high. The industries bring with them associated offices and commercial and professional services. Prosperity attracts more shops, and transport services are developed. Hence industrial expansion and the number of jobs multiplies. However, prosperity brings problems and the big towns in these areas may suffer from housing shortages, traffic congestion and overloaded educational and welfare services.

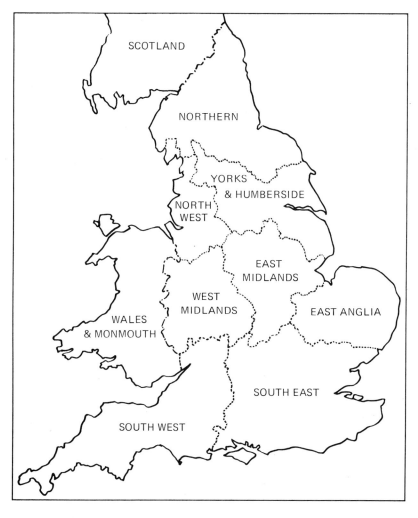

Fig. 39 Economic Planning Regions

Thus in some areas of the country, labour and other resources are wasted, while in others, the pressure of demand on resources is too great.

The primary aim of regional planning is to secure the balanced development of the country's resources within the broad framework of national economic planning. In pursuing this aim, regional planning seeks: (a) to alleviate high local levels of unemployment and to make full use of the resources of labour and capital in those areas which have lagged behind the most prosperous regions; (b) to assist in solving the problems of areas where the pressure on resources and services is high due to changes in the distribution of industry and the population as a whole.

Regional planning machinery
For regional planning purposes, the country is divided into ten regions (eight for England and one each for Scotland and Wales see Fig. 39).

Each region has: (a) an Economic Planning Council consisting of representatives from industries, local government and the universities; (b) an Economic Planning Board consisting of civil servants.

The main tasks of the Councils (assisted by the Boards) are: (a) to work out broad objectives for each region; (b) to advise on the formulation of national policies where these can significantly affect the regions; (c) to advise on the application in the regions of national policy.

Each Council has produced a study of its region based on an analysis of its resources, needs and problems. The studies cover major topics of regional development and include, for example, population, employment prospects, industry, transport, fuel and power and housing. The regional studies provide the basis of long-term regional planning.

QUESTIONS

Write *short* answers to the following:
1 What does 'planning by direction' mean?
2 What does 'planning through the market' mean?
3 What is the essential difference between the two forms of planning?
4 Name two characteristic features of economic planning.
5 Name the two forms of economic planning used in Britain.
6 What is 'Neddy'?
7 What are the 'Little Neddies'?
8 When did the government take over the main responsibility for national planning?
9 Which period was covered by the National Plan?

10 Why did the National Plan fail?
11 What was the principal aim of *The Task Ahead*?
12 In what way was *The Task Ahead* an improvement over the National Plan?
13 List three benefits of national economic planning.
14 What are the obstacles to successful economic planning?
15 What is the primary aim of regional planning?
16 Describe briefly the machinery of regional planning.

Write answers to the following:
1 Why do governments attempt some control of the economy? What are some of the methods used? (Oxford and Cambridge)
2 Explain the aims and difficulties of national economic planning. (Oxford and Cambridge)
3 Describe the aims and methods of conducting regional economic policy. (Oxford and Cambridge)

PRACTICAL WORK

1 The first steps towards the establishment of a prices and incomes policy in Britain were taken in December 1964. Since then the pattern of development has been as follows:
    1965 National Board for Prices and Incomes established
    1966 Prices and Incomes Act
    1967 Prices and Incomes Act
    1968 Prices and Incomes Act
    1971 National Board for Prices and Incomes replaced by the Office of Manpower Economics
    1973 Establishment of the Price Commission and the Pay Board
    1977 Establishment of reorganised Price Commission
  (a) Using reference books find out the changes and developments brought about by the events listed above.
  (b) Keep a record of developments after 1977.
  (c) Draw up a list of difficulties in establishing a prices and incomes policy in Britain.
2 Ask at the library to see the study of the economic region of the country where you live made by the regional Economic Planning Council. Make brief notes on the main topics covered in the study.

21
Public Finance

As a result of growing state intervention in economic life, the government has become the greatest spender of money in the country. This huge volume of expenditure enables the government to exercise a great influence on the economy of the country.

Government expenditure

The main items of government spending are as follows:

social services such as education, health and welfare, and social security;

defence, that is, the cost of maintaining the armed forces;

environmental services, that is, spending on roads, transport services, law and order, housing, and the arts;

National Debt interest, that is, interest payments on money borrowed by the government.

Government income

In order to provide for its expenditure, the government obtains finance in the following ways.

1 *Taxation.* Taxes may be classified as direct and indirect. Direct taxes are levied on a person's or a firm's income or wealth; indirect taxes are taxes on spending on goods and services. Thus direct taxes are paid directly by the person or firm on whom the assessment is made, while indirect taxes are paid indirectly by consumers in the form of higher prices. Direct taxes are collected by the Inland Revenue whereas indirect taxes are generally within the province of the Customs and Excise Department. Direct taxes cannot be legally evaded but indirect taxes can be avoided in the sense that people can reduce their purchases of the taxed goods and services.

2 *Borrowing* in the form of

(*a*) government stocks (stocks which are dealt in on The Stock Exchange under the popular title of gilt-edged securities);

(*b*) Treasury bills;

(c) National Savings, e.g. national savings certificates, premium savings bonds, etc.;

(d) Ways and Means advances from the Bank of England.

The Budget

The government makes a budget every year. It is an estimate of government expenditure and income for the coming year and this statement is usually presented to Parliament by the Chancellor of the Exchequer in April. He reports also on the actual expenditure and revenue for the year which has just ended (1 April to 31 March) as compared with the previous Budget estimates. Budget Day is the normal occasion when taxation changes are announced.

How does the government forecast the amount of money it will have to spend during the next financial year?

The first step is for government departments to calculate how much they will need for their work, and these figures are called the estimates.

Table 25   An example of Budget Estimates

Consolidated Fund	£ million
Revenue	
Taxation	16217
Miscellaneous receipts	545
Total	16762
Expenditure	
Supply services	13871
Consolidated fund standing services	575
Total	14446
Surplus transferred to National Loans Fund	2316
Loans from the National Loans Fund:	
To nationalised industries	982
To other public corporations	157
To local and harbour authorities	885
Other	28
Total	2052
Less Consolidated Fund Surplus	2316
Net borrowing of National Loans Fund	− 264

When the estimates have been approved by the Treasury (the government department which ensures that the proposed spending is in line with agreed policy), they go before Parliament for approval.

Table 25 shows that the government's revenue and expenditure are administered through two funds, namely, the Consolidated Fund and the National Loans Fund. Both Funds are held by the Bank of England.

The *Consolidated Fund* is used to receive government revenue (including receipts from taxation) and to draw out government expenditure. The bulk of the expenditure goes on Supply services which account for the day-to-day spending by government departments. This expenditure requires annual approval from Parliament. The other item of expenditure is Standing Services which do not have to be voted annually by Parliament. They are mainly the balance of the interest on the National Debt (see page 273) which is not offset by interest receipts on government loans.

Expenditure is balanced against revenue in the Consolidated Fund to yield a *surplus* (or a *deficit*). A surplus is transferred to the *National Loans Fund* which conducts the bulk of the government's lending and borrowing. Loans are made to those corporations and local authorities which need to borrow in order to finance expenditure on capital projects such as the building of power stations, schools and houses. The Fund is fed from the repayments of and interest on its loans; from the government's own borrowing; and from the surplus (if any) from the Consolidated Fund.

A surplus of revenue over expenditure from the Consolidated Fund reduces the amount which the government has to borrow to finance the loans which it makes. On the other hand, if expenditure should exceed revenue so that there was a deficit instead of a surplus, the deficit would be covered by an advance from the National Loans Fund and thus increase the amount which the government had to borrow.

The Budget and the economy

The original purpose of the Budget was to enable the government to raise sufficient revenue to cover expenditure in the same financial year. However, with the development of government control of the economy, the Budget has become an important instrument of economic policy. In broad terms, it has two main purposes, namely, the regulation of the economy and the redistribution of income between the various sections of the community.

1 Regulation of the economy
One important function of the Budget is to produce a balance between

the total goods and services which are likely to be available to the community and the total claims which are likely to be made on them. Thus, before the Budget, the government forecasts (a) the potential growth of output and of imports in the coming year and (b) the growth of demand for them which is likely to arise from consumers' personal spending, spending by the government and local authorities, investment by private firms, and exports. The Chancellor budgets for a surplus or a deficit, depending on the economic situation at the time.

If the situation revealed by the forecasts shows that demand is growing too slowly, action may be taken in the Budget to increase demand. Thus, the Chancellor may stimulate demand by a reduction of taxation. A reduction in taxes on incomes, for example, places more money in the hands of consumers; if consumers increase their spending then demand for goods and services is stimulated. On the other hand, taxes on goods and services may be reduced in order to lower prices so that consumers will be encouraged to buy. Alternatively, the government may increase its expenditure in the hope that more spending power will stimulate demand. This increased spending may take a number of forms. For example, the government may decide to increase the rate of investment in the nationalised industries, or in new roads, school building and so on. Another possibility is the expansion of government spending in the form of increased social security payments such as higher retirement pensions or more unemployment pay. Thus when demand is judged to be insufficient, the government plans for a Budget deficit by spending more than is raised by taxation.

On other occasions, the forecast may indicate that total demand is likely to rise too quickly. It will be necessary, therefore, for the government to either reduce its own spending directly or to restrain personal consumption by means of tax increases. Less money in circulation may reduce demand by consumers for goods and services. In these circumstances the government plans for a Budget surplus by raising greater sums in taxation than are used as government expenditure.

2 Redistribution of income

A reduction in the inequality of incomes in Britain has been achieved by a system of progressive taxation, that is, taking a higher proportion of income from the higher income groups in personal taxes. A progressive system of taxation makes saving more difficult and this fact combined with a capital transfer tax, the rates of which are progressive, has greatly reduced the size of inheritances.

Inequality of incomes is still further reduced by the provision of social services which, though available to all, are generally of most benefit to people in the lower income groups. Expenditure on the social services consists largely of transfer payments. This means that part of the revenue collected from taxpayers in taxes or National Insurance contributions is redistributed in the form of old age pensions, child benefits, sickness and unemployment benefits, and other social services. The entire cost of these services is not borne by taxpayers because part is met by the National Insurance contributions of those who benefit from the expenditure. Nevertheless, the social services do undoubtedly raise the disposable incomes of the recipients. The redistribution effects depend upon whether the bulk of taxation is paid by the wealthier members of the community. Certainly this is true of taxation on incomes and wealth, but there is doubt (as will be explained later) as to whether it is true of taxes on spending.

Drawbacks of fiscal policy

Fiscal policy, that is, the use of the Budget as an economic regulator, has a number of disadvantages.

In the first place, it lacks flexibility. Some fiscal changes become effective only after a considerable time-lag. For example, the benefit of a reduction in personal taxation announced early in April is not felt by taxpayers until three or four months later. Thus this method of control is unsatisfactory if an immediate change is desirable.

Secondly, the effectiveness of tax reductions depends on people's willingness to spend the extra income at their disposal. If the additional income is saved, then nothing is done to increase demand. Similarly, additional personal taxes may be paid out of money which otherwise would have been saved, in which case higher taxes will not reduce consumers' expenditure.

Thirdly, if the Budget surplus or deficit is achieved by changes in government expenditure rather than by taxation changes (for example, a surplus can be achieved either by reducing government expenditure or by increasing taxation), these changes may involve major changes of policy and cannot, therefore, be quickly revised. In addition, political factors are involved in decisions to either significantly increase or decrease government spending.

Changes between annual Budgets

Occasionally measures have to be taken between annual Budgets to meet changing economic circumstances. For example: *(a)* a supplementary Budget can be introduced, *(b)* use can be made of the Customs and Excise Regulator which permits the Chancellor to make a ten per cent increase or decrease on the Budget rates of a number of indirect taxes, *(c)* various measures may be introduced during the course of the financial year rather than on Budget Day. For example, changes in hire purchase arrangements can be made such as, for example, restrictions on hire purchase finance, or higher initial deposits and shorter periods of repayment. Other measures could include increases in National Insurance contributions or pensions and other social security benefits.

Taxation

In Britain the main *direct* taxes are as follows.

Personal Tax. Tax is charged at higher rates on successive ranges of taxable incomes above the basic rate band.

Corporation Tax. This tax is levied on the profits of companies.

Capital Transfer Tax or *Gifts Tax.* This is a tax on *(a)* wealth given away during a person's lifetime and *(b)* wealth owned at death. The tax was introduced in 1974 and replaced estate duty.

Capital Gains Tax. This tax is payable on certain types of assets (including shares) which increase in value between the date of purchase and the time of selling.

The principal *indirect* taxes are as follows:

Customs Duties. These are taxes on certain goods imported from abroad, chiefly tobacco and alcoholic drink.

Excise Duties. These duties are charged on certain home-produced goods such as beer and spirits.

Value Added Tax (VAT). Whereas customs duty (which is collected at the port of entry) and excise duty (which is collected from manufacturers) are levied at one point only in the production process, value added tax is levied on firms at all stages of the production process. Each manufacturer, wholesaler or retailer is accountable for tax on the value of what he sells, but credit is allowed for tax already paid on purchases. Put very simply, the tax works the following way:

(a) A shoe-maker buys leather worth £20 from a tanner for which he pays £20 plus VAT at 10 per cent, or £22 in all. The tanner pays the £2 to the tax collector.

(b) The shoe-maker sells his shoes to a retailer for £40 plus VAT of £4. Half the VAT £2 is passed on to the tax collector, while the other half £2 compensates the shoe-maker for the tax he paid to the tanner.

(c) Customers buy the shoes for £60 plus VAT of £6. The retailer keeps £4 of the tax (the same amount paid to the shoe-maker) and pays

the remaining £2 to the tax collector who thereby ends up with the full £6 VAT.

Licences. A motor vehicle road fund licence is another form of indirect taxation and payments for television, gun and dog licences comprise further examples.

Betting Duties. Duties are levied on a wide variety of gambling activities including football pools.

Both direct and indirect taxes have particular advantages and faults.

Advantages of direct taxes

1 Equality of sacrifice
Direct taxes are usually assessed in accordance with a graded scale so that the rate of taxation rises in relation to income. In addition allowances are made for family responsibilities. These taxes, therefore, make for equality of sacrifice on the part of taxpayers.

2 Redistribution of wealth
Direct taxes have considerable appeal to a government with a social policy of redistribution of wealth. Rates of personal tax and capital transfer tax are both progressive, that is, the tax rates increase more than proportionately with income or the size of the estate. Thus the wealthier members of the community are taxed heavily in order to finance government expenditure on behalf of the poorer members of the community.

3 Revenue
The yield from personal taxation is fairly certain and can be calculated reasonably accurately in advance. Taxpayers make annual returns of income to the Inland Revenue so that statistics can be compiled of income groups and the numbers within each group. From these figures, the yield from personal taxation can be worked out.

Drawbacks of direct taxes

1 A deterrent to work
A high rate of personal taxation may cause people to work less hard. A progressive rate of tax means that over a certain income people may prefer to have leisure rather than extra earnings because a high proportion of the latter is taken by the government. The practical results in industry may appear in the form of absenteeism; a reluctance to work overtime, and an unwillingness to seek promotion to a better-paid job. Similarly the owner of a business may decide that the net

266

amount received in profits from an expansion of his business does not compensate for the extra work required. If these conditions appear, then high rates of personal taxation will discourage the production of extra goods and services.

On the other hand, higher rates of personal tax may have the opposite effect in certain circumstances. For example, a family man with fixed commitments such as mortgage and hire purchase repayments may work harder, since more money must be earned to maintain the standard of living.

2 A deterrent to saving

A high rate of personal taxation may reduce consumers' ability to save since it leaves them with less money to spend. Indeed the effect might lead to a reduction in savings by people who are determined to maintain their present level of expenditure. However, the purpose for which people are saving will be a significant factor in this respect. The particular aim—perhaps a house or a car—may be so important that increased taxation may cause people to spend less in order to maintain the same rate of saving.

3 A deterrent to enterprise

Corporation tax is a tax on the profits of companies and such a tax may stifle enterprise. If a business project is successful, the government taxes the profits, but if the enterprise fails, the government offers no form of compensation. In other words, the government gains from the success of a business and loses nothing from its failure. As a result, enterprise may be checked and economic progress hindered.

Advantages of indirect taxes

1 Freedom of choice

Whereas an increase in the rate of personal tax simply reduces a wage-earner's net disposable income, an increase in indirect taxation leaves earning unaltered, and a wage-earner can choose whether or not he wishes to buy the goods and services subjected to higher tax rates.

2 Voluntary payment

Payment of indirect taxes is voluntary in the sense that consumers can choose to avoid expenditure on taxed goods and services.

3 Administration

Indirect taxes offer certain administrative advantages. Customs and excise duties are paid by importers and manufacturers while value added tax is collected from manufacturers, wholesalers and retailers.

Thus, compared with the very large number of people who pay direct taxes, those on whom the Customs and Excise officials have to keep a check are comparatively few. Hence indirect taxes are more difficult to evade and easier to collect than direct taxes.

4 Selectivity
Indirect taxes may be used selectively to achieve particular aims. For example, the retail price of fuel oil may be increased by a tax in order to stimulate demand for other kinds of fuel.

5 Regulation of demand
Indirect taxes are altered more easily than direct taxes. Generally, indirect taxes operate from the day of their announcement. In addition, the Chancellor has power to alter the rate of tax on all or any of the four main groups (tobacco, alcohol, petrol, VAT) by up to ten per cent between Budgets. Thus such taxes are more flexible than direct taxes which may take a considerable time to show any results.

Drawbacks of indirect taxes

1 Regressive
Indirect taxes are regressive, that is, they fall more heavily on people with low incomes than on those with high incomes. Both wealthy and poor consumers pay the same rate of tax and since those who are poorer tend to spend a greater proportion of their income on buying goods and services, they pay a greater proportion of their income in indirect taxes.

2 Limited application
If the price of an article is raised by the imposition of a tax, it is possible that demand may fall and so the revenue raised turns out to be much smaller than anticipated.

3 Cost of living
An increase in indirect taxes can raise retail prices and hence the cost of living.

4 Effect on demand
An increase in price brought about by indirect taxation will decrease demand to some extent. Consequently, the industry concerned may be forced to contract for artificial reasons created by the government's taxation policy.

Principles of taxation
No tax is ideal, especially as many people object to paying taxes, but taxes are inevitable if the government is to obtain revenue to pay for its

expenditure. All taxpayers want to be satisfied that taxes are fair and reasonable and the following are some desirable qualities of a tax.

1 Equality of sacrifice

A person's tax liability should be related to his ability to pay. The latter is determined by (a) income and (b) personal circumstances.

Taxes which require the same payment by the poor as by the rich are unfair in the sense that the lower-paid pay a higher proportion of their income in tax than the higher-paid do. Such taxes are called *regressive*. Two examples are a flat rate tax (that is a tax of a fixed sum per head) and a proportional tax. A proportional tax is fairer than equality of payment because it takes away a greater sum in tax from a large income than from a smaller income. For example, if the rate of proportional tax is 10 per cent, a person who earned £10000 per annum would pay £1000 and a person earning only £500 would pay £50. But this system does not equalise the burden imposed on taxpayers. The loss of a tenth of an income of £500 is likely to be felt much more than the loss of £1000 on a £10000 per annum income.

This fact has led to general acceptance of the principle of *progression,* whereby taxation takes a larger proportion of people's incomes the higher their incomes are. Under this system the amount of tax to be paid increases more than proportionately with income. For example, if on an income of £500, £50 has to be paid in tax (i.e. 10 per cent), on £1000 per annum the tax might be £150 (i.e. 15 per cent) and on £10000 it might be £4000 (i.e. 40 per cent).

In Britain personal taxation is a progressive tax. On the other hand, expenditure taxes on beer, on tobacco and on petrol are regressive because lower-paid people often spend as much on these products as the higher-paid.

Ability to pay is also dependent upon personal circumstances such as family responsibilities. Recognition of this is implicit in the system of allowances incorporated in personal taxation. There is an allowance, for example, for a single person, a larger one for a married man and also allowances for dependant relatives.

2 Certainty

This principle means that there should be certainty with regard to the amount to be paid. Taxes should not be too complicated for taxpayers to understand and each taxpayer should be able to calculate precisely his tax liability.

3 Convenience

The time and manner of tax payments should be made as convenient to taxpayers as possible. The Pay-As-You-Earn (PAYE) method of collecting personal taxation, under which an employer deducts tax on behalf of his employees and pays it to the Inland Revenue authorities is a good example of this quality.

PAYE is convenient for the employee because he knows that he is not building up a tax bill. (On the other hand, self-employed people and companies have to put aside money reserves to pay the tax due when they are assessed).

4 Economy
The cost of administering a tax should be small in relation to its yield so that the net loss to the government is as little as possible. Thus taxes should not be of a kind where the cost of collection is excessive. Some taxes may appear very sensible in theory but be very expensive to administer, so that in extreme cases, the cost of collection might amount to more than the revenue collected.

Conflict between principles
If British taxes do not conform to each of the principles outlined above, it may be because the principles themselves are in conflict. For example, in order to be acceptable to public opinion, taxation should comply with the principle of equality of sacrifice. Unless a tax is accepted by the public there will be large-scale evasion. In an attempt to be fair to people in widely differing situations, the personal tax system provides a number of allowances. As a result the completion of forms for the annual return of income and claim for allowances can be difficult and complicated. Thus the principle of certainty with regard to the amount to be paid and that of equality of sacrifice may come into conflict.

Local taxation
In addition to the taxes considered above, occupiers of property have to pay *rates* to the Council of the area in which they live.

The amount of rates payable is worked out as follows. Every type of property—houses, shops, factories, cinemas, theatres, public houses—within the area of the local authority is given a *rateable value*. The latter is an estimate assessed by the Inland Revenue of the rent that might be charged on the property and is worked out at approximately five-yearly intervals. From the rental value a deduction is made of a sum estimated to be the annual cost of keeping the property in good repair. The net figure is called its rateable value. For example, if a house is considered to be worth a rent of £390 a year and £120 represents the annual cost of keeping it in good order, then the rateable value is £270.

Every year a local council (like the central government) makes an estimate of its expenses called a budget. When the amount of money that has to come from rates to meet this expenditure is known, each ratepayer's share of the cost is worked out in proportion to the rateable value of the property which he occupies. For example if the sum required from rates is £1 500 000 and the total rateable value of all property is £3 million, then $\frac{£1\,500\,000}{£3\,000\,000}$ = £0.50 will have to be paid as rates

for each £ of rateable value. Thus if the rate is £0.50 in the £ and a shop has a rateable value of £450, the owner will have to pay £225 a year in rates.

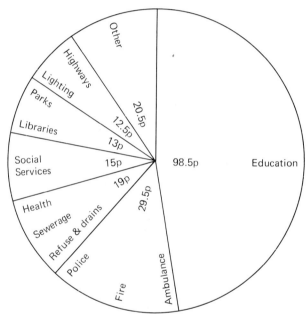

Fig. 40 How a Rate Might be Spent

As a council's expenses increase or decrease so the rate in the £ rises or falls. Where does the money go?

Local government services
The cost of each service varies from district to district according to the amount spent on it but the main services are as follows:

(a) education
(b) fire brigade
(c) housing

271

(d) libraries and museums
(e) environmental services (e.g. water supply, refuse and sewage disposal, drainage, maintenance of parks)
(f) police service
(g) public health
(h) roads and public lighting
(i) social services (including care of children, the aged and handicapped).

In order to meet the cost of these services a local authority obtains money from three main sources.

1 Government grants Each year part of the central government's revenue from direct and indirect taxation is handed over to local councils as grants to be spent on their local services. Grants are either (a) specific grants allocated for a particular service, such as police expenditure, or (b) rate support grants, which are not allocated to a specific service. The latter are often called 'block grants' and the majority of grants to local authorities are in this form.

2 Miscellaneous services Councils operate a number of services which provide income such as council house rents, market rents, charges for the use of car parks, tennis courts, and swimming baths. The money, raised is used towards payment of the total cost of services.

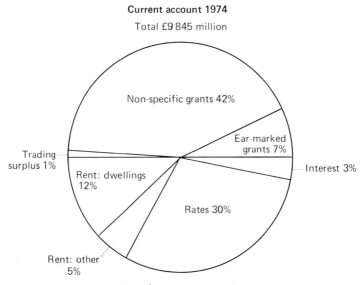

Current account 1974

Total £9 845 million

Fig. 41 Local Government Finance

3 Rates The balance of expenditure, after deducting government grants and income from miscellaneous items is met by a rate.

The National Debt

When revenue received from taxation is insufficient to meet government expenditure, money has to be borrowed. The accumulated value of annual borrowings by the government is known as the 'National Debt'. When there is a Budget surplus of revenue over expenditure, the government can repay part of its Debt.

The National Debt comprises two main types of debts, namely *deadweight* and *reproductive* debts. They are distinguished by the purpose for which the money was borrowed.

Deadweight debt is unsupported by any real assets and most of the National Debt is of this kind. It has been accumulated in financing Britain's wars since the end of the seventeenth century. Money was borrowed from the public during wartime in order to finance the purchases of arms and materials essential to the war effort. Those purchases were used up at the time and so this debt is a deadweight to the government because it does not represent any kind of tangible asset.

Reproductive debt represents money borrowed to finance some important project such as, for example, the building of an additional airport. The debt is balanced by some real asset which will benefit the community. When an industry has been nationalised the previous owners received compensation, the total of which increased the National Debt. However, the state received in exchange the assets of the nationalised industry and the debt is, therefore, a reproductive debt.

Table 26   National Debt: a summary

	Per cent
1 *Short-term debt* e.g. Treasury bills, government stocks with a life of up to 5 years.	37
2 *Medium and long term debt* e.g. government stocks with a life of 5 years and over.	43
3 *Non-marketable debt* e.g. national savings holdings, ways and means advances	20
	100

Table 27   The Increase in the National Debt

Date	National Debt	Significance of date
1914	£650 million	Beginning of First World War
1918	£7435 million	End of First World War
1946	£23 637 million	End of Second World War
1973	£35 839 million	
1976	£56 577 million	

The burden of the National Debt

Each year the government is obliged to pay interest on the National Debt. The source of this payment is revenue from taxation. Hence the interest payments on the Debt are a considerable burden on taxpayers. The actual extent of the burden depends largely on whether it is an internal or an external debt. The *internal debt* is that part of the National Debt owed to people and institutions (such as banks, building societies and insurance companies) in this country. Sums owed to foreign creditors comprise the *external debt*.

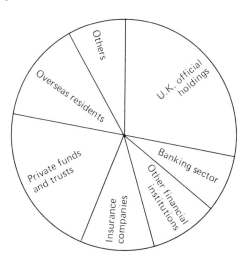

Fig. 42 Holders of the National Debt

It is debatable whether the internal debt can be considered to constitute a burden at all. Certainly it is necessary to raise taxation to pay interest on the debt and the greater the debt the greater the amount of taxation required to provide the interest on it. However, in the case of the internal debt, interest payments (raised from taxation of the community) are paid back to members of the same community. In other words, they are transfer payments and do not affect the total wealth of the community. Generally, the people who contribute as taxpayers to interest payments also receive part of that interest either directly (for example on National Savings Bank balances or on government stocks), or indirectly as subscribers to life assurance and pension schemes, since the managers of these funds invest part of them in government stock.

The true 'burden' of the National Debt is the amount of interest that has to be paid to overseas creditors. These payments have to be made in foreign currencies. In order to earn foreign currencies, it is necessary for exports to exceed imports. Consequently production has to exceed consumption in order to provide either (a) foreign currencies or (b) goods and services to overseas creditors if and when they wish to spend the sums owed to them. Thus overseas holdings of the National Debt represent a British liability to the rest of the world.

Public expenditure
Public expenditure means payments for those things which are provided collectively rather than in return for payment by private individuals.

Table 28   The Main Areas of Public Spending

	per cent
Defence (and external relations)	
including aid, diplomatic service, etc.	13
Commerce and industry	
including nationalised industries and agriculture	12
Local and environmental services	
transport, roads, housing, law and order, etc.	21
housing	
Social services	
education	42
health and welfare	
benefits, pensions, insurance, assistance	
Debt interest	10
Other spending	2
Total	100
of which: central government	61
local authorities	30
public corporations	9

The Budget does not cover all public expenditure. It covers only expenditure by the central government, including grants to local authorities, and loans and deficit grants to nationalised industries.

Public expenditure comprises expenditure by:

(a) the central government—approximately 60 per cent of the total;

(b) local authorities—approximately 30 per cent of the total;

(c) nationalised industries and other public corporations—approximately 10 per cent of the total.

Thus the total of public expenditure is very much greater than the total of central government expenditure shown in the Budget.

About 60 per cent of public expenditure is spent directly on items such as (a) the salaries and wages of the armed forces, police, teachers, nurses, and civil servants, (b) the running costs of schools, prisons, and the National Health Service, (c) the construction costs of hospitals, schools, houses, police stations and roads.

The remainder represents transfers of money to people and companies who make the final purchases themselves. The largest transfer item is retirement pensions, and others include supplementary benefit, sickness benefit, child benefits, and also various grants and loans and interest payments.

Public expenditure is financed from the following sources:

(a) taxation

(b) national insurance contributions

(c) rates

(d) interest, rent and dividends (from publicly owned property)

(e) trading income of nationalised industries

(f) borrowing.

QUESTIONS

Write *short* answers to the following:

1 What are the main items of government expenditure?

2 Name the principal ways in which the government obtains income.

3 What are the differences between direct and indirect taxes?

4 What is 'the Budget'?

5 Name the Accounts which administer government revenue and expenditure.

6 What was the original purpose of the Budget?

7 In what ways can the Budget be used to regulate the economy?

8 How can fiscal policy assist in the redistribution of income?

9 Briefly describe three drawbacks of fiscal policy.

10 List the main direct taxes levied in Britain.

11 List the main indirect taxes.

12 Give some advantages of direct taxes.
13 What are the drawbacks of direct taxes?
14 Give some advantages of indirect taxes.
15 What are the drawbacks of indirect taxes?
16 List the qualities of a 'good' tax.
17 Give an example of a conflict between some of these qualities.
18 What is the meaning of 'rateable value'?
19 Make a list of local government services.
20 What are the sources of local authority finance?
21 What was the origin of the National Debt?
22 What is the difference between 'deadweight' and 'reproductive' debts?
23 Define public expenditure.

Write answers to the following:
1 Giving examples, explain what is meant by (a) progressive taxes and (b) regressive taxes. Why does the government levy both these types of taxes? (WJEC)
2 What do you consider to be the qualities of a good tax? How far do these qualities conflict with one another in practice? (WJEC)
3 John White, a married man with two children at school, earns a weekly wage of £25. What type of taxes is he likely to pay, and in what ways does he benefit from government expenditure? (SUJB)
4 Discuss some of the ways in which Government expenditure and taxation policy tends to distribute the National Income more equally among the population. (SUJB)
5 'Taxation may become a weapon of economic policy, as well as providing the government with its revenue.' Explain this statement, choosing examples from both direct and indirect taxation. (SUJB)
6 Explain, with appropriate examples, the advantages and disadvantages of raising revenue by (a) direct taxation and (b) indirect taxation. (U/L West Africa)
7 What are the major sources of central government income? Does central government taxation policy help in any way to reduce inequalities in the standard of living being enjoyed by various sections of the community? (AEB)
8 What economic principles ought a Chancellor of the Exchequer to have in mind when considering new taxes? Illustrate your answer with examples. (AEB)
9 'Taxes provide revenue for the government'. What other reasons for taxation are there? (JMB)

10 Discuss the relative merits and demerits of direct and indirect taxation. (JMB)
11 How can the government use the taxation system to reduce economic inequalities between British citizens? (Oxford)
12 What is meant by the Budget in Britain? Must we have one every year? (Oxford and Cambridge)
13 (a) From which major source does the government derive its income? (b) Why is it said that the government 'transfers' income? (U/L)
14 Describe the main economic objectives of public expenditure in your country. (U/L West Africa)
15 Discuss the various economic and financial factors which a British government. takes into consideration when it frames a modern budget. (JMB)
16 What is meant by a 'budget surplus'? Under what conditions is a government justified in attempting to achieve such a surplus? (Oxford)
17 What are local rates and how are they levied? Do you consider them to be a 'good tax'? Justify your views. (AEB)
18 The following data relates to public sector expenditure in the United Kingdom: 1963—£11 666 million; 1973—£31 979 million.
   (a) Account for this rise in spending.
   (b) How is the expenditure financed? (AEB)

PRACTICAL WORK

1 Study the financial pages of a newspaper and make a list of government stocks. Classify them into (a) dated stocks (show the repayment dates) and (b) undated stocks. Find out the difference between dated and undated stocks.
2 Consult an economic history book and read about the growth of government expenditure during the twentieth century.
3 Find out: (a) why the government proposes to replace the main tax allowances by a tax-credit scheme; (b) how the scheme will work.

22

National Income

The National Income is an estimate of the value of goods and services made available as a result of the country's economic activity over a given period. Detailed information regarding the National Income is given in a book published annually by Her Majesty's Stationery Office and called *National Income and Expenditure*. This publication is usually referred to as the 'Blue Book'.

The task of measuring the National Income is approached by government statisticians in three ways, each of which acts as a check on the others. The value of goods and services produced can be measured by adding up either the *incomes* received for producing them, or the *total spent* on their purchase, or the sum of the *products* of the various industries. As indicated in Fig. 43 this method involves measuring the circular flow of money three times, as it changes hands from business firms to members of the public and back again. Whichever of these

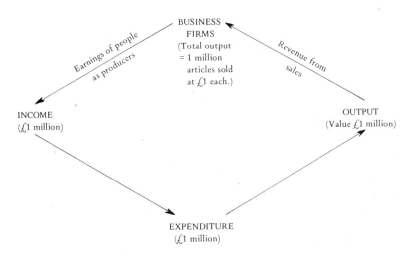

Fig. 43 The Circular Flow of Income

three ways—income, expenditure or output—is used to estimate the National Income, the same total should result.

The procedure and problems involved in each of the methods are outlined below.

Measurement by factor incomes

Table 29 reproduces the tables of Incomes from a Blue Book. The figures used to compile this table are obtained from personal tax and corporation tax returns to the Inland Revenue, and from the accounts of public corporations.

The majority of factor incomes comprise *personal income* from employment or ownership of property, and take the form of wages and salaries, rent, interest and profit. All income (before taxation) received from the production of goods and services must be counted.

A large group of incomes which must be excluded are known as 'transfer incomes'. They include unemployment benefits, child benefits, retirement pensions, student grants, sickness benefit, redundancy payments and interest on the National Debt. These sums represent a transfer of income by means of taxation from one group of people to another. They are not incomes received from productive work. Similarly, private transfers or private gifts (e.g. payment of 'pocket money' to children by parents) do not qualify as factor incomes. The inclusion of transfer incomes in the National Income would result in double-counting of income.

The total of personal incomes obtained from tax returns includes profits distributed by companies to shareholders, but account must be taken of *undistributed profits*. The *trading surpluses* of public corporations must be treated in the same way, since both items represent income generated in production.

Business profits can include a figure which represents 'stock appreciation'. If, during the accounting year, prices rise, then there will be a profit on stocks of goods or raw materials held over from the previous year. Such stock appreciation does not arise from any physical increase in the quantities of stocks and so the amount must be deducted from the total of factor incomes.

The total of personal incomes plus retained profits less stock appreciation represents *Gross Domestic Product* (GDP) at factor cost. It is an estimate of the output of the factors of production in this country.

Another source of income to people in Britain is dividends and interest received from investments abroad. Similarly, people abroad have investments in Britain and payments to them of dividends and

Table 29 Factor incomes in the Gross National Product

£ million

	1965	1966	1967	1968	1969	1970	1971	1972	1973	1974	1975
Factor incomes											
Income from employment	21292	22814	23751	25408	27160	30425	33506	37598	43291	52494	68181
Income from self-employment	2510	2671	2835	3110	3377	3774	4383	5415	6707	7897	8705
Gross trading profits of companies	4741	4610	4663	5275	5314	5669	6585	7732	9872	10783	10387
Gross trading surplus of public corporations	988	1042	1132	1363	1451	1447	1520	1681	2062	2520	2898
Gross trading surplus of other public enterprises	112	106	110	132	153	151	177	140	141	123	114
Rent	1896	2087	2287	2525	2877	3276	3595	4118	4862	5912	7144
Total domestic income	31539	33330	34778	37813	40332	44742	49766	56684	66935	79729	97429
less Stock appreciation	−318	−361	−194	−570	−734	−1162	−1076	−1335	−3180	−6091	−5203
Residual error	−	136	342	214	−115	−91	381	−381	−308	−127	920
Gross domestic product at factor cost	31221	33105	34926	37457	39483	43489	49071	54968	63447	73511	93146
Net property income from abroad	435	387	378	333	498	556	500	551	1383	1392	949
Gross national product	31656	33492	35304	37790	39981	44045	49571	55519	64830	74903	94095
less Capital consumption	−2869	−3107	−3287	−3589	−3908	−4445	−5092	−5823	−6897	−8391	−10907
National income	28787	30385	32017	34201	36073	39600	44479	49696	57933	66512	83188

Source: *National Income and Expenditure*

281

interest reduce the National Income. If the sum received from abroad exceeds the amount paid to people overseas there is a *net property income* from abroad. When this sum is added to the value of the Gross Domestic Product, it provides the *Gross National Product* (GNP) at factor cost. This figure represents the total income earned by British owned factors of production whether situated at home or abroad.

At the bottom of Table 29 there is an item for *capital consumption*. An alternative term is *depreciation* and it represents the portion of income which is used every year to replace worn out or obsolete capital e.g. machinery, buildings, etc. (see Chapter 14, p. 178). The amount of income devoted to these purposes makes no addition to the quantity of goods and services available. It is deducted, therefore, from the Gross National Product to give the *Net National Product* (NNP) at *factor cost* and this is known as the *National Income*. The allowance for depreciation is difficult to estimate and the Inland Revenue lays down an arbitrary figure. For reasons of accuracy, therefore, the Gross Domestic Product or the Gross National Product figures are more commonly quoted than the Net National Product.

To summarize:

Gross Domestic Product =Personal incomes + retained profits – stock appreciation

Gross National Product =Gross Domestic Product + net property income from abroad

National Income =Gross National Product – depreciation

Measurement by expenditure

Table 30 shows Gross National Product by Expenditure.

Total domestic expenditure, that is, spending by those resident in Britain comprises the following.

1 Final expenditure by private consumers and public authorities on goods and services for *consumption*. Since it is impossible to include every item of spending made by every consumer, expenditure surveys are conducted for representative samples of the population. Figures for public expenditure are obtained from the accounts of the various public authorities.

2 Private and public *investment* expenditure on (*a*) fixed capital such as buildings, machinery and houses and (*b*) increases in the amounts of finished goods and raw materials held in stocks.

In calculating *total domestic expenditure,* only spending on goods and services at the final stage of purchase is included, for example, at the

282

Table 30 Expenditure on the Gross National Product

£ million

	1965	1966	1967	1968	1969	1970	1971	1972	1973	1974	1975
Expenditure											
Consumers' expenditure	22845	24211	25428	27338	29102	31644	35165	397	45044	51832	63373
Public authorities' current expenditure on goods and services	6041	6572	7272	7727	8088	9095	10344	11772	13403	16578	22907
Gross domestic fixed capital formation	6504	6922	7523	8200	8590	9453	10515	11680	14148	16633	20510
Value of physical increase in stocks and work in progress	496	339	336	471	449	442	118	57	1163	1144	-1349
Total domestic expenditure at market prices	35886	38044	40559	43736	46229	50634	56142	63225	73758	86187	105411
Exports of good and services	6592	7061	7264	8813	9871	11275	12667	12278	16888	22390	26093
less Imports of goods and services	-6869	-7145	-7708	-9184	-9683	-10887	-11865	-13408	-18557	-26718	-28248
less Taxes on expenditure	-4959	-5421	-5997	-6809	-7771	-8412	-8788	-9262	-10092	-11342	-14046
Subsidies	571	566	808	901	837	879	915	1135	1450	294	3906
Gross domestic product at factor cost	31221	33105	34926	37457	39483	43489	49071	54968	63447	73511	93146

Source: *National Income and Expenditure*

retail stage in the case of goods and services for consumption. If intermediate stages were counted, then duplication of spending figures would occur.

Further, only spending on new goods is included in the calculation. The purchase of second-hand goods such as a car or a house, is merely the transfer of an existing asset from one person to another. The transaction does not represent new assets coming into existence through production.

Another adjustment is necessary because total domestic expenditure is affected by international trade. Some of the money spent by the population is used to buy imported goods, while some of the money received by firms is from the sale of exports. Therefore in order to arrive at the value of the Gross National Product, it is necessary to deduct spending on imports and to add on the value of exports.

Thus total domestic expenditure plus exports less imports is equal to the *Gross National Product* at *market prices*. Spending must necessarily be valued in terms of market prices, but the latter are often either artificially raised by indirect taxes or reduced by government subsidies paid to producers. In order to calculate spending at *factor prices* it is necessary (a) to deduct the amount of indirect taxation from total expenditure and (b) to add on the value of the subsidies.

As with the Measurement by Factor Incomes method, a deduction for *depreciation* is made from the Gross National Product in order to calculate *National Income*.

To summarize:

1   Total domestic expenditure   =   consumption + investment

2   Gross National Product   =   total domestic expenditure +
    at Market Prices   exports − imports

3   Gross National Product   Gross National Product at
    at Factor Cost   =   Market Prices − indirect taxes +
    subsidies

4   National Income   =   Gross National Product at
    Factor Cost − depreciation

Measurement by output

Table 31 shows the contributions of industries and services to the Gross National Product. It would not be practical to try to obtain complete

Table 31   Gross National Product by Industry

£ million

	1965	1966	1967	1968	1969	1970	1971	1972	1973	1974	1975
Agriculture, forestry and fishing	1027	1061	1106	1113	1193	1241	1372	1585	1877	2193	2527
Mining and quarrying	708	707	713	691	652	731	808	933	995	1130	1645
Manufacturing	10624	11003	11194	12003	12813	14120	15428	16974	19745	21763	26726
Construction	2153	2260	2388	2577	2699	2855	3176	3861	4738	5507	6411
Gas, electricity and water	1006	1069	1145	1300	1388	1376	1559	1747	1940	2272	2866
Transport	1984	2079	2087	2349	2476	2706	3021	3341	3948	4503	5753
Communication	646	703	753	813	930	1045	1190	1358	1654	2087	2809
Distributive trades	3605	3756	3910	4055	4168	4467	5193	5882	6664	7516	9159
Insurance, banking, finance and business services	2092	2183	2408	2725	2893	3380	4021	4779	5970	6709	7727
Ownership of dwellings	1395	1542	1693	1866	2118	2411	2627	3024	3546	4509	5535
Public administration and defence	1805	1973	2117	2263	2461	2761	3270	3688	4124	5210	7107
Public health and educational services	1430	1574	1703	1845	1995	2256	2641	3180	3590	4669	7154
Other services	3651	3998	4349	4752	5005	5571	5899	6892	7539	8854	10430
Total	32126	33908	35566	38352	40791	44920	50205	57244	66330	76922	95849
Adjustment for financial services	-905	-939	-982	-1109	-1193	-1340	-1515	-1895	-2575	-3284	-3623
Residual error	-	136	342	214	-115	-91	381	-381	-308	-127	920
Gross domestic product at factor cost	31221	33105	34926	37457	39483	43489	49071	54968	63447	73511	93146

Source: *National Income and Expenditure*

figures from every firm in the country each year and so the basis of the Blue Book statistics is the Census of Production. A Census is taken by the Department of Industry every few years and the figures obtained record the output of each industry. During the period between Censuses, regular returns are requested from a sample of firms.

The major problem in measuring output is that of double-counting. If the total value of every firm's output was simply added up, then double-counting would occur because part of the value of any firm's output is the value of the raw materials or components which have been used. These would have been counted already as the value of the final products of the firm supplying them. The output of the steel industry, for example, is included again in the products of many other manufacturing industries.

Double-counting is avoided by including in the output figure only the 'value added' by each firm during the process of production. For the individual firm this is found by deducting the value of other firms' products or services from the value of its own sales.

A second problem arises because only those goods and services for which payment is made are included in the output total. Thus some goods and services, such as, for example, the value of fruit and vegetables grown in a person's garden, the work of housewives, and the value of decorating and maintenance services which people do for themselves, are excluded from the output total. They are not paid for and do not have, therefore, a market price. On the other hand, if these same goods and services were produced by paid gardeners, housekeepers, builders and decorators, they would be counted as output and would form, therefore, part of the Gross Domestic Product. Whether payment is made for these goods and services or whether it is not, the *volume* of goods and services provided would remain unchanged. Thus the system of counting only goods and services which are paid for, as part of total output, results in some anomalies.

The value-added outputs of all industries and services makes up *Gross Domestic Product* at factor cost. Once again, the total of *Gross National Product* at factor cost is obtained by adding net property income from abroad (i.e. the 'output' of property owned abroad); and *National Income* is calculated by deducting *depreciation* from *Gross National Product* at *factor cost*.

Residual error
Although the figures from the three totals of Income, Expenditure and

286

Output should be the same, it will be noticed that Table 29 and Table 31 each contain a figure for 'residual error'.

It is a recognised fact that errors and omissions must occur when statistics are collected on a large scale. Hence a balance between the totals of income, expenditure and output rarely occurs in practice. The residual error item is introduced as an accounting device to bring income and output totals into line with that for total expenditure. Although the actual sum involved in the adjustment may appear large in itself, as a percentage of the total it is very small.

Uses of National Income calculations

1 Changes in the standard of living

The term 'standard of living' is difficult to define. In a broad sense, living standards depend not only upon the possession of material objects such as food, clothes, cars and houses, but also upon the *quality* of life. Health, freedom or leisure time and many other factors are important in this respect. However, economics is a science and is concerned, therefore, only with things which can be defined precisely and, if possible, measured. Hence an economist limits the meaning of 'standard of living' to things which can be valued in terms of money; the standard of living refers to the material standard of living. The greater the quantity of goods and services available for purchase, then the higher is the standard of living available to a community.

The most widely accepted measure of the standard of living is *Gross National Product per head*. The figure is obtained by dividing the Gross National Product (i.e. the total value of goods and services produced) by the total population. Changes in the standard of living can be assessed by comparing the figures for Gross National Product per head over periods of time.

In making comparisons between different years, it is important to use figures based on *real* terms rather than on *money* terms. The latter relates to prices but the real Gross National Product measures physical quantities of goods and services. An increase in Gross National Product due simply to a rise in prices leaves the community materially no better off. Thus in order to compare Gross National Product figures at different dates, allowance must be made for changes in prices. This is achieved by using a method similar to that used for compiling index numbers. By this means, the output of a given year is valued at the prices of a chosen 'base' year, so called because it is the year on which comparisons are being based. For example, if 1973 is the base year then the value of Gross National Product in succeeding years is estimated at constant (1973) prices. Even so, the comparison may not be very accurate, for the construction of index numbers is a problem with its own particular difficulties, as shown in Chapter 15.

A comparison based on Gross National Product per head is subject to the general limitations of arithmetic averages. For example, it reveals nothing about the *distribution* of goods and services. A rise in the average figure per head does not show whether the increase has gone to a small number of very wealthy people, leaving the rest of the community in exactly the same position as before—or whether the increase was shared equally by everyone.

Secondly, the Gross National Product per head figure reveals nothing about the *composition* of the goods and services available to the community. For example, an increase in the Gross National Product may be due to a rise in spending on military equipment for defence purposes. Hence, while the statistics will suggest a rise in the standard of living, in fact, the extra production does not comprise goods and services which improve economic welfare. Similarly, if the Gross National Product figure is increased because of a rise in the output of producer goods (machinery, factory buildings, etc.), the figure per head will give an over-optimistic impression of the standard of living. It is the output of consumer goods and services that determines the current standard of living, although investment in producer goods allows a higher standard to be enjoyed in the future.

2 Comparison of standards of living in different countries.
Gross National Product per head figures are used to compare standards of living in different countries. Such comparisons are useful for a variety of purposes.

(*a*) They provide an indicator of those countries which are in need of economic assistance.

(*b*) They provide a basis for assessing each country's financial contribution to international institutions. For example, the contribution of the United Kingdom to the European Economic Community budget was worked out in this way.

(*c*) They provide estimates of the value of joining an alliance of other countries or of the strength of a potentially hostile nation.

However, a comparison between countries based on Gross National Product per head can be misleading.

In the first place, each country's Gross National Product is expressed in terms of its national currency, and a comparison requires conversion of the currencies involved. Either one country's currency is converted into that of another country or both are converted into a third currency. Unfortunately, the use of the exchange rate quoted in the foreign exchange market is bound to be somewhat arbitrary. The rate varies from day to day and so the Gross National Product figure may appear as different totals on different dates. In addition, the foreign exchange rate does not always accurately reflect relative price levels in the countries concerned. For example, if £1 is equal to 13 francs in the foreign exchange market, it does not necessarily follow that one pound would purchase the same quantity of goods and services in Britain as 13 francs would in France. Thus Gross National Product figures may be falsified by conversion into foreign currencies for the purpose of comparison.

Secondly, a comparison takes no account of different patterns of living caused by climate or social customs. For example, in poorer countries most people perform services for themselves which, in richer countries, are carried out for money payments. Restaurants, laundry services and tailoring are typical examples. When services are paid for, they are included in the Gross National Product, but if they are not valued in terms of money, their value will not appear in the Gross National Product. It seems likely, therefore, that the real Gross National Product per head in poorer countries is understated by their Gross National Product figures. Again, a person's requirements will differ widely as between, for example, a country in the equatorial region and another in the temperate zone. The inhabitants of the former have no demand for centrally heated homes, winter clothing, etc., all of which make a significant contribution to the Gross National Product calculations of temperate zone countries. Thus the kinds of goods and services produced in different countries can vary a great deal, and a comparison of standards of living is, very often, an attempt to compare unlike things.

Thirdly, some of the considerations mentioned earlier apply to international comparisons. Thus (a) if prices rise faster in one country than in another then an international comparison is distorted; (b) comparative figures refer to countries as a whole and do not reflect the distribution of incomes within each nation. Thus an average figure per head may conceal gross inequality of wealth, as for example in a country where a small number of people are very wealthy and the majority are relatively poor. In another country, the same Gross National Product per head figure may be shown and yet reflect a much more even distribution of income.

3 Regulation of the economy

The statistics published annually in the Blue Book on National Income and Expenditure play an important part in the determination of the government's economic policy. For example, the Blue Book provides details of changes in three important variables, namely, saving, investment and consumption.

Saving represents the proportion of incomes which is not spent on goods and services. The economic importance of saving lies in its relationship to *investment,* that is, the production of producers' goods such as new factory buildings. Saving is a necessary pre-requisite of investment. *Consumption* means the total output of consumers' goods and services. Details of these changes are essential for any form of government economic planning.

Factors determining the National Income

A number of influences help to determine whether a country has a large or a small National Income. The main determinants are described below.

1 Natural and human resources

The quantity and quality of a country's resources provide one of the most important influences on its National Income. For example, fertile soil, ready sources of power, easily worked mineral deposits, a favourable climate, navigable rivers, etc., will have a beneficial effect on a country's productive capacity.

Capital equipment may range from simple hand tools to the most up-to-date forms of industrial machinery. Generally, the achievement of an increasing output of goods is associated with increased investment in capital equipment. For example, a miner can extract a greater quantity of mineral resources from the earth with the aid of machinery than with only a pick and shovel. Thus the effectiveness with which natural and human resources are used depends to a large extent on the capital equipment available.

The size of the working population is determined by factors such as the population age structure and social attitudes. For example, the social attitude towards women is important in this respect. If the community judges that 'a woman's place is in the home', then the talents of many women may be wasted.

The quality of the labour force will depend partly on the innate intelligence of the people and partly on the skills acquired through education and training.

Entrepreneurial skill, that is, the ability to make decisions, calls for sound judgement and some courage. The availability of this skill will affect the use of resources and hence the size of the National Income.

2 Technical knowledge
New methods of production and new ways of utilising resources may increase the output of goods and services. A community which is keen to try out new ideas or inventions in industry and commerce is likely to enjoy a higher standard of living than a country which is slow to adopt new ideas.

3 Political stability
Political stability is essential for the expansion of business activities. War and internal revolution interfere with production because they add to normal commercial risks. Thus peace and a stable government promote confidence and encourage production.

4 Terms of trade
Trade benefits all countries which engage in it, but the degree of benefit enjoyed by a particular country will vary according to changes in the price levels at which it sells its exports and imports. Favourable terms of trade occur if the prices of imports fall relatively to the prices of exported goods. This means that a larger quantity of imports can be obtained for a given quantity of exports. Hence more goods are available and National Income is increased.

5 Foreign investment
A net income from foreign investment means that the creditor country can obtain goods and services from debtor countries without having to give goods and services in return. Thus if two countries have equal Gross Domestic Products, then the country with the more favourable net return from foreign investment will have the higher National Income.

Economic growth
The term 'economic growth' is generally taken to mean the annual percentage rate of increase of the real Gross Domestic Product, that is, the total annual value of home produced goods and services at constant prices. During the decade 1960-70 the Gross Domestic Product of the United Kingdom increased by more than two-thirds in *money* terms, but the rise in *real* terms was much smaller, as over half the increase was the result of rising prices. Hence a statistical correction has to be made to

allow for changes in prices and in order to obtain the *real* growth of output.

Significance of economic growth

Economic growth provides the increased resources which are needed for the following purposes.

(*a*) To develop industrial production through the modernisation, replacement and expansion of factories and equipment.

(*b*) To improve services provided by the government (e.g. education, health, etc.) and paid for in taxes and rates.

(*c*) To raise material living standards through the availability of more goods and services.

(*d*) To finance Britain's role in world affairs. In co-operation with other countries, Britain seeks to maintain international peace, security and economic progress through spending on defence and overseas aid.

The pursuit of economic growth is a prime motive of government economic policy. Policies designed to produce or accelerate economic growth have become part of the philosophy of the main political parties. The prevailing preoccupation with growth is reflected in the frequent presentation in newspapers of 'league' tables showing international growth rates.

QUESTIONS

Write *short* answers to each of the following:
1 Define the National Income.
2 Which publication provides detailed information regarding the National Income?
3 Name three ways of measuring the National Income.
4 What are 'transfer incomes'?
5 Why are transfer incomes excluded from the National Income?
6 What does 'stock appreciation' mean?
7 What is 'depreciation'?
8 Complete the following to illustrate the measurement of the National Income by factor incomes:
  (*a*) Gross Domestic Product = _____ + _____ - _____
  (*b*) Gross National Product = _____ + _____
  (*c*) National Income = _____ - _____ .
9 Name the items which make up total domestic expenditure.
10 Why is spending on second-hand goods excluded from total domestic expenditure?
11 What is the difference between market prices and factor prices?

13 Complete the following to illustrate the measurement of the National Income by expenditure:
  (a) Total domestic expenditure = _____ + _____
  (b) Gross National Product
      at Market Prices = _____ + _____ - _____
  (c) Gross National Product
      at Factor Cost = _____ - _____ + _____
  (d) National Income = _____ - _____ .
13 What is the major problem in measuring output?
14 How is this problem avoided?
15 How is the standard of living measured?
16 Briefly describe the limitations of this method.
17 State why a comparison of international standards of living can be useful.
18 Briefly describe the problems which would arise from such a comparison.
19 What are the meanings of (a) saving, (b) investment and (c) consumption?
20 State the main determinants of National Income.
21 What is the meaning of 'economic growth'?
22 Why is economic growth important?

Write answers to the following:
  1 What is meant by the National Income? What are its components, and what determines their growth? (SUJB)
  2 In attempting to compare the standard of living in Britain in the immediate post-war period with the present-day standard of living, why would it be misleading merely to compare the figures of the Gross National Product at current prices? (SUJB)
  3 Examine the factors which determine the size of a country's national income. (JMB)
  4 Explain what is meant by National Income and briefly indicate the three methods which can be used to calculate it. What is the value of making such a calculation? (JMB)
  5 If wage rates in Britain and in a certain foreign country are the same, does this necessarily mean that the standards of living of the inhabitants of these two countries are identical? (JMB)
  6 What do you understand by economic growth? What indicators would you use to measure the growth of the British economy? (Oxford and Cambridge)
  7 Briefly explain what is meant by the National Income and how it is

distributed. If the National Income increases does it follow that the standard of living increases at the same rate? (JMB)

8 Explain carefully the meaning in national income accounting, of the following terms: *consumption, saving, investment, depreciation.* (Oxford)

9 (a) State which of the following items would be included in a calculation of the national income, and give reasons for your answers.
(i)   A £25 000 win on premium bonds
(ii) £15 which a housewife received as a weekly allowance from her husband
(iii) The incomes paid to employees in service industries
(iv) The estimated value of a do-it-yourself painting job.
(b) What are the problems encountered in calculating the national income of a country? (JMB)

10 What do you understand by the term 'the standard of living'? How has the standard of living in Britain changed since 1945? (SCE)

11 Suggest reasons why the difference in living standards between lower income and higher income groups in the United Kingdom is less than it was twenty-five years ago. (LCC)

12 Explain why National Income can be defined as the total of all factor incomes. (LCC)

PRACTICAL WORK

1 Economic growth can be achieved through either (a) increasing the supply of, or (b) utilising more efficiently, the factors of production. During your study of economics you should have read about a number of ways of achieving these aims. For example, the efficient utilisation of the labour force means that workers must be occupationally and geographically mobile. Draw up two lists showing ways in which (a) resources can be increased and (b) resources can be utilised more efficiently.

2 Each year, usually in March, an official estimate of the National Income is published in the form of a White Paper. The more detailed Blue Book appears in September. Obtain a copy of each and compare the latest figures with those shown in Tables 29 – 30.

Index

296